LAWRENCE E. TYSON AND
PAUL B. PEDERSEN

Critical Incidents in School Counseling

Second Edition

5999 Stevenson Avenue
Alexandria, VA 22304-3300

Critical Incidents in School Counseling
Second Edition

10 9 8 7 6 5 4 3 2

American Counseling Association
5999 Stevenson Avenue
Alexandria, VA 22304

Director of Publications
Carolyn C. Baker

Cover design by Spot Color

Library of Congress Cataloging-in-Publication Data
Critical incidents in school counseling / edited by Lawrence E. Tyson, Paul B. Pedersen. — 2nd ed.
p.   cm.
Includes bibliographical references.
ISBN 1-55620-209-1 (alk. paper)
1. Educational counseling. 2. Student counselors. 3. Critical incident technique. I. Tyson, Lawrence E. II. Pedersen, Paul, 1936-   . III. American Counseling Association.
LB1027.5.C248   1999
371.4—dc21   99-41169
                                                  CIP

DEDICATION

This book is dedicated to my wife Patricia who has always stood by me and encouraged me when I needed it the most; to my parents Harry and Lola who continue to inspire me; and to my children Erin and Jordan who are my shining lights.

This book is also dedicated to all the professional school counselors who go to work everyday, knowing they make a difference in the lives of their students.

Thank you, Paul, for this opportunity.

—Lawrence E. Tyson

This book is dedicated to Ray Corsini, a valued mentor and hero for me and my work on multicultural issues. Also, this book is dedicated to the faculty and staff in Counselor Education at the University of Alabama at Birmingham, Dr. Patricia Sheets, Dr. Linda Holloway, Dr. William Crunk, Dr. Lawrence Tyson, Juanita Turner, and Rebecca Sandoval who provided support and encouragement. Finally, this book is dedicated to Richard Pearson at the Counseling and Human Development Department at Syracuse University and Allen Ivey and Mary B. Ivey at the University of Massachusetts at Amherst who worked on early drafts of this book.

—Paul B. Pedersen

TABLE OF CONTENTS

PREFACE

Experience is a pretty good—if not perhaps the best—teacher. This second edition of V. F. Calia and R. J. Corsini's (1973) *Critical Incidents in School Counseling* demonstrates how the problems manifesting in schools are both similar and different over this 25-year period. We continue the premise developed in the original book: "The basic idea of a critical incident book is simple: obtain sample incidents in any field and then obtain comments on these incidents from a variety of qualified people" (p. vii). We position the incidents themselves as the primary focus of this book, keeping commentary on those incidents to a minimum. Although the incidents and commentary are grounded in counseling theory, the "data" in this book are the incidents themselves, allowing the reader to test many theories by attempting to explain counseling behaviors in the school context.

The purpose of this book is to describe the incidents or situations encountered by school counselors and to reframe those incidents into learning opportunities. Each problem or crisis we encounter as school counselors has something to teach us in preparation for the next crisis. If we can teach ourselves to learn from these incidents, we may better learn from the problems we encounter. This collection of incidents is designed to blur the boundaries between the classroom and the community in which school counselors work. The incidents are collected from situations that school counselors might typically encounter and are accompanied by at least two other reactors experienced in working with school counseling who comment on the incident and what it has to teach us.

The critical incident technique is closely related to the case study method, which evaluates the behavior of a person in a clinical or decision-making setting, examining background, behavior, and changes of behavior. Case data describe and interpret impressions about the subject from a qualitative/subjective rather than a quantitative/objective viewpoint. Sigmund Freud made the case method the foundation of his theories, whereas Carl Rogers, Gordon Allport, and other therapists have frequently used the case method in psychological analysis.

As part of every Practicum or Internship course, practicing school counselors are brought into the classroom to discuss what they learned about counseling after they graduated from the program. Inevitably, they proceed by telling stories or incidents that have happened to them and how they have responded. This book is an attempt to highlight those field-based experiences in a published resource particularly for students in Practicum and Internship courses. We maintained the same criteria for selecting incidents that were part of the first edition, including only those incidents that were relevant, did not duplicate one another, demonstrated frequently occurring problems, and offered an opportunity for learning about the real world of school counseling. In addition, we surveyed the books used in school counseling and programs. The categories chosen are representative of the current perspectives regarding the essential components of a school counseling program. The most difficult decision was which of the many additional critical incident areas to omit. A surprisingly large number of incidents and commentaries from the first edition are highly relevant today.

We endorse the suggestion by Calia and Corsini (1973) that the reader become an active rather than a passive participant by following four important guidelines. First, while reading each incident, ask yourself how you, as the school counselor, would have viewed and handled the situation. Second, tell the writer of that incident how he or she should have handled it. Explain to him or her as carefully as you can how he or she should have viewed and dealt with the problem. Compliment the writer on what he or she did right and criticize him or her for what he or she did wrong. Third, turn to the several reactors and listen to what they say and how you agree or disagree with them. Listen carefully to the incident or reaction before you offer your ideas and suggestions. Finally, enter into a debate with the contributors, explaining once again how you might conceptualize the situation differently.

Calia and Corsini (1973) highlighted five areas of influence that contribute to the dilemma of school counselors 25 ago that are still relevant today:

1. The school counselor's need to please individuals in positions of power and influence for reasons of self-interest;

2. The school counselor's theoretical–philosophical orientation;

3. The expectations and demands of faculty and colleagues;

4. The wants and needs of the student; and

5. The demands of parents and others outside the school system.

The school counselor is in a unique position with regard to the informal, out-of-classroom learning that occurs in the school context. This book is an attempt to illustrate the learning opportunities presented by those critical incidents for the school counselor and others in the school context as a springboard for discussion. Although many critical incidents have been added, the reader will quickly identify important problems or populations that have not been included. We hope that this broad selection will provide a sample of the many problems that arise in school counseling and that the reader will generate many new critical incidents to fill in the gaps for preservice and in-service discussion by school counselors.

—Lawrence E. Tyson

REFERENCES

Calia, V. F., & Corsini, R. J. (1973). *Critical incidents in school counseling.* Englewood Cliffs, NJ: Prentice Hall.

ACKNOWLEDGMENTS

The editors would like to thank the following individuals for their contribution to the success of this book: Dr. Tommie Radd, Dr. Craig Cashwell, Dr. Walter Roberts, Jr., Chris Still, Emily Phillips, Amanda Costin, Dr. John Stewart, Dr. Carolyn Stone, Dr. Jim Whitledge, Dr. Doris Coy, Dr. Christopher Skinner, Dr. Edwin Bordin, Dr. Allen E. Ivey, Dr. Rudolf Dreikurs, Dr. Judy Ettinger, Dr. Marilyn Brookwood, Dr. Scott Young, Dr. Gary Goodnough, Melinda Huhnhenn, Robert Milstead, Amy Skinner, Jill Holston, Dr. Jackie M. Allen, Dr. Richard Pearson, Mary A. Barber, Dr. E. G. Williamson, Shoshana Hellman, Galy Cinnmon, Dr. Tom Hohenshil, Dr. Don C. Locke, Tammy Cashwell, Dr. Rachelle Perusse, Linda Foster, T. Antoinette Ryan, Angelo V. Boy, Dr. Don C. Dinkmeyer, Dr. Carlen Henington, Dr. Susan B. Wilkie, Kristie Rankin, Dr. Rick Morton, Dr. Greg Brigman, Dr. Chari Campbell, Dr. Nancy Nishimura, Dr. Russ Sabella, Dr. Kitty Niebuhr, Elyse Watras, Lee Hinton, Dr. Cecilia Pierce, Kacy Pierce, Carla Mulkey, Dr. Patricia Sheets, Pamela Sanders, L. Edwin, H. S. Lawrence, L. C. Hand, and Harry Steven.

The editors would like to thank Rebecca Sandoval and Whitney Boling for their tireless editing efforts, and Dick Cecil for his retrieval skills on the computer.

Thanks also go to Richard Pearson from Syracuse University, Allen Ivey from the University of Massachusetts, and Mary Ivey from Microtraining Associates who assisted in producing earlier drafts of this book.

ABOUT THE EDITORS

Lawrence E. Tyson, PhD, is in his third year as clinical assistant professor at the University of Alabama at Birmingham (UAB) in Birmingham, Alabama. He is the advisor to the School Counseling Program in the Counselor Education Program in the Department of Human Studies, School of Education. He received his master's degree from Rollins College, Winter Park, Florida; his doctorate is from Mississippi State University in Starkville, Mississippi. He has been a teacher of emotionally handicapped students for 6 years and has served as guidance director and school counselor for 15 years in Florida before coming to UAB. He currently writes a column for the *Peer*

Facilitator Quarterly of the National Peer Helpers Association regarding ethics and standards pertaining to peer-helping programs. He has served as president of the Florida School Counselor Association, president of the Florida Counseling Association, and secretary/treasurer of the Florida Peer Helpers Association. He is an active member of the Association of Counselor Education and Supervision and the Association for Specialist in Group Work in the American Counseling Association and the American School Counselor Association.

Paul B. Pedersen, PhD, is a professor at the University of Alabama at Birmingham in Birmingham, Alabama. Dr. Pedersen is in the Counselor Education Program in the Department of Human Studies, School of Education. He has been a faculty member at the University of Minnesota, the University of Hawaii, and Syracuse University and for 6 years in Indonesia, Malaysia, and Taiwan. He is a Fellow in Divisions 9, 17, and 45 of the American Psychological Association and an active member of AMCD and the Association of Counselor Education and Supervision in the American Counseling Association. He has published over 26 books, 44 chapters, and 76 articles on various aspects of multicultural counseling and communication. He is currently participating in a 1-year leave of absence after being awarded a Fullbright Scholarship and is currently in Taiwan.

Addiction in the Home: "What's Behind the Door?"

CRITICAL INCIDENT

Background

I was in my 5th year as an elementary school counselor in a suburban area. I was responsible for the guidance program in three large elementary schools; the student enrollment of each school was approximately 400 to 500 students. Each school had its unique profile. One school was in the one of the most exclusive areas of our school district. The large majority of those students were from upper-middle-class to wealthy professional families. The second school was in the older section of the school district.

This area included the business strip, which was the main avenue between two cities, motels, lower priced older homes, rentals, and low-income housing. The large majority of those students were from lower income families. One third to one half of the students that started school would move before the end of the school year. The third school was in an area of newer homes. The majority of students were from predominantly lower to middle-class blue-collar families.

Buildings 1 and 2 had a very supportive elementary principal who worked closely with me. The elementary principal in Building 3 was neutral in program support. The parent organizations were fairly supportive of the school at all three buildings. All schools had a few families of color, but the majority of families were White.

Although I was in each school 1 to 2 days per week, each building and all of the students received a comprehensive guidance program. I rotated in each classroom, facilitated a guidance activity, and left a follow-up guidance plan with the classroom teacher. By the 5th year I knew all the teachers very well. Some teachers were more able than others with their follow-through. As a result of this comprehensive guidance approach, I knew all of the students and many of their families.

During my 4th year, I was invited and had decided to become involved with a community chemical intervention program that included parents, high school students, and various administrators, teachers, and counselors K–12. Various groups and teams went for training regarding chemical dependency and addiction. Every group was asked to educate others to help stop students from becoming involved with drugs and alcohol because the problem was becoming bigger and more apparent in the high school and junior high.

One program that was developed as a result of this community intervention movement was an enrichment program for all fourth-grade students in the school district. After extensive training and planning, three to four high school students, who had signed "no chemical use contracts," visited each fourth-grade class one time a month to present information and then create small "family" talk groups with six to eight fourth-grade students. I coordinated the program in each of my three elementary buildings. I observed the information presentation and circulated between the fourth-grade classes during the "family" talk groups. The fourth-grade and high school students were very enthusiastic about the program.

Two important ground rules were established as a part of the small "family" talk groups. As the high school students talked about the topic presented, if any of the fourth-grade students started to discuss anything confidential, the high school students were to stop the students and ask them to talk individually away from the group. Second, the fourth-grade student was to be referred to me immediately so that I was aware of the situation and could work with the student during my individual counseling time.

What started to happen was overwhelming and troubling. My suspicions of possible addiction problems in the homes of many students and families were confirmed. Many more students were identified. In all three schools, students began talking with me about the use and abuse of drugs and alcohol by siblings, parents, other family members, and in a few cases of themselves! In addition, some of the students reported problems from families who were employed by the school district! Some of those school personnel had been either unsupportive or neutral of the program.

Incident

One of the many students who emerged during this process was Sharon. Sharon was an outstanding fourth-grade student who attended the third school building. Her parents were married, and her father had been a high school teacher in our district and now was teaching in a neighboring school district. Sharon's mother worked in the home, attended parent organization meetings, but was not involved with the community intervention program. Sharon was one of those students who are great to have in class. She always did her work, had straight A's, and could not do enough to help others and the teachers.

Sharon was the middle of three children. Her younger brother, Mark, was in second grade. He was smart, did his work most of the time, received low to average grades, and demonstrated acting out behavior that would disrupt the other students. The teacher reported liking him, but they got very tired of his clowning around, pestering the other students, and working below his ability. Mark was popular despite his behavior and had friends because he was outgoing and did well with sports. I knew Mark because I visited his classroom for guidance and his teacher had consulted with me regarding his behavior.

Sharon had an older sister, Margaret, who was an honor student and a junior at the high school. Margaret was not a part the high school teen group. Because I was in the school district just 5 years, I did not know Margaret.

Initially, Sharon became an active participant in the fourth-grade program that visited her class once a month. She enjoyed having a teen to talk with and participated in the "family" talk groups. She reported a close relationship with her sister in high school. The high school teens told her that they knew her sister from some of the high school activities.

As the monthly programs progressed, Sharon began to change and became more and more removed during the meetings. She was polite but contributed very little. By the fourth meeting in January, Sharon reported not feeling well after the presentation and asked to go to the office. Her teacher questioned if she was really ill. The teen group leader had reported a change in her from the first group meeting.

After the program was over, I followed up on my concerns and the concerns of the teen group leader and teacher. Sharon was lying down in the clinic. She looked pale and appeared depressed. I asked her if I could talk with her. I explained that I was concerned about her, had noticed a change in her, and wanted to be of help. I let her know that we could talk then or I would be happy to talk with her during my next day in the school.

At first Sharon did not respond. She appeared to be hundreds of miles away in thought. Then she said that nothing was wrong; she just did not feel good. I told her that if she decided there was something she would like to discuss, she could write me a note and put it in my student referral box. Also, I asked her if I could check with her the next time I was in the building. Sharon said that she would see me in guidance class, that she would use the "note box" if she wanted to talk, and that I could check with her the next time I was in the school. Then, she asked, "Who do you tell if we did talk?" I assured her that what we said would be in confidence unless she or someone else would be in danger. She said nothing else. I thanked her for allowing me to talk with her, hoped she would feel better soon, and restated our agreement that I would check with her the next time I would be in the building.

My experience and intuition told me that this was a student with a deep internal conflict. I wasn't sure of the details, but I strongly suspected addiction problems in the home. That evening I called the counselor at the high school to ask her if she knew Margaret and anything about this family. I explained that Margaret's sister was in the fourth-grade program and I suspected that something may be happening in the family and that everything on the surface appeared fine with Sharon until the teen meetings. I shared that I planned to check with Sharon again and wanted to have as much information as possible before seeing her. Also I shared my plan to talk with the family and the building principal about their observations of Sharon and what may be bothering her.

What I learned from the high school counselor was that Sharon's father, who had taught in the high school, always seemed fine at school, but "loved to party" after school and on weekends. It was suspected that at times he would become violent toward Sharon's mother and the children, but there was "only one" incident when the police were called to the home. Sharon's mother had appeared fine on the surface and never let on about her husband's drinking problem. Even though everyone at the high school knew about the problem, it was never discussed with the family or Margaret. Some teachers enjoyed drinking with him; others did not want to put their nose in where it didn't belong. No one knew the reason the father changed school districts. Now, the father was in another school district and the high school counselor did not know about the family situation. The counselor stated that Margaret appears fine at school, is succeeding in the classroom, and has friends.

Discussion

The next time I arrived at the school I spoke with the building principal regarding Sharon. This principal had always been neutral toward the guidance program, thus it was difficult to know the level of support that I would receive. I asked him if Sharon had been in the office. I explained the concern of the teacher and the teen talk group leader regarding changes seen in Sharon. The principal said he had observed no behavioral changes in her. He stated he knew Sharon's father from a summer ball league to which they both belonged, and her mother was involved with the parent organization. Both parents seemed fine. I was not told not to see Sharon or talk with Sharon's mother, but it was obvious that I would receive little support from the principal if a problem were to result.

I then checked with Sharon as I had promised. She seemed back to her "old self." When she came to my office, after a short time, she began to discuss her fears of her father and the drinking and violence that occur at home. She was often told that she is not to talk to anyone about what goes on at home. Whenever there is a problem, her father tells the children that if they behave they will not need to get "straightened out." Her mother asks the children to stay in their room and stay out of the way of their father, and tells them that all will be fine. After Sharon learned more from the teen program and after difficulties during the holidays in December, she did not know what to do. She begged me to not tell anyone. She acknowledged that there is occasional violence when her father drinks but thinks she is safe in her room.

I asked Sharon if I could talk with her mother. Sharon stated that she would be afraid that if I talked with her mother she would get in trouble. Then, I asked her if she wanted to talk to her mother and father. She stated that she would be afraid because she loves them both and hope everything will just get better. Also, she did not want her sister's friends at school to find out about the problems at home.

QUESTIONS

1. What would be the most helpful thing for the counselor to do for Sharon and the other children? What are the possible consequences of doing nothing? What are the possible consequences of meeting with the mother? What are the possible consequences of meeting with both parents?
2. Explain the best way to involve the building principal, who has discouraged the involvement of the counselor with the family and this problem. What is the best way to involve the teacher? the teen group leader? the high school counselor?
3. What signals did the three children display that were indicators of possible addiction in the home. What are ways to help students who display these signals? How does the grieving process relate to addiction incidents like Sharon's?
4. Tell ways you can address the hurtful chemical behavior of adults in the lives of students—the parents, school employees, or other community leaders. How do you handle your chemical use and the chemical use of colleagues? What community resources are available to help? How does the approach in this case affect the teen program? How do you support people and families such as Sharon's to get involved?
5. What is the probability of Sharon, Mark, and Margaret becoming addicted? What skills and information would they need to prevent this from occurring.

RESPONSES TO THE INCIDENT

Paul Pedersen

There is likely to be a "code of silence" protecting faculty who are within the school family from embarrassment and disclosure. The implicit contract seems to be, "if I protect you from getting into trouble, then I can expect you to protect me if and when I should ever get into trouble." We have seen the code of silence applied to police protecting other police, but the same principle applies here also, with teachers protecting other teachers. This counselor is facing not just the problems of troubled children in the school or addiction and violence in the home but also serious professional risk from the principal and other faculty on whom the counselor would usually rely for help and support.

The counselor has done a good job using attending and observation skills to uncover the problem as being more than a personal and individual problem of Sharon's behavior. The counselor has taken the initiative to inquire and take a lively interest in what others knew about the problems Sharon was facing. The counselor has done this at some personal and professional risk, even working against the advice of the principal who wants to put a lid on the problem. This counselor is willing to spend considerable time on the possible (but yet unproven) problems of one particular student, even though the counselor is working in three different schools and no doubt has a heavy caseload already. It seems clear that we have a dedicated and competent counselor working on this case.

Who is the client? That is a difficult question to answer, especially as the network of relationships leading to Sharon's situation comes to light. It is clear that helping Sharon manage her problems will be impossible without involving the family. It is also clear that involving the family will be controversial, especially if there is clear evidence of abuse and family protective agencies need to be notified. The counselor is obviously reluctant to alert family protective agencies and the police, although the evidence of abuse seems clear and the counselor has a legal and ethical responsibility to notify the authorities.

The legal, ethical, and emotional consequences of this critical incident are going to be painful for some or all parties (including the counselor) involved. The counselor needs to first inform Sharon that the authorities must legally be notified. This will result in a painful situation for Sharon, but it is also the only long-term solution to the problems faced by Sharon and the family. If possible, it would be good to have Sharon's support in that duty or at least her understanding of the necessity. However, with or without Sharon's permission, the counselor has no choice. Once the authorities have been notified, the counselor will be able to separate the legal aspects of the case from the counseling aspects. This will involve working with Sharon, and probably with counselors from other schools where her siblings are students, helping the family or providing referrals to agencies where the family can be helped, and working with the principal and other teachers and colleagues of the parent who may well resent the counselor's interference. This will involve a large commitment of time by the counselor.

It is important that the counselor document every step of what is done and why the situation should result in legal action. Counselors are more and more frequently being called on as advocates, giving up their role of objective neutrality in the face of social issues. This critical incident is a good example of where advocacy is an appropriate counseling intervention.

Linda Foster

In this incident, a school counselor has a duty first and foremost to protect Sharon and her siblings. The counselor is in a position that unfortunately involves many aspects. The clear-cut position involves the safety and well-being of Sharon and her siblings. However, care must be taken to be tactful in handling this incident. School administrators at the building and district office level may hamper the school counselor's duty to warn. The consequences of doing nothing outweigh the hassle from the administration. In the event the counselor took no action and some harm came to Sharon, her siblings, or Sharon's mother, the counselor could be held negligent. Rather than refrain from action, the counselor must step forward and take responsibility for the safety of Sharon's family.

After advising the administration of the situation, the counselor should meet with Sharon and her mother. Sharon needs encouragement to talk to her mother without fear. By meeting with Sharon and her mother, the counselor can be the advocate for the family. The counselor can explain to Sharon's mother the resources available for treatment of addictions and encourage the mother to seek help. Help for the family can take place in several ways through groups such as Alcoholics Anonymous. Sharon's mother also can be referred to a local counseling center for family therapy. The school counselor needs to be very clear with Sharon's mother regarding her role as a child advocate. There are possibilities that a meeting with Sharon's mother could be very beneficial or could have a negative outcome. However, the issue of a counselor's duty to warn supersedes in this incident.

Because the principal has already voiced his concerns over becoming involved in Sharon's family problems, the counselor must be firm with the principal and educate him as to the serious nature of addiction in the home. The principal must recognize the counselor's adherence to a code of ethics and the safety issues involved. The teacher can be consulted regarding Sharon's performance in the classroom but should not be expected to be drawn into this family problem, nor should the teen group leader at this point. The high school counselor should be consulted and advised to talk with Margaret to see if she has experienced any difficulties at home. Issues of confidentiality and disclosure must be examined, and permission from Sharon would be appropriate if any other people were to be involved.

Sharon's behavior change from an active, willing participant to a withdrawn quiet child was most likely due to the subject matter being "too close to home." Sharon's helpfulness, cheery attitude, and good grades were perhaps coping mechanisms to deal with her father's addiction of alcohol. The younger brother Mark also displayed acting-out behaviors along with underachievement. Margaret, the older sister, found her place of belonging by being an honor student. Sharon and her siblings' avoidance of discussing their home life indicated something was troubling them. Children such as these need to be encouraged to seek guidance from teachers and counselors.

The hurtful chemical behavior of adults in the lives of children should be discussed openly and in a nonjudgmental tone with children. Students need to learn how a home environment can be affected by addictions. Children should also be educated to call on their peers for help when needed. Just as children need peer support, colleagues within the school setting also need support and assistance. One way to support and assist would be to confront a coworker with concerns regarding addictive behaviors. The counselor can bring in community resources such as Alcoholic's Anonymous, emergency room nurses and physicians, representatives of community mental health centers, and drug treatment facility counselors.

Bringing in speakers and educators from the community can strengthen teen programs such as the one in Sharon's school. Workshops for parents using the same community resources will educate parents regarding substance abuse and, one hopes, encourage parents to have a stake in their child's future.

Unfortunately, Sharon, Mark, and Margaret have an increased likelihood of becoming addicted. Through education and training, they can learn resistance techniques to drug and alcohol abuse, and also learn about the serious nature of being genetically predisposed to alcoholism. During elementary school years, children need to learn the dangers of alcohol abuse and be taught the skills necessary to resist becoming addicted.

Addiction in the home is a serious problem that affects many school-age children. The only safe place some children will have is at school. The school counselor must be a refuge and a safety net for children who may not have another alternative. The school counselor is truly a child advocate and must do what is necessary to protect students from dangers such as addition in the home.

Advocacy: "The Case of the Phony Genius"

CRITICAL INCIDENT

Background

I am a high school counselor. One day I received a term paper from a teacher with a note, "What do you make of this? Do you think the kid is crazy?" The term paper was titled "New Directions in Electronics," and although written in fairly good English, it sounded like a mishmash of physics, psychology, and neurology. I quote one sentence that gives the flavor of the 12-page essay, "Lasar-like emanations occurring from the distal end of the energy tube fluorescence against the rhodium shield and will generate nerve impulse speeds close to the speed of light." The general theme of the paper was that a race of superhumans could be created by shooting rays, call "Z-rays," during what the writer called "the primal science."

I went to see the teacher about the writer. I learned that Herman, who was a high school sophomore, had received the highest grades in two objective tests given in the class. He was, however, as the teacher stated, "a pain" during discussions. He dominated the class, and the flavor of his comments was, like the essay, a mixture of advanced knowledge and speculation, generally irrelevant to what was going on in the class. "We either have a genius or a nut, or maybe both," the teacher told me. "He sure is strange. He always has a tie, sits right up front, is alert, always has his hand up; however I am growing to fear him and his remarks."

I looked up Herman's records and found his grades for the first year followed the most unusual pattern. Of the 12 grades, 5 were A's, 5 were D's, and 2 were F's. On the various objective tests, his uniform score was in the 99th percentile.

My next step was to call Herman for an interview. He was a slight, pale, intense, neatly dressed, and formal child. I soon learned that he had no friends, he did not play games ("they are for children"), he wanted to become an atomic scientist, he wanted to solve the genetic secret of life, and he read college physics for a hobby. He complained about the physics teacher who, he said, belonged in Newton's and not Fermi's era. He informed me he did not care for literature, history, art, music, or physical education but he intended to become a scientist, and that was all he lived for. I listened with an accepting attitude and encouraged him to be well-rounded, pointing out if he wanted to go to college he had to have good grades in all subjects. Herman informed me he had no intention of going to college, and he was only going to high school because of legal requirements. When he finished high school he was going to start a laboratory of his own and support himself by advanced inventions. When he left, I still did not know precisely what the problem was, but I scheduled a home visit with his parents.

The family lived in a fairly prosperous part of town. The father was a successful businessman. The mother was a short, overweight, and nervous woman. With great pride they showed me Herman's laboratory, which looked like something out of a science fiction movie. He had cages of rats, electronic gadgets, and miles of wires, rheostats, capacitors, and half-completed radios. In talking with them, I learned the family had moved to the present town from a large city in another state. And in this city, a citywide intelligence test had been give to all students in the school system from the fourth grade up, and Herman had received the highest score while in the sixth grade. He had been referred in the local paper as a genius, and the newspaper clipping which the parents proudly showed me had the headline "One in a billion, psychologists say." Out of 20,000 school children, Herman had been first by a wide margin on this college entrance intelligence test, his score being in the 99th percentile of college freshman. It became clear that in the bosom of this family was another Einstein, and both parents were dedicated to the nurturing of this genius. Apparently this was not a question of a *folie á trois*, for I learned the whole family—grand-parent, uncles, aunts, and cousins—were all convinced their fami-ly had been marked by fate to bring forth a person of the most superior ability, who was destined to lead mankind to greater glo-ries. Because the parents did not understand what their son was talking about or doing was evidence to them of his consummate superiority. I left the house a bit shaken, not quite knowing which end was up.

I went back to the physics teacher and asked him whether he had come to any conclusion about Herman's ability, and I was told he felt Herman was either a genius or a nut, or probably both. He also informed me that unless Herman calmed down and went along with the rest of the class, he was inclined to flunk him. It appeared that Herman had flatly refused to do the standard experiments called for in this first-semester high school physics course, but he wanted to bring in some of his own equipment and do some nuclear research. The teacher had informed him he either should conform or would flunk. "I have just about had it with him," the physics teacher told me with finality. I told him about my experience with his parents, and the teacher replied: "My God, they're all crazy." He agreed not to do anything until I completed more research.

I brought the whole problem to my supervisor, a clinical psychologist, who looked over the evidence and suggested I see a university physicist and show him Herman's paper. Right on the spot he called up Dr. X and made an appointment, after telling him briefly and in a neutral manner what the problem was. Within minutes I was on my way to the university, and within a half-hour, Dr. X had read the paper.

"Sheer nonsense," was his comment. "this is kid's stuff, putting together unrelated and half-digested concepts with big words. On top of it there is plagiarism." He looked through some journals on a bookshelf, leafed through one of them, and finally said, "Read this paragraph," I read a technical paragraph which did not make much sense, and then Dr. X showed me the same paragraph in Herman's article.

"What he apparently did," said Dr. X, "was to take a number of paragraphs from various sources and assemble them with some filler material. You can tell the student is bright, but this whole essay is just a confused mishmash. I wonder if it is not the same kid I heard about recently who tried to break into a nuclear society meeting a couple of months ago? It seems they had a meeting recently and this boy, a little fellow with glasses, got up and began talking about his theories of the origin of life or something. Sure sounds like him."

I went to my supervisor with this information, and I asked him what I should do. "It looks as though we sure have a sticky situation here, which could develop into a real problem for this boy. From what I gather, he has received a lot of recognition for being a genius through getting a high score on an IQ test. All the members of the family have equated a high IQ with him being a genius, and this poor boy is saddled with an instant reputation which he is trying to live up to. If we try to contradict them, we are just jealous of him. Any teacher who fails him is a fool. This student thinks he is superior to all of us. The situation has to be handled with great tact. I recommend we have a conference with the parents, inviting as many people as possible, including the physics teacher and Professor X, and try to bring them back to reality."

I made the arrangements. About a week later we had a conference that included the parents, the principal, Dr. X, the college professor of physics, the high school physics teacher, the school psychologist, and myself.

Incident

I facilitated the meeting by saying we were all interested in Herman and wanted to be of help. I went over what I had found, Herman's high score on a college level intelligence test, his elementary and high school grade pattern, the opinion of his high school physics teacher, the opinion of Dr. X, and the general agreement that Herman was very bright. We all believed he could contribute considerably if well-handled and had been apparently put on the spot by his parents and relatives by being considered a genius, which was leading him to a completely unrealistic conception of himself.

To my surprise, after making what I thought was a reasonably moderated and accurate summary of the facts, the father accused us all of being jealous of his son, and he informed us he knew we were plotting against the boy and the family, that we were prejudiced against genius, and we were intolerant of those who were superior to us. Both parents were shaking with rage at this "assault" on Herman. The meeting lasted for an hour. When Dr. X read the two paragraphs, one written by Herman about 2 weeks before and one published about a year ago, it had no effect on the parents. In the middle of the session, the father got up, followed by his wife, and left the room. The rest of us were speechless. We all realized that we had failed in our attempt to clarify matters.

Discussion

After Herman's parents left, the principal got up and ran down the hall to stop them. He came back later and informed us they had refused to talk to him, had picked up their son, who had been waiting in the hall, and had driven off. The principal rejoined us, and we all tried to figure out what had happened and what we had done wrong. All we could think of was we had done everything right but that the whole family was crazy. Later I found out Herman's parents had sent him to relatives and he had enrolled in school in another city. I have not followed the case and often wondered what happened to him.

QUESTIONS

1. Did I do anything that might be viewed as inappropriate or unsound? What else could I have done?
2. Is it possible that Herman was a genius, and perhaps he had memorized a paragraph from a technical journal? Were we jealous of him and unable to understand him?
3. How can one handle unrealistic parents, people who just cannot be talked to? Was the conference too threatening?

RESPONSES TO THE INCIDENT

Rudolf Dreikurs

This example clearly shows the bankruptcy of our educational system. Instead of helping the student in trouble, we criticize and condemn him. It is tragic if the school ruins a student with unusual abilities. What is worse is most teachers and counselors, confronted with such a situation, would act in the same manner, without any understanding of the problem. This is the consequence of the inadequate training teachers and counselors receive in many colleges and universities.

Here we have a boy who received the highest scores on tests given in the class, who, in the sixth grade, received the highest score on a citywide intelligence test, who had been first in the college entrance intelligence test scoring (in the sophomore year) at the 99th percentile of college freshman, and who had to be taken out of the school because nobody knew what to do with him. Apparently, no adult dealing with him had the slightest understanding of the situation.

Let us see what happened. In physics he wrote an essay that perplexed the teacher because of its grandiose and unfathomable language. Was he "a genius or a nut?" Throughout this report, this was the only question that seemed to bother everyone. One had to consult with a university physicist to find out that he was not only "putting together unrelated and half-digested concepts with big words" but also plagiarizing. Neither counselor nor supervisor knew what to do about it. They considered it to be "a sticky situation, which could develop into a real problem for this kid." And sure enough, they endeavored to make it a real problem. They found out the whole family treated him like a genius. And instead of helping him, they blamed the parents. Their inability to understand the boy's behavior prevented them, the educators, from coping with him. Let us see how he behaved.

He was a "pain" during discussion, dominated the class, always sat right up front, and always had his hand up. The teacher grew "to fear him and his remarks." Here the trouble started. The teacher could not see how this overambitious youth always had to be first, on top, the center of attention. There is not the slightest indication in this report that the teachers tried to cope with this undue demand for attention and display of intellectual superiority.

There were many other indications that a trained teacher could have recognized as Herman's overambition. "Of the 12 grades, 5 were A's, 5 were D's, and 2 were F's." Instead of recognizing this as the typical pattern of overambitious students—they are either the best or the worst—the teacher called it "the most unusual pattern." Because the boy refused to do the standard experiments, wanting, rather, to do nuclear research, the teacher threatened to flunk him if he would not conform. In other words, the teacher got himself solidly engaged in a power conflict, from which he could not extricate himself. But apparently it made no impression on the counselor when the teacher told him "with finality" that he "just about had it with him." Neither did he recognize the significance that the boy had no friends, that he did not play games ("they are for children," and he was too superior for that), that he wanted to become an atomic scientist and to solve genetic secrets of life, and that he was much too advanced for college. After all this significant information, the counselor states "I still did not know precisely what the problem was." So he contacted the parents, as if they could do anything about it.

Now the fun really started. The counselor brought the problem to the supervisor and to a clinical psychologist, who could do nothing except suggest that a university physicist be consulted. He, of course, verified that the essay was "just a confused mishmash."

Now they contemplated what to do. They realize that Herman "thinks he is superior to all of us" and is making his own world.

But what did they decide to do about it? They came to the conclusion "that we have a conference with the parents, inviting as many people as possible, including the physics teacher and Professor X, and try to bring them back to reality." What was this reality? They all agreed the boy was very bright and could contribute considerably if well handled. Amazing, how close they came to the real problem! But the reality of which the counselor spoke was different. The boy was "put on the spot by his parents and relatives by being considered a genius, which was leading him to a completely unrealistic conception of himself." And on top of it, the counselor expressed surprise that the parents left when the physicist tried to prove to them that their son had plagiarized. Now "the rest of us were just speechless. We all realized that we had failed in our attempt to clarify matters." He continued that "we all tried to figure out what had happened, and what we had done wrong. All we could think of was that we had done everything right, but that the whole family was crazy." Even after their complete failure, none of them realized their own mistakes, and they blamed the trouble on the parents.

Now let us come to the questions:
1. What could the counselor have done? He should have dealt with the real problem of the Herman's overambition, his conviction that he had to be the best, even by deceitful means. Instead, the counselor was concerned with the insignificant question of whether the essay was real or fake. Instead of finding out what the boy was, he should have understood what he was up to, his direction, his movements. Providing Herman with insight into his goals is still the best and most indispensable corrective approach. This can be done in individual consultations but, even better, through group discussions. Herman's problem was his relationship to others, to the world. This was the issue to be concerned with. And this the counselor, psychologist, teacher, and supervisor failed to do.
2. There is no question that Herman was a genius. Telling the parents that he was not was not only an insult but was incorrect. They were right in their contention that all his educators

were unable to understand their son. Instead of helping the parent to "understand the situation" (it is not quite clear what the parents could have learned to understand), the educators needed to understand the boy and to know what could be done with him.

3. As long as one blames the parents, one cannot expect any cooperation from them. This is particularly true when one considers them unrealistic; but it was the educators who were unrealistic. The boy was a genius and the parents knew it; only the educators failed to see it. The use the boy made of his superior intelligence is a different matter. This was the problem to which the educators should have addressed themselves. Their failure to cope with it and change it led to the traumatic experience for the boy from which he may never, or at least not for a long time, recover. The school has missed its chance to save a child and thereby deprives society of the contribution of a genius who, instead, moved even further toward antisocial attitudes.

Allen E. Ivey

Confrontation may be defined as the meeting between people holding opposing viewpoints in a struggle for power. In a typical confrontation, no one listens to the other and only one point of view can prevail. This might be contrasted with communication, which is an exchange of views, often a friendly exchange, but with no effort at behavior change or accommodation. It is represented by what happens in the sensitivity training, or "T" group. Encounter is confrontation with communication where both parties recognize the need for a decision, listen respectfully to one another, and then mutually arrive at a resolution.

Unfortunately, confrontation was the model chosen by the counselor in this case. One cannot question his observations and conclusions; he did a fine job identifying many facts about Herman and his parents. Few people, however, enjoy being labeled. The counselor and the many professionals he consulted had built a good case. Only one dimension was missing: an understanding of what

Herman and his family were trying to accomplish. Were they listened to? What happened in other school settings? The counselor, his supervisor, and fellow participants apparently never bothered to do the lengthy, time-consuming detail work of discovering the depth and nature of the family, what types of experiences they provided, or what type of learning they felt should be provided for their son. This is the type of work that should be done by the counselor over a period of time. It does little good to confront someone with true facts if satisfactory alternative routes are not presented carefully. The counselor in this case appeared to be concerned primarily with his objective data and seemed little concerned with Herman as a person.

One cannot help but wonder why the counselor did not talk with the high school physics teacher who demanded that Herman "conform" even though he far outranked his classmates on all objective tests. The counselor, for example, could have visited the class and advised the teacher how to work more effectively with Herman. Possibly Herman should have been working as a teacher-aide instead of taking the course. It seems sad that some teachers have trouble accepting the fact that inevitably they will work with students brighter than themselves.

In this type of case, the teacher has an opportunity to show what true excellence in teaching is, helping the student reach beyond the teacher. A skilled counselor-consultant could have been of real value to the teacher and the student in this situation. The counselor may even use this situation to help the teacher grow and gain new skills in communicating with bright students.

In addition, the counselor should want to know why Herman received D's and F's. Were they for nonconformity or for lack of performance? One of the most dehumanizing aspects of the schools today is the time-honored curriculum that demands conforming participation in a series of often irrelevant experiences and then fails to reward actual learning and performance. From this frame of reference, the school, as well as the parents, may be equally responsible for Herman's difficulties. This case clearly illustrates, again, the importance of the counselor working within the school system to change it and make it more responsive to human needs.

It is possible, of course, that Herman was a genius. More important, however, was that he was a bright and promising human being. By placing undue emphasis on his intelligence and the possible incident of plagiarism, the counselor reinforced the emphasis on Herman's intellectualism. If the counselor had dealt, instead, with Herman's humanity and his feeling of frustration with a school and family unable and unwilling to understand him, a common basis for encounter between Herman and the counselor might have occurred.

In summary, difficult situations such as this cannot be resolved through objective data and threatening parent–school conferences. Rather, a depth-encounter approach is called for that demands a real commitment of time and skill from the counselor. Some may object to the approach suggested here, saying that the counselor does not have enough time in his busy schedule to spend this amount of time with one individual. However, the time spent with the physics teacher may help that teacher assist future students more positively, thus preventing some future referrals to the counselor. Through working with the parents and helping them learn to work with the school, the counselor himself will learn new skills that will enable him to work more effectively with other parents, his colleagues, and the school. It is suggested that by applying himself more fully in this case, the counselor may, in the long run, be saving time for himself and for his students.

It is recognized that the encounter or "listening with action" approach suggested here may not be successful. No counselor ever can marshal enough subjective and objective information so that his or her decision is always right. The counselor in this case did, in fact, do many things well.

He is to be complimented for a sincere, but incomplete, effort. One must tune in to all aspects of a complex situation such as this, evaluate one's actions, and then move forward to use these data more effectively in encounter with new situations.

Bullying: "Help, I Don't Know Where Else to Turn"

CRITICAL INCIDENT

Background

This public junior high school (Grades 6, 7, and 8) serves students diverse in ethnicity and socioeconomic status. Teacher salaries in this district are low compared with other districts in the area, and recruitment and retention of strong teachers is an issue. The school administration is supportive of a comprehensive developmental school counseling program.

As the only school counselor in a school of 700 students, my ability to work with each student individually is limited. As such, most of my direct service to students is through group counseling and classroom guidance lessons. A limited amount of time is available for individual counseling and consultation with teachers and parents to address emotional and behavioral problems of students.

Over the past 6 months, there has been some racial tension in the school. Two groups of students—one African American group and one White group—have loosely organized. In staff meetings, the term "gang" has been mentioned in reference to these groups. Other staff assert that it is simply a formation of cliques, not uncommon for students at this developmental level. As one preventive strategy, I prepared and delivered a series of classrooms guidance activities on appreciation of diversity. Although this was well received overall, some of the students who were participating in the various "gangs" appeared to be less receptive to this information.

Incident

Just after lunch on a Wednesday, I heard of an incident that had occurred behind the gym. As the story was related to me, two White students had enticed John, an African American student of small stature, outside of the gym. There, a group of White students (perhaps as many as 12 students) were waiting and beat John up badly. John was taken to the hospital, as it was suspected that he had suffered broken ribs and possibly a broken nose. In addition, his mouth was badly bloodied and his eyes were swollen almost shut. At the point in which the incident was related to me, the principal and the assistant principal were handling the situation and I had not been called in to consult.

Later in the day, Kevin, a student who was currently participating in a "Children of Divorce" group asked to see me individually. We seemed to have built a strong rapport, so I thought it strange that he was so anxious as he began talking. He related the following: "I don't know if I should tell or not, but somebody's got to do something. If you tell I told, I'll get hurt ... this could get bad."

I asked Kevin to take a deep breath and relax for a bit before continuing. After doing so, his story was clear: "The boy who got beat up today. That was just the start. You think that these gangs are harmless, but they're getting ready to go off. They almost got into it at the mall this weekend, but the police came and broke it up. Word is there is gonna be a war after lunch Friday out behind the gym. Some of the Black kids are saying they ain't gonna wait 'til Friday if they can get one of us alone." After reflecting in a few moments of silence, I gently asked, "Kevin, how do you know all of this?"

He looked away from me before answering haltingly, "I was there today ... I thought they were just talking big. When they got John outside, they just started kicking him and beating him." Kevin began to get agitated and tears welled up in his eyes. "When I saw it was really happening, I just ran off. That's how come I didn't get caught. You gotta do something."

Discussion

After helping Kevin to calm down, I informed him that while I would have to tell others about what he had told me, I believed that I would not have to identify him as the source of the information. Although he was torn between knowing that people needed to be informed and fearing for his own safety, he agreed that I should "get help."

QUESTIONS

1. How and with whom should I consult about what Kevin has told me?
2. Am I justified in breaking the confidentiality of my counseling relationship with Kevin? If so, is it appropriate to withhold the source of the information? Relatedly, what should I do if administrators "push" for the source of the information?
3. Should my decision making about handling this issue be influenced by the fact that Kevin participated in the planning aspect of the assault, fleeing only when the first punches were thrown?
4. Was informed consent obtained? What might have been done differently regarding informed consent?
5. What types of actions are needed in the school to prevent more violence from occurring?

RESPONSES TO THE INCIDENT
Walter Roberts

The concept of duty to warn and the sacredness of protecting client confidences have, in many ways, been turned on their heads as a direct result of the nature and increasing severity of school violence within the past 5 years. The school counselor is faced with making a professional judgment call when in receipt of information pertaining to potential for harm to self or others: Is the information credible? In instances wherein the answer to the question is yes, the professional school counselor is required to act. State statutes typically require human service professionals of all disciplines to break client confidence in such cases.

Ethical canons are clear when confidences must be broken or consultations made that the information shared with third parties should be as factual as possible, providing only the details necessary for the implementation of a successful intervention while at the same time doing everything humanly possible to shield the release of minutiae that would make specific identification of the individual likely. In schools, particularly smaller ones, this is often an impossibility. Students make it their business to know everything about everybody else's business. Often the most minimal release of details related to a particular incident or person is enough to distinguish the individual in question.

A clear duty to warn exists in this instance. The information released by Kevin certainly seems credible. One terribly violent assault—and let's call it what it is—has occurred. Kevin's demeanor, presentation style, and depth of information about the increasingly tense atmosphere in the school environment can in no way be dismissed. To fail to act in the face of this level of a believable disclosure would be negligence.

Who should be consulted? Good question. The first priority in a duty-to-warn situation is to safeguard the individual threatened with harm. But in this situation, just who is that person? No one single individual was indicated as a designated target. The implication is that violent activity is planned between two specific groups and that random single individuals might be targeted if the opportunity exists. An additional factor must be addressed. Large-scale violence between groups in a school setting has the potential to escalate into an uncontrollable situation. Innocent bystanders may be and often are victimized—possibly directly and, most certainly, vicariously— in the chaos surrounding violent incidents. The potential exists in this instance for an extremely dangerous event if what Kevin has shared with his school counselor is true.

Cross-validation of the information Kevin has revealed to the school counselor is in order, and the school counselor is most likely the best individual in the school setting to be able to meet individually—*individually!*—with other students known to be associated with the recent behaviors under discussion. The school counselor should calmly inquire (as school counselors can do so well without inflaming or making informed sources overly defensive) of those students known to be associated with the groups in question as to their knowledge of any future violence that may be planned on campus, what rumors are floating around among the student body, exactly who might be targeted for such violence, while at the same time placing urgent emphasis on the fact that such behaviors are both against school rules and, most likely, subject to prosecution in court. My guess is that the school counselor will get the information necessary to make the professional judgment that, indeed, Kevin's information is accurate. Unless specific targets or locations are identified during the school counselor's cross-validation, the information gained through the process should remain confidential.

Certainly, chief school administrators within the school must be alerted that generic information has surfaced about planned potential violent acts occurring on school grounds and the exact location (if known) of the intended behaviors. Likewise, all school staff should be notified as to the generic information that is known, but that is the function of the school administration, not the school counselor. Doubtlessly, the administration knows the identities of some of the students involved in the pending mayhem as a result of the beating meted out to John. That list serves as a good reference point for school staff to begin a more measured inquiry as to who knows what about the rumors at hand.

It must be stressed: Information shared in duty-to-warn situations must still maintain as much of the vestiges of client confidentiality and privacy as can be preserved. School counselors must be able to walk a fine line and avoid saying too much during consultations with third parties, which includes both school staff and students, even in predicaments of potential for harm to self or others.

As previously discussed, enough credible information exists in this instance to warrant consultation with third parties over an issue of potential for harm to others. In the best of all worlds, informed consent from the student should follow the disclosure. However, the potential for harm to other students in the school setting and the believability of the source of information far outweighs the obligation to maintain the client's confidence in this scenario.

What becomes more complicated for professional school counselors is how to share confidential information and still protect as much of the client's confidences and privacy as possible, particularly with school administration whose views of the school environment may be skewed more toward discipline and order. The school counselor in this case could proceed to share what he knows in the following manner.

• • •

Professional School Counselor (PSC): "Look, don't ask me for what I can't tell you, okay? You know I wouldn't be down here if it wasn't important in light of everything's that's happened today."

Chief School Administrator (CSA): "Yes?"

PSC: "Well, here's the deal. Rumor has it that the fight with John has been brewing for a long time. Apparently, we have two groups of students in school who have started to gang up and go after one another both in and out of school. There was an incident last weekend at the mall in which a fight almost happened, but the police broke it up. I called the police and checked on that. It's true. What happened to John is linked to both that incident and the ganging activity we've been seeing recently."

CSA: "Are you saying this is a legitimate gang-related incident?"

PSC: "At this stage, I don't know what to call it. It may be, but it might also be just normal cliques getting out of hand. We can figure that out later. There's a bigger problem for us right now. The buzz is that this Friday behind the gym there's a fight planned between these two groups. However, it may not wait until then and we may have some attacks directed at students at random by these kids if the opportunity presents itself. And it may be a racial thing between these two groups. That we will have to figure out as we go along. The bottom line is, I think the story's legit, I think the staff needs to be alerted as soon as possible so that we can increase supervision—but without pushing any panic buttons—and I think we have also got to somehow figure out a way to calm the student body as soon as possible. This thing could get out of control quickly if we don't act proactively."

CSA: "And your source of information for all of this is?"

PSC: "Sorry. You know how we do this. Don't ask me, okay?"

CSA: "But I need to know. Did you get this from an individual student? I've got parents and the police breathing down my neck to get this thing solved."

PSC: "Look. Trust me on this one, will you, like you've always trusted my judgment in the past. I believe the information is accurate, I've checked out enough of the story to see if the pieces fit— they do—and, besides, if you squeeze me about the source of information you may place that individual—or those individuals— at risk for being attacked. Just work with me on this, will you?"

CSA: "You know I don't like it when you do this to me."

PSC: "I know, but you also know me well enough to know that I'm going to do everything I can to work with everybody so that we all walk away winners."

CSA: "So what am I supposed to do now?"

PSC: "Do you have a list of names of the boys who attacked John today?"

CSA: "Some. Not all. He couldn't identify all of them."

PSC: "Well, you might start with the names you have, call them in again, and ask them what they know about a fight planned for this Friday behind the gym. Ask them what's been brewing the last few weeks around town. See what kind of reaction you get. I'm sure you'll get more information and names before the afternoon's over. Then make sure the staff knows about the rumors so that we can tighten the supervision the rest of this week and the next until we get a handle on things. I'll be willing to get into all the classrooms as fast as I can and talk about respect, diversity, and remind everyone about our violence prevention initiatives. Sounds like a good time for a reminder."

CSA: "You could make my life a whole lot easier if you'd just give me a name to start with."

PSC: "I've seen you work your magic before. I think you'll get to the bottom of things sooner than you think. If I run across anything else that I can share, I'll let you know."

• • •

Breaking the confidence does not necessarily mean identifying the source. It is possible to share need-to-know information obtained confidentially in a duty-to-warn situation while maintaining client identity. Disclose only what is necessary and do so only when there is no choice. However, let's be clear. Certain situations may demand full disclosure of all information and identity in certain cases of high-risk harm to self or others.

The school counselor's primary concern is to the welfare of the client. The immediate decision-making factor involved in the fact that Kevin was an on-scene participant in John's beating is just that—knowledge that Kevin was there, was a witness to what happened, and left the scene when he discovered that the talk and bravado were more than just talk and bravado. Kevin is, in his own way, a victim of the day's events, and his victimization is just beginning. No other judgment should be attached to Kevin's behavior in those early moments of intervention. There will be plenty of time to explore with Kevin the meaning of his participation in the assault and his responsibilities with regard to reporting his involvement in the days and weeks to come.

The school counselor's relationship with Kevin is important. It is obvious that Kevin sees the school counselor as a person to turn to in his time of trouble. Kevin is scared. He is afraid of being punished by school authorities and the police for his participation in the events leading up to John's beating. Likewise, he is probably afraid of receiving the same kind of punishment that John received earlier in the day from members of his own group if they were to discover that he had "narced" on them. Most likely, Kevin understands the ramifications of the day's events extremely well. He did, after all, run away from the scene of the assault once it began and did report to the school counselor information about future planned violence. As far as we know at this point, none of the others involved in the beating did so.

The school counselor must assure Kevin that he did the right thing by coming forward with his concerns. The school counselor acted responsibly by informing Kevin that he would have to inform others, presumably school authorities, about the information Kevin shared related to the potential for further school violence. What is unclear is whether the school counselor explored with Kevin the full progression of what might happen to him from this point forward as the school moved ahead with its investigation of the assault on John. Kevin needs to understand that, at some point in the future, he will have to explain himself to school authorities, that his actions will undoubtedly be revealed as the investigation continues, and that there will be consequences attached to his presence at the beating—all the more reason for both the client and the school counselor to fully understand the importance of informed consent on the remediation process.

It is clear that the school counselor informed Kevin of his obligation as a school official to report some of the information just shared. Contained in the school counselor's notification to Kevin of his need to disclose information was the implied promise that efforts would be made to keep his identity in confidence.

What is not certain here is whether it was explained in full to Kevin what also might happen—that it might not be possible to keep his identity a secret—and if the school counselor explored the depth of Kevin's comprehension about what might proceed from this point forward. It is not enough to "tell" clients about the limitations to confidentiality and their right to privacy. Good faith

efforts must be made to ascertain whether the client actually understands what informed consent is all about. For instance:

•••

PSC: "Kevin, you know this is one of those subjects we've talked
about before in our divorce group. This has to go 'outside the
room.' It's bigger than the two of us because it's about information
which, if something's not said to the principal and teachers, some
other people might get hurt later today or tomorrow or next week,
just like what happened to John today."

Kevin: "I know."

PSC: "Help me out with this, will you? Would you give me permission to talk to the principal about some of what you told me? I
will do everything I can to protect your identity by only giving him
the basic information, but I can't guarantee that he won't figure it
out in the long run. At some point in the future, anyway, we've got
to work on a plan for you to accept your responsibility for what
happened to John today, but that can wait for now. I'm more concerned about preventing other students from getting hurt in the
immediate future."

Kevin: "You can tell the principal some of this, but I'm afraid about
what's going to happen to me."

PSC: "Me, too, both for you and for the rest of our students. That's
why we have to work together to try and make this situation better as quickly as possible."

Kevin: "What are you going to do now with what I've said?"

PSC: "Let me know what you think I've said about talking with
the principal."

Kevin: "You'll tell him just the stuff about what's been happening
the last few weeks and about the fight planned this Friday."

PSC: "Should I tell him who's involved?"

Kevin: "No. He's going to know who did it anyway. John
told him."

PSC: "Okay. So you don't want me to mention names, but

you don't mind if I talk about location and the rumors about future attacks."

Kevin: "Yes."

PSC: "Do you know if anyone in particular is going to be attacked soon?"

Kevin: "No, but then I didn't think anything was going to happen to John. He just happened to be in the wrong place at the wrong time."

PSC: "And what did we say about what might also happen when I go to see the principal?"

Kevin: "He might find out everything."

PSC: "Yes, he might figure things out about who told me this information even if I do my best to keep it confidential. And you know we're going to have to eventually deal with your involvement in today's events, anyway, right?"

Kevin: "Yes."

PSC: "Alright. Are you ready for me to do my part?"

Kevin: "I know you have to do something."

PSC: "I'll do my best and I'll check back with you before the day's out about how it went and how you're doing. You come and see me, too, if you need to before the day's out, okay?"

Kevin: "Okay."

• • •

Unless there is evidence of client comprehension, which is best expressed in the client's own words, an argument must be made that informed consent was not successful.

Students in school settings should be given informed-consent opportunities from the get-go. Explanations about confidentiality, privacy, limitations on both, and basics about mandated reporting procedures and responsibilities of the professional school counselors should be printed in both the student and parent handbooks. Typically, schools send such handbooks home and require parental signature acknowledging receipt and review of the materials. Additional informed-consent opportunities arise during individual and group counseling sessions with students. Some school counselors have resorted to printing and posting such information on the walls outside and inside their offices as yet another source of disclosure to students. However, it is imperative to remember this: Informed consent must be based in language most likely understood by the clientele for which it is intended. Elementary school children need elementary language, and secondary school students need age-appropriate language for secondary students. Cultural considerations regarding language as well must be taken into account if true communication about informed consent is to be most effective.

Violence in American society is ubiquitous. Children and adolescents are exposed to it through everyday news coverage, recreational video media, and themes in popular music, television, and movies. Violence is often portrayed as the most efficient method to get what one wants. And kids do not only learn about violence vicariously. All too often they experience firsthand verbal and physical abuse in the home or neighborhood.

Children and adolescents have absorbed the American culture of violence into their everyday lives. One of the most frequent manifestations of this exposure to such destructiveness is through bullying, teasing, and other outwardly aggressive behaviors. Underlying the mechanics of such conduct is simple: "The use of overwhelming power toward those less powerful gets me what I want. If I can get it through verbal or intimidating mannerisms, then I do it. If I am able to use physical strength to overwhelm my target, then I will hit until I get what I am after. If carrying or using a weapon increases my power, then I am likely to get more from those on whom I prey."

Counteracting student perceptions about the usefulness of aggressive behaviors must begin early in a child's school life and permeate the entire K–12 school environment. The message within the school community must be clear: Violent and aggressive behaviors are not acceptable here, and those who violate this rule will be held accountable for their actions. The school counselor in this scenario has been a part of the school's overall efforts to increase appreciation for diversity in his classroom guidance lessons throughout the year.

In the immediate aftermath of the attack on John, the severity of the attack, and the scuttlebutt about future similar acts occurring, the school has no choice but to respond vigorously and promptly. The problem is schoolwide. All students are at risk because of the nature of the threats. Whether the behavior was perpetrated under the aegis of a true gang or a porous and poorly defined clique of gang "wannabes" makes little difference at this moment. The bottom line is that a group of bullies, some more connected to the act than others, violently attacked a student and inflicted serious injury as the result of the assault. The attack was premeditated and involved multiple students. The possibility exists of repeat occurrences. This is clearly a situation warranting a full school staff response.

The professional school counselor can play a major role in helping decrease the tensions associated following such incidences. Besides immediate responses in such ways as conferencing with the students involved and their parents (always make that link to parents whenever possible because they must be included as a part of the solution), long-range efforts include increased classroom guidance presence and delivery of lessons on a wide variety of topics: respect and tolerance for diversity, deescalation of violent situations, and ways to avoid bullying and intimidation ("bully proofing" one's school). The formation of conflict mediation groups under the guidance of the school counselor would be another potential form of long-range intervention.

Lawrence E. Tyson

In this scenario, the counselor has an ethical and perhaps legal duty to warn. The question is, to whom? I believe, in this case, the counselor should immediately share his information with the appropriate administrative personnel within the school. Information such as this, within the context given, should not be kept confidential. The counselor in this case is in no position to affect specific change because the consequences of the previous violent act may indeed affect the entire student body, faculty, parents, and community. There is no indication that the counselor is adept at mediation or conflict management skills, has a background in multicultural sensitivity training, or has other "expertise" in similar areas other than providing classroom guidance activities relating to cultural awareness and appreciation. It would be appropriate for the counselor to play a part in whatever "plan" the administrative team devised, as he does have a rapport with many of the students and seems to be considered approachable.

In this case, the counselor is justified in breaking confidentiality with Kevin. In many states, school counselors are not "bound" by a legal definition of confidentiality. In fact, the term *confidentiality* has many definitions with many interpretations. Confidentiality is an ethical term that implies a guideline or framework from which to act in a particular situation. The counselor in this case should not let a guideline dictate what he should or should not do. The code of ethics from which the counselor is operating is a format from which to make a "best practice" decision.

Another issue that comes to mind, especially in school settings, is "Whom am I responsible to?" It is necessary for the school counselor to "come to terms" with who these people are: students, parents, faculty, administrators, school board members, and/or the superintendent. Functioning within an ethical framework, the counselor may operate on a need-to-know basis with these different factions. However, the counselor is in a precarious position when determining who these might be. Before making such a decision, the counselor could confidentially consult with other counselors whom he holds in high professional esteem. Another issue is the professional relationship the counselor has with his principal. It is hoped that the principal views this counselor as a key professional within his or her administrative staff. This could make all the difference in how information is relayed while protecting students whose names might not need to be revealed.

Another issue that needs to be examined is the counselor's ability to think rationally and not emotionally. The situation described in the incident is potentially chaotic and dangerous for all members of this school and the community. The counselor needs to remember to think and act in a calm, clear, and professional manner. The decision by the counselor in terms of how to handle the situation should not be influenced by Kevin's actions. The potential is great for individuals to react and act in highly emotional states. The counselor will serve his students, teachers, parents, and administrators best if he has the ability to think and act in a calm manner.

Informed consent in school settings is usually obtained through the many school mailings that are sent home to parents. Students and parents should always be informed, before counseling occurs, what counseling means, what can be expected of services, the client's responsibility, the counselor's responsibility, confidentiality, duty to warn, and so on. This should also be stated in appropriate counseling brochures obtained in the guidance office. Many school counselors provide parents information regarding their counseling programs at initial "open houses" or parent–teacher association meetings that are held on a regular basis. Sometimes information such as this is also sent home the first few days of school through the student.

An obvious action is the development of conflict management curriculum within the various disciplines. Also, a peer mediation program would seem to be a significant contribution and would provide immediate results in terms of resolving immediate conflicts. Another idea would be to start holding parent meetings in the community. Parents can and should be contributors in their children's education, and they should be involved in planning activities to reduce violent acts in their neighborhood and school. Ways in which school personnel may become more visible should be explored. Also, plans for integrating students in activities, both in and after school, should be investigated.

Classism:
"I Never Wanted to
Come Here Anyway"

CRITICAL INCIDENT

Background

After graduate school, I promptly found a job in the local school system with which I was fairly familiar. I was fortunate the school that hired me as school counselor was one of the best in the city. My first full year was eventful and very challenging. The next year was one of change. To distribute more of the city's educational resources, the school system decided to redistrict all the schools in the system. Our school, once a bastion of the elite upper class, would receive students from a lower socioeconomic status (SES) area. There were not many new students who would be making the transfer from that area, but the repercussions of that transfer would eventually be felt.

A transfer student who was assigned to my caseload was Matt. He was 16 years old and would be an incoming junior. His transcripts showed him to be a fair but unmotivated student. My initial thought was that it would be unlikely he would be able to sustain average grades at this school because he was coming from a more disadvantaged one. As a courtesy, the discipline files of students now attending our school had been sent by the student's previous school. Matt's records showed that he had been reprimanded on a couple of occasions, but nothing particularly troubling or serious. All in all, he appeared to be an average teenager. However, life in the first month at his new school was different. His grades did suffer. After only a month, Matt had been involved in a fight with a couple of upperclassmen who had been at the school for a number of years.

Prior to this incident, I had learned that an argument had occurred a week earlier involving Matt and one of the same upperclassman he had been in confrontation with. As a result of the fight, both students were suspended. Before leaving that day, they were instructed to come speak to me. The upperclassman reiterated to me he had nothing to do with starting the fight. When I talked to Matt about the incident, he was unresponsive and answered tersely when he did speak. I asked Matt how he thought school was going, and he responded indifferently. He gave the same answer when I asked him how he was adjusting to life at this school. He seemed unconcerned when I spoke of his sliding grades. Matt left my office having given me little information to work with. I could not decide if he was preoccupied with other thoughts or if he was really as ambivalent toward the recent events as he seemed.

Incident

Both boys returned from suspension 3 days later. Much to my surprise, Matt stopped by my office to talk. He apparently been involved in another fight because he had a cut on his lip and was walking with a slight limp. He would not discuss exactly what had happened, but he did tell me of some things that had transpired during his first month in school. He said that he and some of his friends had been repeatedly harassed by some boys whom he referred to as the "rich guys." He said they constantly taunted him and his friends, using names like "scum" and "poor boys," and frequently told them there was no room for them at their school. He seemed much more comfortable speaking to me now.

At the end of the discussion, though, he made a remark that disturbed me. I had asked him if he would tell the principal the same things he had told me, and he responded, "That won't help. I can take care of myself. There won't be anymore troubles." I felt that in such a context and by the tone of his voice, I had no choice but to take that as a threat. I recommended that Matt's locker and belongings be searched. Matt was escorted from class and the search was conducted. In his bag, they found a small buck knife. Matt insisted that he used that bag for hunting and that he had not realized he left the knife in there. Regardless of his explanations, Matt was suspended again and referred for expulsion according to the school board policy pertaining to a weapons violation. Before being picked up by his father, Matt, in an angry and disappointed voice, told me he never regretted anything more than trusting me and, because of that, I had ruined his life.

Discussion

Matt was eventually granted a transfer to another school but dropped out after only a week. In the months to come, Matt's friends and upperclassmen were involved in yet more altercations. Punishments were handed down, of course. Before the school year had ended, two of Matt's friends had followed his path and dropped out.

QUESTIONS

1. Everyone has to adjust to new environments. Were the events that transpired here predictable? If so, should I have done more to alter these predictable events?

2. Although Matt was guilty of breaking school policy, was it proper to speculate as to his intentions and take action? Colleagues have suggested that I acted in a biased manner by jumping the gun and assuming that Matt was a risk.
3. Could some form of group session between the conflicting parties been of some help after the initial confrontations?
4. What could have been done, if anything, to facilitate a smoother transition for the new students from their old school to the new one?

RESPONSES TO THE INCIDENT

Emily Phillips

Rather than take the questions in order, I believe that addressing the later questions will help illuminate the answer of whether the events were predictable. To me, assumptions made both by the school and the counselor added to the predicament.

Assumptions Before Matt's Arrival

It appears to me that an assumption was made by this counselor that Matt would not be able to get adequate grades in the new school. This assumption was based on written data that were narrow in focus (transcript) and the counselor's belief that Matt's apparent lack of motivation would follow him to the new school. Is the counselor saying that the school is too "elite" for those who get passing grades? Is there no room in this school for a "fair" student? What does "fair" mean? Must everyone get "A's" to be acceptable?

There are many factors that may have affected Matt's grades and motivation that can only be assessed through discussion with the student in order to understand his world view. For example, maybe he appeared unmotivated because receiving good grades was not prized in his peer group or social network. Perhaps his parents were pleased that he was passing everything and getting a high school diploma. Perhaps this family had so many social problems going on that paying attention to Matt's academic successes was a low priority as long as no one was failing and there were no complaints from the school. Finally, perhaps the grades Matt is receiving are better than anyone in his family has ever received and they are pleased. Obviously, there are many cultural lenses through which to view his grades and, without this level of exploration, the counselor is left with assumptions only.

Assumptions Regarding the Counseling Relationship

This counselor did nothing to establish a counseling relationship with Matt. The first time the counselor talked with Matt was following a fight, immediately before being picked up for his suspension—not a good time to try and establish positive rapport. The counselor stated that Matt appeared indifferent about his grades and that this attitude was accepted by the counselor. Is this counselor assuming that education is not a priority to Matt just because an adolescent speaks to an adult from a voice of indifference, especially when he is waiting to be picked up by a parent on a disciplinary action? Is there any reason for Matt to trust this counselor?

Assumptions During the Process of the Incident

This counselor asks if bias was involved in assuming risk or in how the teens were treated. There is a bigger issue here, I believe, that includes possible bias on the part of the entire school. On the broader level, the school itself may have fostered class bias. This counselor was familiar with the school district and believed it to be "one of the best." A school that can be described as a "bastion" (fortress, protected?) for the elite may create an elitist attitude toward any who are "them." The counselor commented that the new "lower socioeconomic status" students were few in number (a minority).

The two teens involved in the fight cannot get along. A 3-day suspension from school to brew over it and to put distance between them does nothing to help form bonds between them. One way to think about the "punishment" for the altercation would be to think about how an opportunity could have been provided to get these students to know one another in a nonthreatening way (e.g., a joint tutoring project, a bulletin board). I suspect much of what happened occurred from ignorance, faulty beliefs, and lack of adult modeling for getting along with others who are different. This is for both boys.

In an attempt to assess bias, one important issue for the counselor would be to look at the differential treatment of the boys who teased and taunted and Matt who stated he could "take care of himself." He made no obvious threat. Matt was humiliated by being escorted from class and having his locker searched and then expelled for having a knife (was this weapons policy written and shared with the transfers like Matt?). If he felt that the principal could not or would not help, then there is a schoolwide image that does not include zero tolerance for aggression, whether it be verbal or physical. Although Matt's locker was searched and a knife found (whether by accident or for self-preservation), the boys who were verbally abusive were not equally treated with action.

Assumptions Regarding Cross-Cultural Encounters

One important question for this school to ask itself is did it regard this new mixture of students as one of cross-cultural encounter? Was this happening predictable? From my view, the answer is yes, and obviously these situations, left unattended, continued until Matt and his friends were driven out.

Regardless of the level of students (elementary, middle, or secondary) or the areas of difference (special education integration, sexual orientation, SES, gender, etc.), efforts that are explicit, comprehensive, and sensitive will help students learn to accept, and perhaps even appreciate, those who are different from themselves. This school may have pretended there would be no problems with this new change or may have unintentionally hoped the new lower SES students would not feel welcome and go away so as not to "ruin" the fortress created. They did nothing to prepare the current students for the change, to help the new students understand the system into which they were entering, or to establish positive contact, supervised by adults who model acceptance, tolerance, and understanding, before the actual start date. This cannot be handled by the school counselor alone but must be addressed by the entire school.

Subtle biases are painful issues for any district to address. It involves staff discussions regarding attitudinal stances and assumptions, as well as tremendous amounts of work developing an equitable and concrete plan for both prevention and intervention.

In summary, Matt was treated as an individual, isolated case of classism when, in fact, this system appeared set up to reinforce isolation and dissension through the lack of addressing classism as a cultural factor.

Amanda Costin

My first impression is that the counselor had a preconceived notion that Matt could not succeed in this new school. The counselor, prior to knowing Matt, characterized him as a "fair but unmotivated student" by looking at his transcripts alone. Characterizing Matt as unmotivated before meeting him is what I would consider somewhat unprofessional. Perhaps he was a hard worker who received fair grades. Similarly, the counselor anticipated that Matt would be unable to sustain average grades at this elite upper-class school before meeting him or evaluating the situation after one semester's grading period. It is clear that the counselor had already decided that Matt probably would not make it in the school. I am guessing that other staff members had similar preconceived notions. Furthermore, the fights and verbal downgrades toward Matt and his friends were predictable events. If staff members were threatened by the impact that lower SES students would have on them and their school, one can easily predict that the elite students of that school would not welcome peers from a lower SES area. It should have come as no surprise to this counselor that upper-class adolescents often times look down on their peers from lower SES groups.

So yes, the events that transpired in this scenario were predictable. First, staff members could have been trained to deal with their own concerns and fears. Second, staff members needed to be prepared for and alerted to likely tension between the two groups of students. Third, a counselor could have been assigned exclusively to these new students and could have met with them weekly to establish a relationship. Fourth, a peer mediator program could have been established with extensive training prior to the arrival of the new student population. Fifth, new students could have been paired with peer helpers or other student leaders in the school to answer questions and provide support. Sixth, a no-tolerance policy for this type of behavior should have been established and carried out by the administration from Day 1.

Although Matt was guilty of breaking school policy, was it proper to speculate as to his intentions and take action? "Colleagues have suggested that I acted in a biased manner by jumping the gun and assuming that Matt was a risk." I feel as if the counselor jumped the gun by requesting a search of Matt and his locker. Matt shared with the counselor that the rich guys were harassing him. The counselor was correct in asking if Matt would talk to the principal; however, the counselor should have expected his hesitancy. Obviously, Matt had no reason to believe that the principal would do anything to support him. It was the counselor's job to ask Matt why he did not feel comfortable bringing this information to the principal. Furthermore, the counselor should have asked Matt what he meant by, "That won't help. I can take care of myself." While building a relationship with Matt, the counselor likely would have been able to learn about Matt's fears in the school and his belief that he was on his own in this environment. It is likely that the school staff had seen Matt and his friends being harassed by the upper-class students and that nothing had been done to stop the behavior.

I do agree that having a knife in school should be dealt with in the most severe manner. However, in this case, finding the knife was just one example of the school's prophecy regarding Matt. I get the impression that the school never wanted Matt in the school and finding a knife was just one example of staff and students saying, "See, look what this type of student does to our exclusive and safe environment." I am fairly confident if Matt was not made to feel insignificant in the first place and was embraced by some staff members initially, he would have continued as an average student in his new school.

Could some form of group session between the conflicting parties been of some help after the initial confrontations? Yes, group meetings after the initial confrontation could have been helpful in making sure future confrontations were not likely to occur. After the first fight, the principal should have met with Matt and the other parties involved to find out what was going on. Again, a no-tolerance policy for this type of behavior needed to be enforced. The counselor, after meeting with Matt and the other student, could have predicted that the rich student would claim no wrong-doing and Matt would be reluctant to talk. Rather than accepting these responses, the counselor could have delved deeper into what was really going on between the two parties. The counselor should have sensed that the underlying issue was that of classism as well as a lack of understanding and acceptance. Knowing this, the counselor could have worked with the two groups as a facili-tator to help them understand their similarities and differences. If the initial incidents were followed up with group discussions facil-itated by a counselor, I feel quite confident that Matt would still be in school. Furthermore, the boys' parents should have been involved in working with their children.

What could have been done, if anything, to facilitate a smoother transition for the new students from their old school to the new one? First, student and staff diversity and conflict mediation train-ing could have been initiated from Day 1. Second, as mentioned earlier, peer and staff advocates could have been paired with new students to help them learn about their new school and act as a contact person if concerns arose. Third, along with student redis-tricting, staff from Matt's previous high school could have been redistricted so that familiar adults were in the new environment. Fourth, more than a handful of new students should have been relocated to the new school. Matt's counselor should have met with him on a weekly basis to develop a trusting working relationship.

It is obvious to me that Matt felt isolated in this school and had little to no support from the staff or students. In closing, I feel relatively confident that the primary reason that Matt and his friends ended up dropping out of school is that they were not welcomed there from the beginning and were treated as less than their peers who had originally gone to the school. It sad-dens me that in this case, the counselor did not advocate for Matt and that the counselor's self-fulfilling prophecies for Matt were met.

Matt, a seemingly average teenager prior to entering this new school, was expelled and then dropped out of school. Somewhere along the line the system failed for Matt. Lack of support from those in his new surroundings along with being made to feel unwelcome laid the groundwork for Matt's demise. By finding a knife in Matt's bag, the school system administrators, teachers, and counselors were able to shift the blame for Matt's failures away from themselves and their own elitism and onto him and his lower socioeconomic background. The counselor did not fulfill his or her role, which was to support Matt, build a relationship with him, find out what was keeping him down in the new school, and help him succeed academically and socially.

Confidentiality:
"I Know What's Best"

CRITICAL INCIDENT

Background

Tara is a 16-year-old sophomore student who has recently transferred into the school. As part of my role as school counselor, I interviewed her when she arrived at the school. The purpose of the interview was to get to know her and to orient her to the school. Tara's parents have separated and she is living with her mother, who resides within the school district. Tara indicated that she really did not want to live with her mother but had no other choice.

Tara was pleasant during the interview and volunteered any information that was relevant to the school orientation. She felt that she had been academically successful in her former school and was maintaining an average in the high 70s. She expressed interest in popular music and art. We developed a good rapport, and I would often stop and talk to her in the halls when we would meet. She appeared to fit into the life of the school and make friends easily. She appeared to have made a successful transition to her new school environment.

About 3 months later, I was in the main school office to discuss some things with the secretary. Tara came in carrying a large suitcase and looking stressed. I asked her if she was spending the weekend at a friend's place. She angrily responded that she was never going back home again. She had a big fight with her mother, who was concerned with the late hours that Tara was keeping. As a result, her mother had imposed a curfew on her. Tara was not going to live with her again if she had to have a curfew. I asked her if she wanted to talk further about this, and she responded by saying there was nothing to talk about. After all, she was 16 and she had the right to make her own rules. She said emphatically that she did not want to talk about this issue and that she could handle it on her own.

She was quite loud during this tirade against her mother. I asked if she had a place to spend the night, and she said she hoped to spend the night with one of her friends. At lunch time during that day, I asked her if she had a place to stay for the weekend and she told me she had. Because I knew the mother of Tara's friend, I took the liberty to call and confirm that Tara was staying there. I was concerned that she may be on the street for the night, and I wanted to help her find shelter.

Incident

About a year later, Tara came to my office. She looked very pale and tired and wanted to know if she could lie down on the health room bed for the rest of the school day. I asked her how long she had been feeling this way. She indicated that she had been tired for the past 2 weeks. I asked her if she knew of anything that might explain her feelings. She did not respond, so I assumed she may have had the flu. I thought I should probe further so I asked her about mononucleosis. She indicated that she had not been to see her doctor. I opened the door to the health room and fixed the blankets on the bed. During this time, she indicated that she had not had a period for 2 months. I asked her if she thought she was pregnant and she nodded. I asked her if she had told her mother, and she instantly said I was not to say anything especially to her mother. She did not want anyone to know if she was pregnant. I asked if she had been eating a balanced diet. She indicated that her diet mostly consisted of Pepsi, chips, and occasionally a burger. She did not like milk and was not taking any vitamins.

I indicated that I felt obligated to inform her mother of the possibility of pregnancy and that this sharing of information would be best for her in the long term. Instantly, she became very angry with me and shouted something about my breaking confidentiality. She was now 17 and could look after herself. It was none of my business and she did not want it discussed any further. Again she reiterated that she did not want her mother to know of her possible pregnancy. I attempted to tell her the limits of confidentiality but she would not listen. She called me several names and immediately left the room, slamming the door as she left.

Discussion

I decided I had to call her mother, which I did. However, I did not discuss the possibility of pregnancy but indicated that Tara was looking pale and was experiencing tiredness. I suggested that she be taken to her doctor and be checked possibly for mononucleosis. I was hoping that if Tara was pregnant, the doctor would detect it. Tara's mother came to the school that afternoon and took her to see the doctor. The doctor confirmed she had mononucleosis and was not pregnant.

QUESTIONS

1. Should I have broken confidentiality with Tara by informing her mother of her symptoms? She was 17 at this time and had the legal right to deal with her medical needs without her mother's knowledge.

2. Should I have been up front with Tara's mother and told her that Tara had not menstruated for 2 months and that she may be pregnant?

3. In terms of looking after a client's welfare, should I be more concerned about Tara's long-term needs that may necessitate overlooking the immediate wishes of the client? If Tara was pregnant, she would be much more healthy if she acknowledged her pregnancy and adjusted her diet to reflect her nutritional needs. Or should I have respected Tara's ethical right to confidentiality? In this incident Tara did not want to discuss her condition any further and did not indicate that she would see me again.

4. Should I have suggested that Tara see her doctor and let it at that?

5. Should I have informed the school principal of the possibility of Tara's pregnancy and let him deal with it instead of contacting Tara's mother myself? It was school policy that the principal be informed of all student pregnancies so that suitable schooling arrangements could be made during the last trimester of the pregnancy.

RESPONSES TO THE INCIDENT

Craig S. Cashwell

There are a number of legal, ethical, therapeutic, and policy issues that interweave to make this a difficult and challenging incident with which to deal. The "easiest" response would be to confront the school counselor about the failure to establish informed consent regarding confidentiality prior to the disclosure by the student. Apparently, confidentiality and the limits therein were not understood by Tara. However, the therapeutic relationship between the counselor and client appears to have been informal, primarily involving brief conversations in the hall. Because a more formal counseling relationship has not been established, it is hard to fault the school counselor for failing to establish informed consent before the disclosure of the possible pregnancy. The counselor attempted to tell Tara about the limits of confidentiality after the disclosure, but as we might expect, attempting to establish informed consent after the disclosure was not well received by Tara.

One issue around disclosure to the mother is whether this is clearly in Tara's best interest. Although information is limited, it appears that Tara did not want to live with her mother after her parents separated, and she has left home on at least one occasion. Also, it seems that the mother has failed to notice physical symptoms (i.e., looking pale and tired) that the counselor noticed immediately. From this, our "best guess" is that the relationship between Tara and her mother may be strained. In addition, no information is given about any contact or relationship between the school counselor and Tara's mother. Thus, at the point at which disclosure was made, there was no foundation on which to believe that Tara's mother would serve as an advocate for Tara if she had indeed been pregnant.

Regardless of the correctness or incorrectness of the decision, the school counselor appears to move quickly into the issue of disclosing to the mother. That is, the school counselor moves into the legal and ethical issues of disclosure without fully exploring the therapeutic issues involved in this situation. It may well be that Tara was "crying" out for help by disclosing that she had not had a period for 2 months, thus hinting to the counselor of a possible pregnancy. Process-oriented questions such as "What do you plan to do now?" or "I sense that you have told me this for a reason. How can I help you?" may be useful to collect additional information from the student. From this, it is possible that there are more solutions than simply disclosing to the mother. For example, Tara may choose to go to see a doctor on her own.

Because Tara was not pregnant, the incident seems to have been resolved. However, there is one major aspect of the incident that likely is unresolved—that of the therapeutic relationship between the counselor and Tara. It is unlikely that Tara will trust this counselor with other personal situations when they arise. Furthermore, Tara may associate this incident with counseling in general and refuse to seek help from any professional helper in the future. Thus, the potential damage from the decisions of this counselor may be far-reaching.

Also, it seems inappropriate to notify the school principal at this point in time. The school policy is geared toward providing adequate alternative arrangements for students in the last trimester of their pregnancy. Even if Tara were pregnant, she would be in the early stages of pregnancy and would not need accommodations for many months.

After consulting with appropriate professionals, I likely would have spent more time discussing the therapeutic issues with Tara. Ultimately, it may have been necessary to give Tara a choice to either pursue medical attention on her own or disclose her condition to her mother herself. Only if Tara were unwilling to do either of these would I consider breaking confidentiality and disclosing to her mother. Allowing more time to discuss the situation with Tara and communicating a higher level of empathy for her situation may have facilitated a more positive resolution of this incident.

Carolyn Stone

This critical incident characterizes one of the most difficult ethical dilemmas that school counselors face: multiple obligations that extend beyond guarding a minor's confidentiality. Ethically, school counselors must provide a confidential, safe environment for their minor clients while simultaneously adhering to school board policy, protecting the legal rights of parents to provide guidance to their children (especially in such important issues as pregnancy), consulting with administration when there is a legitimate need to consult or inform, and guarding against a breach in duty to warn and the resultant possible charges of negligence. Laws, policy, ethics regarding pregnancy, and abortion counseling are often open to interpretation, leaving school counselors to wrestle with each case in context. As this critical incident demonstrates, the complex ethical principle of informed consent, which is dependent on the competency of the client and the determination of clear and imminent danger and duty to warn, is complicated with minor clients.

Complicating Factors

Parental rights and responsibilities to minor clients. Confidentiality of minor clients is often the most difficult ethical dilemma facing school counselors, as this scenario illustrates (Isaacs & Stone, 1998). This school counselor is confronted with the challenge of balancing Tara's right to confidentiality with the legitimate right of her mother to be involved in guiding Tara in life-altering decisions. The primacy of confidentiality, clear in the code of ethics and standards of practice for the American Counseling Association (ACA; ACA 1995 Ethical Standards, Section B: Confidentiality B.1) and the American School Counselor Association (ASCA; ASCA 1992 Ethical Standards for School Counselors, A: Responsibilities to Students and B: Responsibilities to Parents), instructs this school counselor to protect Tara's privacy while simultaneously complying with all laws and policies pertaining to confidentiality. Both ACA and ASCA suggest collaboration with Tara's mother, representing the endeavor to establish a cooperative relationship with parents to facilitate the maximum development of the counselee (American School Counselor Association, 1992, p. 2).

Duty to warn. This critical incident outlines one of the most difficult, yet all too common critical incidents faced by high school and middle school counselors: a pregnant teen who legally has the right to handle her medical needs regarding pregnancy. However, ethically, and in most states, legally, school counselors need to discern if pregnancy and abortion constitute a duty-to-warn situation. It is difficult for school counselors to determine when a minor client is mature enough to handle a potentially dangerous situation. The chronological age of this student is a primary consideration, as courts may give a 14-year-old immature minor's status allowing limited self-governance. More importantly, and harder for this school counselor to discern, is Tara's developmental age and the possible impact of disclosure on the relationship and further therapeutic progress. Will Tara flee, effectively eliminating anyone's chance of helping her, or will informing her mother help Tara develop a stronger relationship with her?

Counselor's values. What constitutes duty to warn and extreme circumstances will be the decision of this counselor in the context of the situation and will likely be influenced by the counselor's religious and personal values. Different courses of action are taken in similar situations involving minor's right to confidentiality, especially with highly charged issues such as teenage pregnancy or prenatal care. In Davis and Mickelson's (1994) survey of school counselors, ethical dilemmas that involve issues of student-client privacy, confidentiality, and parents' rights received less than 50% agreement regarding the preferred ethical or correct legal choices. This counselor can guard against imposing his or her personal values on Tara, but no counselor leaves their values at the schoolhouse door.

Informed consent. School board policy and community standards may necessitate breaking confidentiality. In the case of this critical incident, this school counselor's professional code binds her ethically to respect the policy of the school board employing her and the principal supervising her. Even when the administrative policies and rules are clear, counselors often experience ambivalence and difficulty following them when the policies and rules conflict with the confidentiality of their minor clients. Informed consent requires client competence to understand the limits of the confidentiality regarding school board policy, duty-to-warn issues, and parental rights. This counselor knew a medical problem was at issue and before probing further should have exercised informed consent, taking care to assess this student's mental state and its effect on preventing her from fully understanding or exercising informed consent. Ideally, the counselor should have obtained informed consent a year prior to this incident and reiterated it before delving into this sensitive area. Early in the exchange, the warning signs were clear that this was potentially a duty-to-warn situation.

Empowering the student. At 16 years of age, Tara should be given the opportunity to explore and problem solve the various courses of action with this counselor. The crux of this counseling situation should be on empowering Tara to make good choices, not on whether to inform the parent. Wrestling with the issues of confirming pregnancy, prenatal care, and the necessity to have support in the months ahead, especially parental support, should have been the focus of counseling sessions, instead of a brief exchange in the health room. Empowering students like Tara to make her own decisions furthers the moral obligation of school counselors to enhance the client's autonomy and the ethical obligation to protect the client's confidentiality. Immediately going to a 16-year-old's parents without first talking to the student is confusing the moral principle of nonmaleficence as protection for the school counselor rather than nonmaleficence in its true meaning, that is, above all do no harm to your client. School counselors often find that the solution in these difficult situations is to help bring the student to the decision to allow the counselor to set up a three-way conference with the parent in which the school counselor is present to lend support and information. Given Tara's history of difficulty with her mother, this may not have been the result but should be the first course of action with a 16-year-old. Counselors find that students are often relieved when parents are informed in this manner, and parents often react more reasonably. If counseling and informational sessions fail to convince Tara to involve her mother or to make responsible decisions regarding her health, then this counselor must make a determination as to whether this is a legal duty-to-warn situation as there is not an expressly written in school board policy guiding counselor behavior in this situation. The school policy in this incident deals with pregnancy only in regards to ensuring suitable schooling for a student in her third trimester of pregnancy. It is unclear as to when the principal should be informed of a student's pregnancy, but it appears unlikely that a suspected pregnancy must be reported. Therefore, this counselor is not hampered, or depending on this counselor's personal point of view, helped by this school policy. In the absence of an expressly written policy, this counselor would not have to inform Tara's mother unless clear and imminent danger is suspected, and the state in which this incident occurs has clear standards regarding duty to warn. However, in every state this counselor must be prepared to give competent advice or refer the student to an outside agency to prevent liability for any damages.

Consultation. Another salient issue when dealing with difficult ethical decisions is consultation with another competent professional as a basic standard-of-care principle. This situation obviously poses many ethical questions for this counselor, who should therefore not make decisions regarding this case in isolation. Consultation is in the best interest of clients and ought to be considered, especially in the unlikely event that charges of negligence be brought against the counselor. The critical question of professional consultation will be asked and, as has been the case in many negligence suits, is a critical deciding factor.

REFERENCES

American Counseling Association (1995). *Code of ethics and standards of practice.* Alexandria, VA: Author.

American School Counselor Association. (1992). *Ethical standards for school counselors.* Alexandria, VA: Author.

Davis, J., & Mickelson, D. J. (1994). School counselors: Are you aware of ethical and legal aspects of counseling? *The School Counselor,* 42, 5–12.

Isaacs, M., & Stone, C. (1998). *School counselors and confidentiality: Factors that mitigate professional choices.* Unpublished manuscript.

Consulting:
"I Know This Subject"

CRITICAL INCIDENT

Background

Bonnie is a new school counselor and is completing her first year at the local high school. She is eager to continue her learning by taking additional courses, attending conferences, and participating in local workshops. Bonnie has an interest in working with adolescents and concentrating on adolescent suicide or attempted suicides. She believes that addressing this topic will assist her as she continues dealing with the suicide of her brother.

While attending a workshop at a college, another counselor overheard Bonnie discuss her interest in adolescent suicide with another colleague. The counselor asked Bonnie if she would be interested in providing an in-service on adolescent suicide for her school district. The counselor stated her system could pay Bonnie $200 for her presentation. Bonnie accepted the invitation but did not request a contract from the district. Bonnie researched the topic; purchased kits, books, and brochures; and prepared the material for the workshop. She also collected handouts from the local Suicide Prevention Center. She developed a list of resources and references that will be used for the workshop. She quickly selected materials that were 4 to 10 years old. One reference was taken from a publication within the past 5 years.

A flyer from the Tarrant City Independent School District was sent to Bonnie that announced Bonnie, a school counselor in the Jackson City School system and an expert in adolescent suicide, would present a 3-hour workshop on the topic of adolescent suicide.

Incident

Bonnie arrived at the Tarrant City School Board for her presentation and was introduced to the participants as an expert in adolescent suicide. She presented an outline of the workshop and objectives for the participants. Being conscientious, she had prepared the material in a coherent manner and had attractive overheads and charts for use in the presentation. Early in the 3-hour presentation, individuals asked questions that Bonnie could not answer. However, Bonnie stated she would find the answers and provide them to the school district. As questions continued that Bonnie could not answer, it became evident that Bonnie was not as well educated on the topic as the term "expert" suggests. To deal with the conflict, she decided to divide the participants into groups. However, she was not prepared to conduct group activities and, at the last minute, provided assignments that were vague and somewhat confusing to the participants. Bonnie became visibly agitated when questioned about the assignments. She became so upset she concluded the presentation early, not allowing for discussion, and left the building.

Discussion

Several weeks passed, and Bonnie noted that she had not received the $200 check from the school district. She called and inquired about the check and was told that the check would not be paid because she did not complete the workshop. Bonnie stated she had an agreement with the professional development chair from the school system to present a workshop. The agreement did not list a time limit, and Bonnie had purchased materials that were used at the workshop. Bonnie believed she did abide by the oral agreement.

QUESTIONS

1. What part did Bonnie "play" in being called an expert in the field of adolescent suicide?
2. What constitutes "an expert"?
3. Whose responsibility was it to determine that Bonnie was an expert?
4. Was the oral agreement binding and to what degree?
5. What, if any obligation, did Bonnie have to complete the 3-hour workshop?
6. Because it was evident Bonnie had done research, purchased materials, and prepared a presentation, what obligations did the school district have to her?
7. What alternatives could Bonnie have taken to remedy the situation from the beginning?
8. How did Bonnie's brother's suicide complicate the situation?
9. What ethical issues does this incident address?

RESPONSES TO THE INCIDENT

Christopher Skinner

Bonnie should not be held responsible for the brochure that identified her as "an expert." However, because the brochure was clearly misleading, Bonnie should have made reasonable attempts to correct this misleading advertisement and she should described her limited training and experience in adolescent suicide and indicated that she was not an expert before beginning the workshop. Bonnie had several options. She should have contacted the school district and demanded that they send a notice or another brochure that (a) acknowledged their previous error and (b) provided accurate information regarding Bonnie's qualifications. In addition, Bonnie could send a copy of her curriculum vitae that accurately described her professional qualifications to the school district and demand that it be distributed to the school and made accessible to possible trainees. Finally, Bonnie should begin her workshop by providing clear, accurate information regarding her qualifications before she began covering the material. While Bonnie may not be responsible for the brochure, she was responsible to make reasonable attempts to correct the misleading advertisement once she became aware of it. If the school district would not comply with her request, she should have declined to conduct the workshop and recommended another presenter (consultant).

Within the legal system, witnesses are sometimes called to testify and a judicial process (e.g., opposing side can question their qualifications) is used to determine if the person is qualified to testify on a specific issue. An additional safeguard is in place as opposing sides can call their own "experts" as witnesses. There is no corollary system of checks and balances outside the legal system. Therefore, it is best to avoid using the term "expert" altogether because it is vague and can be misleading. Instead, individuals should provide information about their training and experience that is clear, specific, and verifiable. For example, someone might report that they have a PhD in counselor education and have worked 5 years as a crisis intervention counselor. They could also indicate specific coursework taken on a topic, workshops attended, and refereed publications and presentations related to the topic area. The goal here is to provide enough clear and precise information so that consumers can judge for themselves whether the person is qualified.

Although the contract should have been in writing, oral contracts can be binding. Whether written or oral, consultation contracts for workshops should contain the following: (a) general goals of the workshop; (b) timeframe for service delivery; (c) consultant responsibilities, including services to be provided, methods to be used (e.g., 1-hour lecture, then 30-minute film, then 1-hour breakout groups, and 30 minutes for debriefing, discussion, and evaluation); (d) agency responsibilities, including fees, expenses (e.g., travel), and materials to be provided (e.g., overhead projector); and (e) an agency contact person who is responsible for bringing in workshop attenders, payment dispersion, supplying materials, and so on. In this case, it is not clear if there is an agreement on what specific services would be provided (workshop is rather vague), for how long (was 3 hours agreed upon?), and whether the counselor had the authority to commit the school district to the contract. Regardless, I believe that Bonnie has an oral contract, but because the contract was vague and oral it could prove difficult to enforce legally. Bonnie also had an obligation to finish the workshop, and the district had an obligation to pay Bonnie. A clear written contract with all the necessary elements could have prevented many of these difficulties.

There are many times when one should not engage in consultation. One of the most obvious times is when one is not qualified to provide the services requested. Bonnie is not qualified because she lacks extensive formal training and supervision in adolescent suicide. Her brother's suicide may further exacerbate mistakes she is likely to make owing to her lack of formal training in this area. To make matters even worse, Bonnie is presenting on an area, adolescent suicide, in which poor training can lead to disastrous outcomes.

This is an interesting vignette because it addresses implementing services beyond one's scope of training, misleading the public (although Bonnie had an obligation to correct this misinformation), personal issues interfering with work-related duties, and contract issues. Although Bonnie may not have received extensive formal training and supervised experience in adolescent suicide, her formal training should have been sufficient to inform her that she should never have entered into this agreement. For these reasons, it is essential that counselors who engage in consultation receive adequate and extensive training in consultation theory and practice, including legal and ethical issues related to consultation.

Furthermore, as this case illustrates, all counselors must be aware of their own professional limitations because failure to do so damages not only their own professional reputation but also the reputation of their fellow counselors.

Jim Whitledge

Consultation is a considered a legitimate function of the role that school counselors play in helping teachers, parents, administrators, and other school-related personnel improve their effectiveness in working with others. Improving the efficiency and effectiveness of student learning is the main outcome that is desired in the schools. Consultation is considered part of a comprehensive guidance and counseling program and is one of the responsibilities for school counselors that the American School Counselor Association (ASCA) includes in its role statement (American School Counselor Association, 1990). In addition, ASCA lists consultation as one of the competency areas in which school counselors should demonstrate skills. In the scenario involving Bonnie, there are certain conditions that must be met in order for effective, ethical consultation to be implemented.

There is an immediate concern in regard to the part that Bonnie took in being called an "expert" in the field of adolescent suicide. Although Bonnie did not initiate the concept of her being considered an expert, she did accept Tarrant City School promoting her as an expert by doing nothing to refute the claim when she became aware of the promotional brochure and when she was introduced at the beginning of the workshop.

An expert is generally perceived as someone who is well advanced in the field; someone who has extensive knowledge, experience, and skill; and someone who is proficient and expected to provide answers on the topic under consideration. By doing nothing, Bonnie allowed others to think that the description of "expert" applied to her in the area of adolescent suicide.

Both Bonnie and the school district have a responsibility for accurately discerning Bonnie's qualifications and experience to conduct the workshop, as well as how the workshop will be accurately promoted. This information should have been determined when initial discussions began in connection with Bonnie conducting the workshop.

Whether the oral agreement was at all binding presents a legal question that is best answered through interpretation of law as part of the justice system. It seems expected, appropriate, and legally binding, however, to have a written contract signed by Bonnie and a person in authority for the Tarrant City School District, based on negotiations between the two parties. A written contract would provide protection for the interests of both parties and describe how much would be paid for specific services delivered.

On the basis of Bonnie's integrity in relation to this scenario, one could argue that she did have an obligation to complete the 3-hour workshop. Even though there was no written contract, the 3-hour obligation could be viewed as implied through promotional material about which Bonnie was aware. At some point, she was probably told about the 3-hour timeframe so she would know how to plan for the workshop. Because there was nothing in writing, the district could have assumed that the $200 fee included Bonnie's research, preparation, and purchased materials.

As implied above, all of the misunderstandings about fees, time limits, obligations, and inaccurate representation of Bonnie's qualifications could have been avoided by adherence to honest negotiations, a written contract, and consideration of ethical guidelines. Bonnie would have had a better idea of exactly what was expected. She certainly should not have presented herself as an expert in an area that was outside the scope of her training, education, and experience as a professional school counselor.

Bonnie's brother's suicide, tragic as it was, could have clouded her decision-making capacities in terms of agreeing to present a workshop and be promoted as an expert on adolescent suicide. Her original interest in the topic was based on her desire to address the topic of adolescent suicide, for it to be a learning experience that will enable her to deal with unresolved issues that she has in connection with her brother's death.

Although there are legal concerns in connection with the lack of binding written contract, there are also ethical issues to address.

Section E.1.c. of ASCA's Ethical Standards for School Counselors indicates that the school counselor "Strives through personal initiative to maintain professional competence and to keep abreast of professional information" (American School Counselor Association, 1992). Bonnie's desire to continue learning through coursework, conferences, and local workshops is admirable and consistent with this section.

There is conflict in the scenario involving the ethical guidelines, however, where Sections E.1.a. and E.1.b. are concerned. These two sections imply that the professional school counselor functions within the scope of their professional competence. Bonnie has a responsibility to not participate in any activity that may lead to inadequate services that might harm a client. In delivering a workshop on a topic in which she does not have the training, education, and experience, she creates a potentially harmful situation to students who may receive service from the workshop participants in the future. The American Counseling Association (ACA) Code of Ethics also supports this premise in Section C.2.a, which focuses on counselors practicing only within the boundaries of their competence, based on education, training, professional and supervised experience, and credentials (American Counseling Association, 1995).

In addition, the ACA Code of Ethics in Section A.10.a. and b. references fees in connection with counseling services. Counselors have a responsibility before entering into the counseling relationship to explain to clients all of the financial arrangements related to professional services. The implication is that in this case, Bonnie is the counselor who is entering into a consulting relationship with the Tarrant City Independent School District. As a counselor, her consultation is a function of what she does in that role and implies the same informed-consent obligation.

There is another ethical issue that may be of concern in this scenario. It is not clear as to when the workshop is being offered in terms of it being a time when Bonnie has an obligation to her counseling job in her school district. There is a question of her ethical responsibility if she is supposed to be working in her school and, if so, what policies are in place that provide approval for her to consult in another school district.

Consulting can certainly be a worthwhile service that school counselors can provide to others to develop a more effective, efficient learning environment for students. As with any function of the school counselor, however, consulting should be delivered with strong adherence to both ethical and legal guidelines.

REFERENCES

American Counseling Association. (1995). *Code of ethics and standards of practice.* Alexandria, VA: Author.

American School Counselor Association. (1990, July). ASCA role statement. *The School Counselor* [Online]. Available: http://www.school-counselor.org/General Info/role.html [1999. July 17].

American School Counselor Association. (1992). *Ethical standards for school counselors.* Alexandria, VA: Author.

Disabilities:
"Fallen Through the Cracks"

CRITICAL INCIDENT

Background

The school district described is in a mid-sized midwestern city that is dominated by a large state university. The district has a good reputation in the state and prides itself on its ability to meet the needs of all students. The student in question, Michael, appeared in the counselor's office at the end of the ninth grade. He is a 15-year-old White male. His grade point average (GPA) was 2.2 at the end of the first semester of his freshman year.

A history of Michael's experiences in school is necessary to understand the context in which the incident occurred. Michael had worked hard throughout the elementary grades but was only moderately successful. He completed his homework on time but did not seem interested or able to put much creative effort into it. While interacting well with his classmates and teachers, he reported a lack of interest and motivation in the classroom. He consistently read one grade below the expected level consistently throughout elementary school and had poor writing skills. Michael received passing grades and, because he did not present behavior problems in the classroom, received little attention from teachers or specialists. His reading skills did not improve as he progressed through elementary school, and his writing continued to be immature for his age.

When Michael entered middle school, his parents became more concerned because he was becoming known as the class clown. In addition, Michael was not completing his assignments and was not utilizing his independent study time to his benefit. His homework was completed but was sloppily done. His three teachers were each approached by his parents, who felt there was something wrong with their son's ability to learn and process information. The teachers, however, uniformly stated they felt the drop in academic skills and his antics in the classroom were typical of a middle school boy who is trying to figure out how to fit in with his peers.

By the end of middle school, Michael was still receiving low grades (GPA was 2.1) but not low enough to attract the attention of the special education staff. Also, his reading and writing skills did not appear to improve with maturity. His parents continued to be concerned but were rebuffed whenever they brought up the possibility that their son had learning disabilities even though he was passing his classes.

Michael fell further behind and started skipping a few classes, upon entering the large high school of 2,000 students. Once again, Michael just seemed to be falling through the cracks. Again, he continued to pass and seemed well adjusted, so he did not receive much attention from student services personnel or from his teachers. His parents, however, decided to have Michael evaluated by a specialist outside of the school district. The specialist found that Michael had a learning disability that prevented him from processing information in an efficient manner. The disability had a direct impact on his reading and writing skills. Michael's parents did finally get the school to agree to schedule him with the reading specialist despite the fact that he was not classified as a special education student.

Incident

Michael was taking a science course required of all freshmen that was very difficult for him. He was in a classroom with a teacher who, according to informal reports from the principal's office, attended more to the needs of the gifted students in the class rather than those who were having academic difficulties. The teacher seemed to have difficulty interacting with boys and tended to deal with them more harshly. Several complaints had been filed by parents but no action had been taken. Because the teacher had not been supportive the entire year, Michael went to several friends for help with his final class project. Upon learning this, the teacher became very angry and publicly accused Michael of cheating, copying from other students, and being a failure in his class. Michael was humiliated, frustrated, and incredibly angry, and he left school immediately. He refused to return to what he described as a very hostile environment. Michael did, however, agree to meet with the school counselor, who agreed to mediate the situation.

Both Michael and his parents felt they had received little support from the school. His parents were also reluctant to put Michael back into a situation that might lead to more humiliation, and they demanded a remedy. They were disturbed by the teacher's treatment of their son, but, more importantly, they wanted services for Michael that would help him meet the academic demands of high school.

Discussion

Even though his grades indicated Michael would not qualify as a special education student, he did have particular learning needs that are included in the 1990 Americans With Disabilities Act, Section 504. His parents were not sure what this legislation meant, but they knew they needed help in interpreting those regulations and then applying them to Michael's specific needs.

QUESTIONS

1. How could the incident with the science teacher be remedied so Michael would pass the class?
2. What did the 1990 American With Disabilities Act, Section 504, have to offer Michael?
3. How had Michael's learning needs fallen through the cracks for so many years?
4. How many other students were in the same situation and needed support before an explosive situation occurred?
5. What could be done systematically in the school to make teachers, staff, and administrators more aware of the support issues of those students, who might have learning disability and need help in succeeding?
6. How could the elementary, middle, and high school work more effectively with parents who have concerns about their son's or daughter's success in school?

RESPONSES TO THE INCIDENT

Marilyn Brookwood

Michael's story reveals a profile typical of the realm of "shadow disability," that is, the presenting problems are easily and frequently mistaken for developmental issues and consequently do not send a critical signal to the professional. The expectation is that the student will catch up as his or her developmental process moves forward, and, in fact, that does happen in many cases. The shadow darkening Michael's performance was one to which a counselor would need to have been sensitized through training or experience. The model for what should have happened could start in elementary school or middle school. Counseling staff, along with consulting learning specialists and, most importantly, the classroom teacher need to always question the small failures in growth as well as the larger, more demanding ones. These difficulties, especially

Michael's written expressive language weakness as evident in his poor writing skills, his mild difficulty in written receptive language noted in his reading one grade below, and especially his failure to improve in middle school, suggest that a screening be done to explore what might have been inhibiting his growth into better performance. The demands of more clear-cut cases, or the desensitization of working with these problems over many years while not really understanding them, may account for such lapses.

When Michael's performance slipped further in middle school, the educational staff seems to have made an assumption along a stereotypical, familiar bias that middle school boys tend to be notably immature. At this point, the parents apparently shared with educational staff their concerns about the possibility of a learning disability. Many educators in middle school and beyond think about learning disability as something that is examined in elementary years and, if it is not found early, it is not there. This risks insufficient attention to the increased cognitive processing demands school presents in middle school and then, again, in high school, which contributed to the problem Michael had in science.

Acting as concerned advocates for their son, Michael's parents' efforts to get some attention for him extended to seeking a private evaluation when he was in ninth grade. While Michael was found to have a learning disability, for reasons that are not clear, he was not presented to the appropriate committee for development of an individual educational plan. A counseling intervention here would have been to inform teachers, confidentially, that this boy was struggling because of specific learning issues; to meet with the parents to focus on what interventions the school could provide, including ancillary services in reading and language skills; and to write a 504 accommodation plan in accordance with the Rehabilitation Act of 1973 if that seemed appropriate. Michael would have benefited from counseling service to examine his learning style and how it influenced his life in school and at home. The failure of these interventions to occur did not lead to the incident but would have provided support for Michael in his crisis.

The incident is a realistic portrayal of something that should never happen, no matter what, and that happens only rarely. The

humiliations to which students are subjected are usually more subtle and frequently involve sarcasm used in the name of "humor" or
"for your own good." It was healthy, perhaps even healing, for
Michael to have raised the level of the school's concern by refusing
to return to the situation with this tormentor (the science teacher).
The counselor is trusted enough to mediate the situation. She will
need to join with Michael in his humiliation and anger, but she will
also need to signal that the school is now able to listen and respond
to the family's concerns about Michael's learning.

There is a paradox in this critical incident that raises a complex
issue of the balance between the school's and the parents' responsibility. For many years, this family sensed something amiss in their
child's learning, repeatedly suggesting to the school that this was
the case. While it is clear the school underresponded to the family,
it is also suggested here that the family was inconsistent in its pur-
suit of a remedy. Finally, the identified patient, Michael, raised
enough concern, but only when he was in high school, when he
was older and more mature. Did the attitude of the school personnel cause the parents' efforts at getting a remedy to be incomplete
or did the not-too-sure, not-too-demanding style of the parents
cause the school personnel not to take them seriously? And what
do parents have to do to raise the ante enough to be taken seriously? Also, the outside specialist had an opportunity to advise the
family how to proceed with the school, but if that happened, it
does not seem the parents changed their behavior.

Tommie Radd

I would like to start this response with the addition and answer of
another question. How could a K–12 developmental guidance and
counseling program support the student and prevent this incident? I
agree with the points made by the first respondent. In addition, I
have found that K–12 developmental guidance systems in the school
can do much to prevent incidents such as this. The social, emotional, academic, and behavior activity experiences taught by the counselor through developmental guidance provide the skills needed for
Michael to communicate concerns. The classroom teacher, with the

support of the school counselor, follows through on the skills taught so that Michael and the other students understand the skill and practice it. These skills become a part of student life skills.

A positive behavior plan that includes class meetings and a democratic environment would provide Michael and others with a safe environment to explain frustrations. Skills learned in the guidance activities would be practiced during the day-to-day activities of the class. An opportunity for ongoing communication and care could be established. Michael would not need to experience little support in elementary school, escalating to "clowning around" in middle school and moving to exploding in high school. Self-talk and self-pictures could be taught in this process. Michael and the other students could learn to use their thoughts and perceptions of self to support learning.

The developmental guidance activities would include this important information beginning in kindergarten and continue throughout Michael's school years. These activities are taught by the counselor and integrated into the classroom and school by the teacher and other professionals. Because Michael is in such a large high school, organizations such as "a school within a school" or extended "family homeroom classrooms" are important considerations. Throughout all of this, Michael's awareness of self and his ability to communicate his needs would have clarified that his behaviors, such as lack of motivation and interest, were not the result of behavior but a learning disability.

After learning concerns were identified by Michael and his family, the counselor would have already known Michael from visits to the classroom. An individual counseling session would have provided a way to gain a clear picture of what Michael was "living" daily. The counselor could become an advocate to help Michael through small-group counseling, a referral to the school psychologist for a complete assessment, peer support with collaboration and cooperative learning opportunities, tutoring, family suggestions for the home and in the community, and additional academic help from the teacher.

Michael's parents entrusted their son to the school because the staff are professional educators. When they asked for help for

Michael but were informed that Michael was fine, they believed the school. If we, as part of the school system, want the confidence of our public, we need to take the extra time needed to provide students like Michael with every opportunity to succeed. His academic pattern needed to be assessed after his parents called this problem to the attention of the teachers. The school counselor could have become involved at this point. A family history could have been taken to determine if learning difficulties were a pattern in the family. We know that each student will have different challenges. As professionals, we have a responsibility to integrate guidance and counseling into the heart of the school. All students deserve support, including students like Michael who "fall through the cracks."

It is a sad day for public education when a family goes outside of the school to assess their child after 9 years of being told that his is fine. Equally sad is the fact that Michael needed to "blow up" because of unfair treatment from his teacher to get the attention of the staff and to involve the counselor. Michael's incident is an example of how professionals can blame students for difficulties that develop but not assume their responsibility as a part of the problem. There had been numerous complaints about the student–teacher relationships in this class, yet the teacher was permitted to continue teaching in a way that greatly contributed to this problem. Michael was cited as the problem when the student–teacher relationship was one of the main contributors. Through mediation, it is my hope that suggestions can be made to assist the teacher in understanding what role the teacher plays in such incidents. All staff members need support with professional and personal growth plans that require teacher improvements in a safe, nonthreatening way. Classroom climate surveys can provide important insight into the relationships between staff and students. Staff development opportunities can be designed with those findings. Approaches such as invitational education can be valuable. The counselor has an opportunity to mediate, advocate, and educate.

Michael's story is a classic example of a student who "falls through the cracks." The system and the student–teacher relationship let Michael and his family down. He was frustrated throughout his school years and achieved under his ability level. What if

Michael was in a family situation without parents who care and who never contacted the school? What if Michael did not get the private learning assessment that defined his limitations? What if Michael did not have parents who could afford to pursue the private assessment? What sociological ramifications do we face as a result of students who fall through the cracks? How do these schooling errors impact our courts, juvenile justice system, and prisons? What is the cost of "missing" Michael?

REFERENCES

Americans With Disabilities Act of 1990, 42 U.S.C.A. § 12101 *et seq.* (West 1993).

Divorce:
"The Circle Becomes Larger"

CRITICAL INCIDENT

Background

I was a counselor intern in an elementary school, and there was a student I worked with closely. I remember him because of how his situation was misinterpreted by the adults around him. Although there was nothing overly distinguishing about the child at first meeting, it became clear to me that he was having some difficulties that were affecting his ability to function well, both in and out of the classroom.

Jason was a fifth-grade student who had attended the same school throughout his education. He presented to me as somewhat shy and easygoing, and this was his manner throughout our time working together. He was of average intelligence and ability and had the reputation as being a reasonably compliant and easygoing child. Suddenly, however, he began to have behavioral problems in the classroom as well as at home. He became noncompliant with his teachers, and his mother would report that he was becoming hard to manage at home (i.e., defiant, angry, at times very nervous). Jason was an only child.

Incident

Jason's homeroom teacher reported that within the preceding 2 months, Jason had begun to not do well in the classroom. She indicated he had initially became more quiet and more withdrawn than normal, which she had asked him about. He said nothing was wrong. After several weeks, he made a 180-degree change in his behavior and became easily agitated, had begun to talk and act out in class by causing disturbances, often did not bring in his homework, and had gotten into a fight on the playground, which was broken up by a teacher and the assistant principal. With me, Jason discounted the seriousness of his change in behavior, saying things were "Fine" and school was "Okay."

Because of the suddenness of the change in his behavior, I invited his mother in for a conference. She reported that Jason was, as she called him, a "gentle child," which I discovered to mean that he was somewhat shy and sensitive and was easily affected by things around him. She reported he had generally been easy to parent but had lately began to be more difficult to manage at home. She reported that he would now openly defy her requests, which he had never done before. She reported that she had given him spankings because of this defiance, but he was still hard to deal with. I would later help her develop a behavior management plan to implement at home, which involved clearly defined rules and the removal of privileges when Jason misbehaved.

After meeting with Jason a few times, he revealed an important piece of information that I was surprised had not been discussed before by his mother or teacher. His mother's live-in boyfriend, whom she had never married, had moved out of the home 2 months earlier after living in the house for 7 years, most of Jason's life. Jason mentioned this change in an off-handed way and suggested it was not that important. Further exploration revealed, however, that this man was in effect Jason's father, as his biological father was not living in the area and had had little, if any, contact with Jason.

Jason knew there were problems in the relationship between his mother and the boyfriend because of the fighting that went on. So he understood that his mother was less stressed without the boyfriend in the home. However, Jason was feeling a good deal of sadness and loss over the breakup and felt a sense of betrayal that the boyfriend had left him. Subsequently, I had the mother come back in to discuss the situation with Jason and how he was experiencing things. The mother tried to make the breakup sound like an unimportant event that should make Jason happier. She had a difficult time seeing that he might be affected by it in a negative way. So she really discounted the seriousness of the experience for both her and Jason. After a bit of discussion, however, I was able to get her to trust my hypothesis that he was reacting to the changes at home. I used a metaphor of a "town crier," suggesting that Jason was trying to tell the news of something that had happened to him but he could not find the words. So, he was expressing himself in other, less productive, ways.

Discussion

After I developed an understanding of what was really going on, my focus shifted from a individual counseling model to a systemic one. I worked to have Jason's mother appreciate the loss that Jason was experiencing and to help her to help him discuss his feelings. I also developed a behavior management plan with his teacher and explained to her some of the difficulties Jason was facing. I realized that from Jason's perspective, his mother's ex-boyfriend was a father figure. Therefore the breakup was synonymous to a divorce for him. I spoke with his mother about the possibility of having Jason spend time with the ex-boyfriend, which she was initially quite resistant to. But she did come to see the benefit that this might be for Jason.

A plan was established whereby the mother would talk with the boyfriend about the possibility of seeing Jason, which he indicated he would be interested in doing from time to time. I worked with Jason on issues of loss, sadness, anger, and the appropriate expression of feelings. Over a couple of months, I was able to help him adjust to the situation at home and in the classroom successfully mostly by helping the adults in his life acknowledge his experience and support him in it.

QUESTIONS

1. This case is a good example of how issues related to dynamics in the home affect a child's performance in school. However, it took the school counselor a good bit of time to figure this out. How might the time it takes to discover the underlying causes of a child's problems be brought to light more quickly?

2. What is the school counselor's role in dealing with parental relationship issues?

3. Do you think it was appropriate for the counselor to have Jason's mother solicit the ex-boyfriend's involvement in working with Jason?

4. Some counselors may have treated this case as a school-based problem. What are the advantages and disadvantages of this approach?

RESPONSES TO THE INCIDENT

Gary Goodnough

This incident is an excellent example of the issues facing children, families, and counselors today. Jason's presentation, particularly his sudden change in demeanor, is important and telling of some significant problem. The school counselor (even as an intern) seems to have had an ongoing consultative relationship with the teacher and was not in the least bit hesitant to involve the parent.

It is vital for school counselors to have this orientation toward the larger systems that influence children, particularly when children are in the elementary school. The counselor's initial orientation to wider systems seems to have paved the way for what appears to have been a successful intervention.

The issue of divorce is prevalent for children and families, and it has been steadily increasing in incidence for the past 35 years. Counselors have been in the forefront in recognizing the destabilizing influence this common family disruption has on children. Jason's case is, in many ways, a telling example of the commonplace nature of single parents cohabiting with significant others. In a worthy effort to be nonstigmatizing toward children who may have family configurations other than nuclear-intact families, the counselor in this incident did not seek information on the family constellation. Counselors sometimes hesitate to ask about fathers in the home for fear of offending mothers. In the changing society in the United States, it is considered "bad form" to ask about fathers because this implies we may believe that mothers cannot raise their children alone. All counselors are aware of single mothers who have successfully raised children. By asking about fathers, some counselors fear that this implies to mothers that the counselor questions their abilities as a single parent. So out of respect we sometimes do not ask. This is a common mistake.

The counselor in this incident did not ask. He waited until Jason shared the information about the boyfriend leaving. The counselor did, however, show an astute understanding of contemporary family dynamics by realizing that a long-time father substitute may be incredibly important to a fifth-grade boy. Students of this age are on the cusp of puberty. Developmentally, they are particularly in need of a close adult male with whom they can identify. Having a loving father (or father substitute) helps the 11-year-old deal with his budding masculinity in a safe way. Research suggests that boys who have been separated from their fathers face many problems of aggression and managing their interpersonal relationships; Jason exhibits some of these very symptoms. Although the counselor discounts Jason's biological father, we do not really know the extent to which the loss of the father substitute exacerbates Jason's sense of disconnection from the important men in his life.

In this sense, the counselor's focus in counseling on issues of loss and betrayal seems appropriate. These are difficult feelings for most people to handle. For an 11-year-old boy, the sadness is not easily managed, certainly not by himself, and almost surely not with his mother, who does not see the precipitating cause as an issue. The counselor does a good job working with Jason and then moving beyond exploring Jason's feelings to real action that is helpful to him and gives him what he needs—a relationship with his father substitute.

Here are some additional thoughts:

1. When meeting with parents regarding children who are having problems, counselors need to ask about any changes that have occurred recently. This "intake," if you will, should include such events as separations, deaths, and so forth.

2. The counselor's role in dealing with parental relationships is only tangential. As school counselors, we must always remember who the primary client is—the student. We deal with the parents' relationship only as it is a factor in the child's development.

3. It seems that the counselor was a forceful advocate with the mother regarding the counselor's interpretation of Jason's behavior. In this context, it is appropriate to brainstorm avenues for promoting change as well as collaboratively to speculate as to the potential of these avenues to meet the needs of the child. Within this context, asking Jason's mother to solicit the ex-boyfriend's involvement seems appropriate. However, as counselors, we must remember that we do not solve our client's problems. Clients must own their solutions.

4. It is true that Jason's in-school behavior is the reason for the counselor's involvement with him. In this sense, there can be an argument made that a behavioral approach to Jason's behaviors in school better meets the counselor's role within a comprehensive school counseling program. While this in-school approach may be an important part of the intervention, by itself it is short-sighted. The counselor correctly makes a systemic intervention.

Melinda Kuhnhenn

Jason could have been questioned casually about home, school, and play. The counselor could have asked about Jason's present and past family (i.e., brothers, sisters, dad, mom). Usually, when I counsel students and inquire about the father, they may tell me dad is not with them, but they have a stepdad, but he left, and on and on. At this point, I usually ask, "Did you like him?" "What did you do with him?" "How long was he with you?" "How did you feel about him leaving?" In this scenario, I feel the counselor spent too much time letting the child talk randomly. For good therapy, and to obtain the information needed, I find that students often need focused questioning. This usually leads me to an Ellis or Glasser approach. Glasser's reality therapy and Ellis's rational–emotive behavioral therapy theories allow the issue of personal responsibility and attention to present behavior to be the focus of my counseling approach with students (Wallace, 1986). Time in a school can be limiting, so I feel a more direct approach would have worked a little more quickly.

The school counselor's role in dealing with parental issues is to first listen to the student's point of view and try to get as many facts as possible. Talking to the parents may help to clarify the more adult issues the child cannot express. I feel that, with permission, the counselor could have talked to the ex-boyfriend, particularly if that was difficult for the mother. But in the end, the role of the counselor is to help the child cope with the loss no matter how it turns out. It is imperative to have empathy for the child, as he may need someone on his "side." A counselor may want to use solution-focused counseling. For example, ask the child what he or she wants. Brainstorm how the child, child and mom, or the ex-boyfriend and child could accomplish their goals. The counselor should ask, "Can I help the child reach some of the goals?" Ask the child how he would feel if this does not happen. In addition, the counselor should help the child learn coping skills that would help with the outcome. It is my belief the counselor should help the child prepare for as many positive and negative outcomes as possible.

I believe the ex-boyfriend should be solicited. It could also be helpful for him to meet at school with Jason and counselor. This could help alleviate any misunderstandings that might occur as a result of the mom's and ex-boyfriend's relationship ending. Referral to a family therapist might also be advisable. I believe if the boyfriend or stepfather did not want to participate, teaching Jason coping skills should be emphasized.

It is also imperative to treat the child as a whole. Nobody lives or functions in a vacuum. What happens at home affects what happens as school and vice versa. The advantages of counseling the child is that he or she can be helped to better cope with problems at home. This will make for a happier and more successful student at school. There really are no disadvantages. Treating the child as a whole does not mean one must be a family therapist or do home visits. It just means you consider the child's whole being and validate his or her life.

REFERENCES

Wallace, W. (1986). *Theories of counseling and psychotherapy: A basic issues approach*. Boston: Allyn & Bacon.

Eating Disorders: "The Perfect Daughter"

CRITICAL INCIDENT
Background

It was at the beginning of my first year as a school counselor at a rural junior high school that I first met Jill. She was smart, pretty, and popular and had never presented a discipline problem in her entire school career. I should have seen the warning signs—the dark shadows under her eyes, her refusal to spend her lunch hour in the cafeteria—but I took for granted that if something were seriously wrong with Jill someone would confide in me.

Jill's parents were successful lawyers in the nearby town and devoted a great deal of time to both their careers and their family. Jill, an eighth-grade student, had been in the same county school system since first grade, as had her two younger brothers. She excelled academically, and her vibrant personality attracted everyone to her. Jill studied dance on the weekends, was captain of the school's girls' volleyball team, and vice president of the honor society.

Incident

One day in early October, the girls' volleyball team was having a practice session to prepare themselves for an upcoming game. During running drills, the other girls on the team noticed that Jill did not look well. When asked about it, Jill brushed off their concerns and told them she had just been up late studying the night before and was tired. This seemed to satisfy them, but a few minutes later, Jill collapsed in the middle of the gym floor. By the time the coach got to her side, she was awake but somewhat dizzy. A few minutes later, Jill was lucid and back to her old self, trying to brush off the incident. She told the coach she had been too busy to eat lunch that day and that hunger had caused her to pass out.

The coach sent Jill to the sidelines and told her she would call her parents. Jill begged the coach not to call her parents and assured her that she was fine and that she would discuss the incident with her mother that night. After much persuading, the coach relented. She brought Jill some crackers and an apple from the school lunchroom, and practice resumed. An hour later, when practice was over, the coach noticed Jill furtively throwing the food away. When confronted, Jill just smiled and told the coach she felt so much better that the food was obviously unnecessary.

The next morning the coach came to me and told me of the incident. I called Jill in to my office and asked her how she was feeling. She said she was much better and that it was silly for everyone to be so concerned about her. I sat down next to her and asked her as gently as I could, "Jill, what have you had to eat today?" She was immediately on guard and replied, "Why? Why is that important?" I told her it was important for me to know and that anything she told me was confidential. "I had a glass of orange juice this morning," she told me. "And what did you have to eat before that?" I asked.

"I had a glass of orange juice yesterday morning," she replied, as her eyes filled up with tears.

I carefully explained to Jill how serious her refusal to eat could be and she appeared to be very concerned, especially when I told her this could end in her becoming quite ill. She told me she had to watch her weight because she had to be perfect and that her weight seemed to be the only thing she had trouble controlling. A friend in her dance class had told her she could control her weight and eat anything she wanted, just by making herself throw up after any meal. Jill told me she had tried that but found it impossible to make herself vomit. She felt that the only way to control her weight was to stop eating.

Discussion

Jill and her mother met with me in my office that afternoon. Her mother was shocked to learn the extent of her daughter's problem with food—Jill had been subsisting mostly on just one glass of orange juice a day for the last 6 months and weighed 80 pounds on her 5 1/2-foot frame. Neither of them knew that Jill's condition even had a name—anorexia—and when I informed them of this, they both broke down. The three of us discussed treatment options, stressing that it had to be Jill's decision to get help. Jill agreed to treatment, and she and her mother left.

I received a call the next day from Jill's father, informing me that they all had decided to send Jill to an inpatient treatment center for the next 6 weeks. I contacted school administration, and they agreed to let Jill make up the work she would miss during summer sessions. Six weeks later a student walked into my office unannounced. It took me some time to realize it was Jill! She had gained enough weight to be in a healthy weight category and looked the picture of health.

QUESTIONS

1. What can be done for Jill to prevent relapse and to support her therapeutic gains now that she has completed her treatment plan and is back in school?

2. What role did Jill's parents, probably unknowingly, play in her acquiring an eating disorder? How can this be acknowledged to prevent it from happening again?
3. What is the probability that other girls in the school will notice Jill's behavior and adopt it to their own lives? Is there a problem with Jill's treatment being so removed from them?
4. What should be done about the other girls in Jill's dance class? Who should be informed about their "dieting" methods? What ethics are involved in this action?

RESPONSES TO THE INCIDENT
Jill Holston

Jill has poor prognostic indicators, such as low weight level, caloric intake, age, and exercise involvement. Primary trigger conditions will be in her exercise domains. Because her involvements in dance and volleyball are probably important to Jill, not allowing her to continue can be harmful to her recovery. To support her continuing in sports and her recovery process, monitoring the times she spends on exercise, the intensity of her workouts, and weight status will be important factors. Defined consequences (that she will have to stop or restrict her sports) if she begins to show signs of relapse can be included. These procedures should be considered a helping tool for Jill's continued recovery and communicated that way to Jill. I would have Jill sign a contract, agreeing to these conditions because compliance to treatment can become difficult unless specifications are clearly documented (because of the distorted thinking individuals with anorexia may have). A second area of support can include monitoring Jill's eating patterns. For example, Jill may require different needs, such as eating at a different time or eating particular foods. This will depend on her current level of food acceptance. The incident implies that she is eating "normally." However, chronic cases of anorexia sometimes warrant a different process of eating. It is hoped that Jill can assimilate to the regular lunch environment, but she may be more able to eat (which is the first concern) with certain specifications. In any event, eating-related issues need to be addressed with Jill to clarify possible eating concerns. Further prevention can entail observing if Jill starts to go to the bathroom more frequently, particularly after eating. Anorexics are vulnerable to develop bulimia, especially if they are being monitored for weight loss. The fear of fatness is a prime motivator in eating disorders, so Jill may go to purgatory behaviors because of her current weight. Jill also had prior attempts at throwing up. Teachers, lunchroom employees, and coaches can be mindful of this potential behavior. Finally, Jill's involvement in promoting the prevention of eating disorders at school can strengthen her recovery process. Together, Jill and the school counselor may consider starting a food-issues support group or design seminars targeting these areas.

The crucial consideration in Jill's treatment plan is to have all the people involved in Jill's recovery (including Jill!) informed of the stipulations of Jill's behaviors at school. Furthermore, it is important to communicate that Jill's illness necessitates certain preventative methods and that soliciting other school members' involvement is a supportive measure. Finally, ongoing sessions with the school counselor is crucial to her continued success. Jill is likely to experience emotional issues (particular anger issues about weight, comments from friends, etc.) during her adaptation to school.

The parents' (as well as the entire family's) roles to the development of eating disorders typically include issues of control, approval needs, adoration of the father, and parental messages about food. The fact that both parents are lawyers suggests themes of high expectations and perfectionist tendencies, both which are classic characteristics of eating disorders. Also, family messages about beauty, money, social standards, and high accomplishments relate to self-worth and esteem concepts. Relevant to Jill's case, her age indicates the developmental time of identity formation. Thus, Jill's concept of herself might be defined by modeling family behaviors that explain her high levels of school performances. A most crucial area is Jill's relationship with her parents, particularly her father. A logical assumption is that both parents have strong personality types indicative of being lawyers. Oftentimes, the parents directly or indirectly expound certain themes that children internalize. If children do not feel that they "measure up" to their parents' beliefs, the internalization process becomes twisted. Thus, the parents are unaware of this process. This development is compounded if the children have high adornment and approval needs from either parent. Particular to fathers of anorexic daughters, characteristics include high work ethics, strong self-will, and emphasis on reason rather than emotions. In turn, girls lack emotional closeness to their fathers, and anorexia becomes a way of coping. For example, the girl might observe what impresses her father and will attempt to copy those behaviors to get his attention. If the child believes "nothing is working," it creates a negative self-concept (particularly self-blame) of not being good enough. This reinforces a low self-esteem, which validates the "I'm not worth it" theme of anorexia. Furthermore, anger issues might develop sometime during this process. Jill's attempt of pleasing her father by being perfect might not be "praised," and she might only receive criticisms for doing too much. Mixed messages of incorporating behaviors that are suppose to be admired and getting "in trouble" for doing them compound the anorexic person's need to control life. Control issues can relate to the father's style of communication with Jill. If the father's involvement with Jill primarily includes "telling Jill what to do" during momentary times in her life, but overall he is uninvolved, Jill might resent her father's input and look toward food to handle these emotions.

Anorexic daughters are influenced by maternal messages about females. Descriptions about weight/beauty, social behaviors, relationship with others (especially males), and styles of personal conduct form the female child's image of womanhood. For this case, I imagine the mother is highly involved in her career and expounds messages of independence and self-responsibility. Her mother's "full load" of having a career and being a mother and wife probably reinforces the normalcy of many responsibilities. Again, Jill observes that being successful in many areas is normal and expected. The deemphasis on emotions is likely to be a main theme inherent in both parental styles. If this is the case, emotions are probably not expressed in the home and thus appear to have no real value. As such, Jill has to find out what to do with her own emotions. "Getting rid of emotions" might be accomplished by "getting rid of food." Food refusal is also a sign of strength. People with anorexia see food as a weakness because it interferes in productivity. Jill probably blames food for her perceived sense of failure, thus the less she eats the better she is. Finally, the oldest child tends to have more "adult" themes placed on them. Thus, Jill might have had adultlike expectations during her childhood years. The "responsibility" theme placed on her at a early age might have prevented her from "just being a child." In addition, her younger brothers might not have had the same adult expectations during their childhood. Thus, Jill might have hidden resentment for her parents' attitudes about her younger brothers.

The parents can be educated to these relevant, anorexic family themes and assess their own behaviors. The parents can take inventory of the family messages that are being presented in their home. They can examine the quality and content of their family togetherness, such as what they do when they are together, how much time is actually spent with Jill, and what kind of attention she receives in relation to her brothers. Most importantly, in order for Jill to give herself permission not to get overly involved in activities, her parents will need to tell her that being too busy or being the best at everything may not be what she needs to do. That is, being highly accomplished in many areas may not be a part of Jill's self-image. The parents might not be aware of how much Jill relies on their approval to define her self-worth. Clarity in what Jill wants to do with her life, what makes her happy, and what she values is important to the family's role in her recovery. This leads to the significance of communicating emotions. Understanding that emotions are of equal value to accomplishments will help Jill understand herself and life. The parents will need to take a honest look at how much emotional support is given in their children's development.

Finally, the apparent dismissal of Jill's weight loss suggests that her parents were either too busy in their own lives or chose to ignore that something was wrong. The parents will need to explore the reasons why they did not notice Jill's behaviors. Ultimately, it is Jill's responsibility to speak up. However, adolescence is a scary and confusing time, particularly for young girls. If girls feel that they cannot reach out to parents, they will seek external sources to find solutions to their problems. People with anorexia find comfort and solutions in food, and the power they experience by "dieting perfectly" leads to fatal states of the illness. Her parents' awareness and recognition of Jill's eating habits would have provided an earlier detection of her anorexia.

Because this age group is the most susceptible to developing eating disorders, there is a high probability that others students will "copy" Jill's behaviors. Although I do not see a problem in Jill's treatment being removed from them, I do think it is important for the school to be involved in educating the other students on eating disorders. Several factors are involved here. First, because Jill has attended the same school for many years, there are probably close relationships among the students. As such, other girls might be confused or even scared about what happened to Jill. This, in turn, might make it more problematic for Jill to return to school. Moreover, people with anorexia are often embarrassed and ashamed of their illness. It might be helpful to Jill if other students understood the seriousness of her condition. Second, other students might tease or make unpleasant comments to Jill about her illness. Boys in particular tend to make weight-related comments to girls. Therefore, the male students might be more prone to make joking comments to Jill that could be extremely damaging to her recovery. Third, Jill might want to talk about her experiences of treatment. Six weeks is a long time to be away, and surely her absence was noticed by the other students. Jill's ability to openly discuss her illness can benefit her own recovery process as well as educate other students. The key is to assess Jill's comfort level and willingness to discussing her treatment process. Explaining this to Jill is important.

Specific to Jill's dance class, it becomes crucial to implement an educational format on eating disorders. Girls of this age and involved in sports (particularly solo sports such as dance) are the ones most prone to develop eating disorders. The education of eating disorders can easily be incorporated into the school. One effective method is asking a person who has developed an eating disorder to speak to the girls. Schools can contact the community for referrals. Typically, individuals who are in recovery desire to speak out for prevention of these illnesses. Local support groups, treatment facilities, or national eating disorder organizations can provide assistance. Sports classes could also design prevention programs by providing daily seminars on healthy eating habits. Most students are unaware of the relationship between proper levels of caloric intake and those they expend in exercise. At this time, facts about eating disorders, such as who is vulnerable as well as the signs and symptoms, can be introduced into the curriculum. Finally, a school's role in the prevention of eating disorders is receiving more recent attention from athletic departments. Schools provide an excellent forum to reach the students who will develop eating disorders. Another advantage is that other students can recognize friends who might be exhibiting signs of abnormal eating habits. Finally, coaches, teachers, school nurses, and school counselors can be trained on eating disorders, which will assist in reducing the clinical cases of these illnesses.

The ethical issues really come down to the extent of the school's role in nonacademic areas. Currently, school institutions are seen as a cogent force to correct problems in the larger society. Social-related subjects to curriculum design includes healthy eating behaviors. The Federal Drug Administration's (FDA) endorsement of healthy eating could be used as the school's rationale for the inclusion of information on eating disorder. The FDA provides a handbook titled "The New Food Label: There's Something in It for Everybody" is specifically structured for classrooms. Prototypes for eating disorder seminars are available and usually involve classroom exercises to monitor weight, develop daily menus, calculate caloric intake, and learn about nutritional needs. School personnel could benefit from this information and assess the school's current food purchases and lunch offerings. Overall health promotion serves to reduce medical complications for students, which can benefit both school and parents.

L. C. Hand

This incident clearly shows the need for a school counselor to be a mental health professional as well as an educator. Jill needs continued individual counseling services, a support group, and a support network that includes friends, family, and other students with whom she can relate. Although it may not be within the scope of the school counselor's job description to provide all of these services, the school counselor can function as a coordinator and referral source.

Policies of the school district dictate the role of a school counselor regarding individual long-term counseling with students; however, consideration must be given to the health and well-being of Jill and the potential liability surrounding Jill's condition. The school counselor's job may involve individual counseling with Jill as one way to monitor her eating disorder. The counselor can use individual sessions with Jill to assist in the transition back to school after being away for an extended period of time. Jill will encounter peer pressure and will need a safe place to escape, and the counselor can provide the needed place for Jill to talk about her feelings. In any situation wherein a student may be harmed on school property, the school district must be aware of potential liability. In Jill's case, problematic situations such as induced vomiting on school property, being injured during a school-sponsored event, or detrimental fasting during school hours could be liability issues for not only the counselor but the school district as well.

School counselors must be knowledgeable about a wide variety of issues. Many times the focus of middle and high school counselors revolves around curriculum issues rather than personal issues of the student. Middle and high school counselors have a duty to their student populations to be cognizant of issues that are important to adolescents. To be aware of these issues, the counselor must be actively involved in the lives of middle and high school students. Eating disorders, drug use, violence, sexual activities, and pregnancy are increasingly becoming more prevalent in schools. A good knowledge base for the school counselor is vital to successful implementation of a comprehensive developmental guidance program. In Jill's case, the counselor recognized anorexia and did what was necessary to help Jill and her family.

Jill's parents were unaware of their contribution to Jill's eating disorder. Highly motivated and successful in their careers, Jill's parents were unable to recognize the pressure they inadvertently placed on Jill. One way to prevent this type of situation would be to use the position of the school counselor to facilitate parent education and awareness focus groups. This could be accomplished by bringing speakers from outside agencies into the school to hold such educational groups. Brown-bag lunch sessions for busy working parents, nighttime parent meetings, or spend-a-Saturday at school meetings would serve to give parents the opportunity to learn as well as be a part of their child's education and life.

The role of educator within the school counselor's job is another vital component to the role of counselor in elementary, middle, or high school environments. Students, particularly at the middle and high school level, are overly aware of others. More than likely, other girls noticed Jill's behavior and may be in similar situations. Classroom guidance lessons may be focused primarily on academic or social skills, but the need for education of personal issues and feelings could also be included in the social development issues of students. Eating disorders, like other issues such as sexual abuse, are too often cloistered and hidden from discussion. Jill's disorder and its treatment are opportunities for education and awareness of students, teachers, administration, and parents. This situation would also be a case for the counselor to provide motivational speakers from outside agencies, such as others with eating disorders who have successfully recovered. This would allow students to gain accurate knowledge, give students the opportunity to ask questions, and gain an awareness of successful recovery.

If Jill could be encouraged to share her experience, it would benefit others who may be having feelings and struggles similar to Jill's. Because Jill is a dedicated dancer and athlete, opportunities for support and sharing will be available to her. Ethically, the counselor may not divulge information without Jill's permission. However, the counselor and Jill together could develop a plan to increase the awareness of other girls, not only in dance class but also in other venues. Jill may find comfort and support from other girls who are experiencing eating disorders but have been unable to discuss their fears and problems. Discussion and sharing among the students and the counselor would help to eliminate the dark secrecy surrounding eating disorders.

Encouraging Jill to seek support of friends and family would help to strengthen and bolster her newfound healthier lifestyle. By increasing Jill's awareness of the importance of support in her recovery, Jill may feel not so alone and ultimately may increase her positive feelings about her appearance and weight issues. The role of school counselor is comprehensive and requires awareness of many social and personal issues affecting the youth of our ever-changing society.

Ethics:
"The Counselor Succumbs"

CRITICAL INCIDENT

Background

Among my various responsibilities in Valley Elementary School, I have the responsibility of deciding whether children should be promoted. I look over the child's records, interview the teacher and the child, and then try to make a decision. I try to keep everything in balance—the child's aptitude for learning, his or her social level, physical status, test results, grades, and so forth.

In reviewing the records of fourth-grade pupils, I found one girl, Yetta, who was a prime candidate for retention. First, her teacher stated that Yetta tried hard but did grossly inferior work and was not learning. Second, Yetta had been tested for intelligence many times. Her most recent appraisal had been conducted a few months previously by a psychologist who gave this statement in his report: "Yetta is too bright to go to an institution for the retarded but unable to profit from the usual school." Third, Yetta was very small for her age, and it was noted that she tended to play with children several years younger than she. Finally, when I talked with Yetta, she indicated she would prefer to repeat the fourth grade because the work had been "too hard."

I talked to the principal before writing my recommendation and was told that Yetta's older brother had graduated several years before with the highest grades. I told him my decision about Yetta. The principal agreed that her interests would be best served by having her repeat the year, although he had some reservations about how her parents would take it. How right he was!

Following the protocol in such matters, before making the final decision I sent a letter to Yetta's parents summarizing the facts, stating that both Yetta's teacher and principal had agreed with me and outlining how the parents should inform Yetta and their other children about our decision to retain her. I ended the letter with the routine "if you have any questions or concerns, please call me or come to see me."

Incident

Two days later, while peacefully working on a report, I heard a scream from the outer office and the sounds of a scuffle. I dashed to the door and saw Millie, my secretary, struggling with a woman who held a small brown bottle in her raised hand. Not knowing what it was all about, but thinking that perhaps the bottle contained acid which the woman intended to throw at Millie, I got into the act, grabbed the woman's hand and removed the bottle, whereupon the woman collapsed. Millie and I examined the bottle and noted a skull and crossbones on the label and the word *iodine* below it. The secretary said, "She said she was going to drink the iodine if you didn't promote her daughter." "Who's her daughter?" I asked. "Yetta," she answered.

The end of this little drama was as follows. Yetta's mother was revived and came into my office. She informed me in a highly emotional manner she would kill herself if Yetta was not promoted. In a reasonable manner, I went over the facts and pointed out that Yetta herself wanted to be left back and that retaining her would be better for Yetta. The mother was adamant and insisted that she would kill herself if Yetta was not promoted. When I asked what the reason for all this drama was, the mother stated that for poor Jews the ultimate pleasure was to have bright children, and the ultimate disgrace was to have stupid children. She informed me that her husband was a business failure, and the one bright light in her life was her son, who had done so well in school. Were Yetta to be left back, it would be a serious disgrace, and she would lose her status in her little community. The mother agreed that Yetta was not bright, had difficulty learning, and loathed school and everything about it. Whenever I would try to explain the various reasons for the importance of keeping Yetta in the fourth grade, the mother became emotional. Finally, I reversed my decision, and the mother sailed out gaily, thanking me profusely.

Discussion

I am still uncertain whether I did the right thing. I suppose that Yetta's mother would not really have tried to commit suicide. However, this incident made it painfully clear to me that, for some families, school failure is a family disgrace. I supposed Yetta would not have learned much more by being left back in the fourth grade. In the fifth grade, the same pattern of delinquency and lack of achievement occurred. We have no special provisions for special education, even though teachers make allowances for individual differences in our school.

QUESTIONS

1. I would like to have some explanations for the mother's behavior, especially since she knew that Yetta was not getting anything out of school.
2. Did I do the right or wrong thing in promoting Yetta? At the time, I simply wanted to get rid of the mother. I did not think things out. Was I fair to the fifth-grade teacher in giving her a child who had difficulty doing third-grade work?
3. Was I fair to Yetta, pushing her ahead because of her mother's demands when she herself preferred to remain in a lower grade?
4. How on earth can one make parents act reasonably in such matters? Every year I run into a handful of parents who think the world is coming to an end if their child does not get good grades or get promoted. I try to explain to them the dangers of pushing a child beyond his or her capabilities, but this makes little impression on them.

RESPONSES TO THE INCIDENT

Mary A. Barber

From the background given, I would assume this situation is one in which the counselor's position is at least quasi-administrative, in which he had too large a caseload to do much personal counseling with individuals and instead performs as a consultant to a number of teachers. Assuming these conditions and assuming that there were no provisions for borderline mental retardation cases within the school, the original disposition of the case sounds like a considered, logical resolution. In the critical incident with the hysterical mother, the counselor's actions possibly were the only way of solving the immediate problem. However, giving in to the mother's selfish wishes represented a disservice to Yetta in the long run, for it meant condemning her to conditions that would probably prolong her failure pattern. If Yetta had only minimal learning ability but was pushed into situations in which she undoubtedly continued to fail and fall farther and farther behind, the prediction is that she would drop out of school as soon as she was old enough or would resort to various kinds of acting-out behavior in response to her unhappiness.

This case sounds like one in which family counseling should have been instituted if such services were available. It is obvious that the child was being used as a pawn in the game of upward social mobility, which the mother was rather unsuccessfully trying to play. Even following the suicide attempt (which was probably not real, because it was melodramatically performed in front of an audience), the mother might have been calmed down by a promise to delay the decision and review the case rather than completely reversing it. If the counselor had made a play for more time, a more constructive resolution might have been possible. There might have been a chance to instigate counseling with the whole family, and the mother might have been led eventfully to a more realistic attitude.

Parents who measure their social status in terms of the achievements of their children are demonstrating the level of their own emotional immaturity. In this day and age, children will eventually rebel in one form or another against the kind of extreme domination exhibited by such parents. Trying to make such parents see the almost inevitable outcome of their actions is not an easy task. It is a function of the social services referral sources to work with these individual cases. Whether the decision to promote Yetta was fair or unfair to the fifth-grade teacher would depend on whether she had the ability, willingness, and time to give Yetta the special attentions she undoubtedly needed.

How to make parents reasonable in such matters poses a very general question, and there can be no satisfying universal answer. Each case, each family, represents a unique combination of personalities and interactions, and where there seems to be a serious degree of unhappiness or instability, counseling with the whole family would be desirable. In this particular case, in which the mother seems so completely self-centered, regards her husband as a complete failure, and perceives her family's successes or failures as reflections of her personal worth, there would seem to be a definite need for protracted counseling. There is not much information

about the father, except for the mother's reference to him as a failure and a disappointment to her, but it could be surmised that he
has many problems too. Ideally, through a continual program of
adequate counseling, they both might be brought to a more accepting attitude toward both their and Yetta's limitations and encouraged to appreciate whatever positive resources they have.

E. G. Williamson

Yetta's and her mother's behavior are rather typical in every
school, and such incidents are common in the life of every school
counselor. Progress for the child in his or her education has become
such a status symbol, particularly for the upward-bound middle-
class and selected members of the lower class, that it is understandable that Yetta's mother would be upset by her being held
back. A more achievable, realistic attitude in the modern school system would be not to care whether she was making progress so long
as she was making an effort to learn and getting satisfaction out of
the school experience, and as long as she was gradually maturing
so that she would become a more serious student. That would be
the end goal that I would hope would emerge.

The counselor asks whether he was right in promoting Yetta. I
think one could argue that the counselor was both right and wrong
in this action. I would say to him: "Under the circumstances you
were not unfair to the fifth-grade teacher in promoting into her
class a girl with third-grade mentality. But you did have an obligation to explain to the fifth-grade teacher why you were doing this
and to give her a chance to express her point of view and her willingness or unwillingness to have Yetta in her class. No, I don't
think you were fair to Yetta in pushing her ahead because of her
mother, but I don't see what else you could have done under the
circumstances, given the necessity for an immediate decision.
Sometimes we have to take the least desirable of the possible alternatives when action is required immediately."

We may look at this problem in another way. To let Yetta remain
in a lower grade too long could produce a whole symptomatic pattern that in itself would be difficult to deal with. The counselor is

between the devil and the deep blue sea. One had to go one way or another, and one had to make the best decision one can, as is true of every situation that calls for judgment on the part of counselor. There is no way I know of that we can make all parents reasonable in such matters because school success for their children is a precious status symbol. They have less than full appreciation for the most part (particularly parents from lower socioeconomic levels) of the intellectual demands involved in the mastery of the subjects, especially at the upper levels of education.

So again I would say to the counselor, "Please be sympathetic with the parents if they use their children's progress as a means to satisfy their own need for status. It is perfectly normal. Every counselor will recognize this if he or she has children of his or her own." Counselors should understand that in some problem situations, such as the one in this incident, there is no clear right or wrong thing to do. We just have to muddle through and pick up the pieces when the world comes apart. We cannot expect people to use logic or rationality in the face of such strong irrationalities as the upward-bound motivations of some parents in relation to their children. It sometimes takes years to get parents to see facts of life. We must keep trying, and unless we have this kind of eternal optimism, we had better get out of the counseling field.

Exceptional Education: "He's Not Coming to Our School"

CRITICAL INCIDENT

Background

Allen, age 13, is a sixth-grade student, enrolling in a new middle school. Allen was born prematurely and weighed just over 2 pounds (0.9 kg) at birth. He was placed in an intensive care for several months. Allen survived this early trauma relatively well, and his developmental milestones (e.g., walking, talking) were reported as normal. According to his mother, Allen was diagnosed as hyperactive in early childhood. On several occasions, his mother had to find other child-care arrangements for him as his preschool providers refused to allow him to continue in their programs because of his excessive activity, noncompliance, and disruptive behavior. Allen was placed on Ritalin at age 4.

Incident

The mother was worried that Allen was going to have a hard time adjusting and succeeding in his new school. Upon finishing the initial paperwork to enroll Allen in school, the mother asked to speak to the sixth-grade counselor. Being available, I asked the mother to come into my office. Introducing herself, she wanted me to understand "what kind of a child" Allen was and the difficulties he has had to encounter.

Allen's mother confided that his father was an alcoholic and had been abusive to her and Allen. She said the child protective agency had been contacted several times when Allen had appeared at school with bruises. She said that although this was embarrassing to admit, she wanted me to know these things so it would help me understand Allen better. She stated although this behavior had been going on a long time, the father had recently agreed to see a counselor and that she felt good about the future. During the past 2 years, Allen had begun to damage property within their community (e.g., bashing mailboxes, beating a parked car with a baseball bat), although she had managed to keep Allen out of trouble by "negotiating" with police informally to pay for the damages he incurred. According to the mother, Allen was suspended one time recently for striking his learning disabilities teacher. I thanked her for having the courage to disclose such personal issues with me, and I told her that I appreciated her obvious concern for her son. I also told her I would welcome further meetings with her and would make it a point to know Allen and to help him succeed. I told her I was looking forward to working with her, and I would attend Allen's staffing meeting that afternoon and looked forward to seeing her there.

The staffing meeting included all of Allen's new teachers, the exceptional student resource compliance specialist (whose job was to ensure that Allen was staffed in the correct program and all forms were legally completed), the disciplinarian for the sixth grade, myself (as sixth-grade counselor), and Allen's mother. Upon request, Allen's mother proceeded to explain Allen's school history and produced several forms which the counselor of Allen's old school had given her. She said Allen began receiving services for learning disabilities in the first grade. Her records also showed that Allen had been retained twice, and his grades throughout school had been very poor. She stated Allen had been suspended several times, and most of the suspensions were due to noncompliance, disrespect for authorities, and for verbal aggression (I remembered our earlier conversation about Allen's physical attack on his learning disabilities teacher). Academic and assessment records indicated Allen was reading at a primer level and recognized only a few words. On measures of intelligence, Allen scored within the low-average range throughout his elementary years. Mathematically, tests revealed that he currently is able to compute simple addition and subtraction problems. In the sixth grade, Allen was placed in a self-contained class of children with emotional and behavioral disorders and learning disabilities.

Allen's mother began to cry, saying since Allen had been placed in the self-contained class, she had not seen any improvement, and in fact, she felt like her son did not receive any help in learning to control his behavior. As I handed her a tissue, I wondered privately about Allen's need for a lot of individual attention and if our personnel were capable of giving Allen what he needed. Our exceptional student education classes were almost overloaded with students.

Furthermore, Allen seemed to have other problems that were not being addressed. The new administration had started a "get-tough" policy regarding student discipline. It seemed obvious to me that Allen would need a very strict, and perhaps individual behavior plan to deal with the issues the mother had shared with me in my office. I also wondered if I should share with the committee Allen's past history, which the mother had talked about with me earlier in the day. I decided not to. There seemed to be enough issues already to deal with. When asked about his positive attributes, the mother stated Allen was an exceptional athlete who had won various awards in wrestling and basketball. She also stated that he loves to play computer games. When he took his medication, his teachers had reported that he was a very likable child.

The meeting ended with Allen being staffed into our program that duplicated the program in his former school. All of the teachers stated they were impressed by the mother's candor, and they wished other parents were as receptive to ideas and supportive as she appeared to be. The sixth-grade disciplinarian thanked her for coming and told her if there was anything he could do, to please not hesitate to call. As I walked her to her car, I also reiterated how impressed I was with her commitment to Allen. She looked at me and said she really hoped this school could do something for him. With all that she was going through at home, she said she could use a break. She wanted me to know that Allen was basically a good boy and that she loved him very much. She told me she felt relieved and knew that I would watch out for Allen. She finished by stating she felt sure she could count on my to help, and she was looking forward to seeing Allen succeed.

As she left, I wondered if I had been too passive at the staffing. There were behaviors that the mother had shared with me the committee might have needed to know. Allen had, on several occasions, displayed violent behavior toward things and individuals. He had issues going on at home that necessitated intense counseling, which nobody had addressed. I decided to hope for the best.

The next morning, after showing Allen to his first class I returned to my office to begin my day. At lunch time the sixth-grade disciplinarian called me to come to his office. Upon arriving, I saw Allen sitting in a chair on one side of the office with another boy, looking like he had been in a terrible fight, sitting on the other side. The disciplinarian was sending Allen home pending expulsion.

Discussion

By all witness accounts, Allen had been teasing Justin repeatedly about his clothes. Allen made fun of Justin's "hand-me-downs" and was very cruel and relentless in his teasing. Things quickly worsened and the two boys engaged in a rather heated argument when they went to physical education. When Justin left to get a physical education teacher, Allen tripped him, causing him to hit his head on the basketball pole. Allen proceeded to hit Justin until he fell to the ground almost unconscious. Allen had to be restrained by one of the physical education teachers. During the time it took to restrain Allen, he bit the instructor on the hand and hit his head against the instructor's mouth, causing a tooth to chip. The disciplinarian had decided to send Allen home and ask that charges be filled against him for assault. The disciplinarian stated that in spite of our meeting yesterday, these types of behaviors would not be tolerated and that faculty safety would be enforced.

When Allen's mother arrived to pick him up, she came to my office. Upon seeing me, she began to cry and said she was wrong to put so much faith in me. Why hadn't I kept an eye on him like I said I would? She said she had been totally honest with us about Allen's troubles and the school had done nothing to assist her or Allen. The mother said she just couldn't take schools not following through with their commitments and that she was going to the School Board to file a complaint against me and the school. I returned to my office shaken at the events of the past several hours and enraged that all of a sudden the behavior of a sixth-grade student was suddenly my fault. In addition, the thought of a parent going to the School Board to file a complaint against me was equally unnerving, especially being a first-year counselor. Was I going to be fired? What had I done wrong?

QUESTIONS

1. Was the information told to the counselor regarding Allen's past physical behavior told in confidence?
2. Was this information valuable information to share with the committee that was assigned to the task of writing an individual educational plan for Allen? Why or why not?
3. If so, how would you have shared this information?
4. As Allen's counselor, are there other intervention strategies you could have introduced in the staffing meeting that might have helped Allen's first day?

5. Does the school have the right to recommend expulsion for a student who has a valid individual educational plan?
6. Does the school have a right to press charges against Allen?
7. Is the school system required to provide Allen his education? If so, how might they do this?
8. Should the counselor have been more proactive at the staffing meeting?
9. Given that the counselor knew more information about Allen, should the counselor have been more proactive during Allen's first day?
10. Has the counselor done anything wrong that might jeopardize his job?

RESPONSES TO THE INCIDENT

Carlen Henington

The information shared by Allen's mother was confidential. However, this information also needed to be shared with other school personnel (e.g., the disciplinarian and the exceptional student resource compliance specialist). The counselor may have been well advised to ask Allen's mother if she was comfortable sharing the information with the other staffing members. It might have been helpful to suggest that important information about Allen's behavior problems (e.g., noncompliance, physical and verbal aggression against property and individuals) should be shared with those directly interacting with Allen in his school setting on a day-to-day basis so that they might be vigilant to warning signs of problems or avoid placing Allen in situations in which problems may be likely to occur. If Allen's mother agreed to share information, then helping her to identify key pieces of information for sharing and the people with whom to share the information would be a logical next step.

If Allen's mother indicated that she was not comfortable sharing the information herself, then she may have been willing to have the counselor share the information. Again, emphasizing the importance of key people having all possible information that will be relevant to Allen's success in his new school would likely be helpful. This should be the least that she would be willing to do because she willingly volunteered the information to the counselor and obviously was seeking the counselor's advice and assistance. If she was still reluctant to share the information with key school personnel, then it might be advised to guide her in understanding the importance of accepting the counselor's advice in this, so that the school personnel might be most effective in helping her and her son.

That said, despite the need for confidentiality in this case, it is also the counselor's duty to protect Allen, as well as other children and personnel in the school. Before any counseling should occur, it is always important to outline the limits of confidentiality (i.e., harm to self, harm to others, court orders). Therefore, if Allen's mother still refused to allow the information to be shared, there are two areas that are relevant to this case that she must know: The counselor is obligated to report (a) abuse of Allen by his father and (b) potential harm to others that Allen might pose. At this time, given the current problems facing schools regarding student violence, the school should have a plan or policy for monitoring students suspected of possible violence. This plan should be explained to Allen's mother and immediately implemented. If the counselor is not aware of such a plan, then consultation with the school principal or disciplinarian or both regarding policy for generic violent behavior by students should be conducted.

If Allen was in a behavioral disorder/learning disability classroom previously, there should have been a behavioral component in the previous individual educational plan (IEP). If there was none, then one should be devised by the current staffing members, and it is important for the counselor and the staffing members to make sure that it is in place. Allen's noncompliance and verbal aggression as reported by his mother would be enough cause to include a behavioral plan. Again, relating back to the response to Question 1, the counselor should already have permission from the mother to share the information or she should be prepared to share the relevant information with the staffing members. This last point will increase the likelihood that some intervention will be in place for Allen should the need arise.

It is preferable to allow Allen's mother to state the information herself, but if she has asked to speak with the members, then the counselor should honor her wishes as to who is privy to the information and what information is revealed, provided that the duty-to-warn and child abuse issues have been covered as federally mandated.

It might have been helpful for Allen, at the very least, to have a classmate with good social skills and peer acceptance to mentor Allen during his first days in his new school. This might be a good policy for all new students. Furthermore, problem solving with his teachers to identify potential times or situations that may be difficult for Allen, such as transition times (in the hall between classes) and less supervised times (dressing for gym class, lunch), may have foreseen difficult times with strategies implemented to address specific instances.

The current federal law states that a new placement or IEP must occur anytime a student's placement changes. The student may be placed on suspension for 10 days before the letter of this guideline kicks in. This must occur and any provisions for behavior management contained in the IEP must also be implemented as would any other intervention for Allen.

Allen can and should be held accountable for his behavior. Furthermore, it is important that Allen's violence be formally documented. This will allow the authorities to properly track Allen's behavioral difficulties, will assist in avoiding future misunderstandings about the importance of a behavior plan for Allen, and may assist authorities in finding a program to help Allen that requires documentation of difficulties.

Given that Allen should have been provided a behavior management plan, and given the discussion during the staffing meeting (note the mother's tearful statement during the staffing meeting that Allen was not getting the help he needed to control his behavior), as well as the conversation between the mother and the counselor prior to the staffing, and that all children are entitled to a free and appropriate education, the staffing members should have the foresight and been proactive in their discussion of interventions and placement plans for Allen. This might have included a discussion of the school's discipline plan, the levels of placement for Allen available within the district, and other resources that the school might have available to assist Allen in his new school.

The counselor should have been more proactive during the staffing. However, the events that occurred during the staffing meeting indicate that the other staffing member had sufficient information to indicate that behavioral issues should have been addressed. They all should have been more proactive.

The counselor as well as the entire staff should have been more proactive during Allen's first day. Again, the school personnel should have a plan of action for violent behavior in the school setting. This plan should have been immediately enacted when Allen began harassing Justin, before the situation escalated to physical violence. A possible first step that might have prevented the escalation is peer mediation. With this type of lower profile intervention, perhaps Justin or another peer may have been comfortable enough to come forward before the incident had gotten out of hand. Peer mediation has been used in many schools with positive results.

Although it is possible that the counselor could be held solely accountable for mishandling this case, the entire staffing personnel should have seen the potential for Allen's behavior. They should have explored Allen's mothers comments about his need for assistance with controlling his behavior and provided a behavior plan for Allen. Potentially, this oversight could have serious consequences for the staffing members, the counselor, and the school district with legal action coming from Allen's family, Justin's family, or the teacher.

L. Edwin

There is no indication that the information told to the counselor by Allen's mother was told in confidence. However, as the mother was not familiar with the school, school policy, or the counselor's ethical stance on such issues, it is clear the counselor should have told the mother under what conditions they were going to have such a conversation (as presented in this incident). If the mother was under the belief that her words were going to be held in confidence, she was mistaken because of the limitations of such confidentiality when the content describes abuse, harm to self, and others. In this incident, the mother has described herself and Allen as being the recipients of physical abuse from the father. Also the mother described Allen as being physically abusive to adults and potentially abusive to himself and other children. This information circumvents the ethical issue of confidentiality and allows the counselor to divulge such information for the protection of Allen, his mother, other students, and faculty members.

The counselor was negligent in not sharing the information learned in the parent conference with the committee. If such information had been shared, then school personnel would have been able to develop, as part of the IEP, a behavioral plan that might have prevented the events from occurring the next day. In reading the incident, I am puzzled as to why the counselor was unable to make a decision regarding the sharing of such important and meaningful information at the staffing meeting. The counselor failed to exhibit a concise and clear ability to make the proper decision regarding information that may have prevented a fight between two boys, a teacher from being assaulted, and a possible personal lawsuit brought about by the parent. It could be argued that the counselor was indeed negligent and responsible for Allen being suspended from school because of the failure to disclose important information at the staffing.

A behavioral plan should have been included in Allen's IEP. However, even a strict behavioral plan is not enough when the adults in charge of the plan are not capable of carrying out such a plan. In this incident, the counselor wonders to herself "about Allen's need for a lot of individual attention, and if our personnel were capable of giving Allen what he needed. Our exceptional student education classes were almost overloaded with students." The counselor should have consulted with key faculty and administration before the staffing meeting to develop a plan of action that could be produced at the staffing meeting. Allen's behavioral, educational, and emotional issues are too many to be addressed in one meeting after school. This is a good incident to examine the need for prestaff meetings to occur among school personnel before an actual staffing meeting with the parent or parents occurs. Of course, much of this is dependent on the counselor sharing information with the appropriate school personnel and necessitates the counselor taking the lead in this direction as student (Allen's) advocate. In my opinion, this is another area in which the counselor failed.

Current school law does not allow the school to expel anyone; only the school board has the right to expel a student. In this case, without a change of placement, the disciplinarian can only send Allen home for 10 days (for the entire school year). In addition, a manifestation meeting between exceptional education personnel, the parent, and school administration must be held to investigate the incident, adjust Allen's IEP, and develop strategies for Allen's future education.

Charges could be filed against Allen by the faculty member for assault. This would be a decision made by the teacher, although in this incident it appears the disciplinarian is promoting this action against Allen.

The school board may not have the right to expel a student who has a valid IEP. In some states, student failure rests solely on the IEP, its implementation, and the individual(s) whose responsibility it is for its implementation. The belief is that if the student is not progressing (or failing) according to the IEP, then a manifestation meeting needs to occur and the IEP needs to be rewritten. The failure does not rest with Allen but with the school officials.

School systems are required to offer Allen an education until age 21 (in some cases). However, where that education is offered is up to the school board. School boards have many options to "traditional" schooling (i.e., home school, alternative school, or modified day). Any one of these options (as well as others) may be open to school officials. However, it is my opinion that Allen's IEP did not provide Allen the structure needed to be successful in the least restrictive environment available to him. Allen will return to this school site for his education. It is hoped that school personnel will do a better job next time.

Faculty Relations: "Shut Up and Sit Down"

CRITICAL INCIDENT

Background

The private school served students from low socioeconomic status (SES) neighborhoods. As school counselor, my job description included consulting with teachers to address students' socioemotional and behavioral problems. Because the school was private, many of the teachers were not certified and did not receive traditional training in classroom management techniques. Despite the nontraditional backgrounds of the teachers, most of them were highly motivated, were intelligent, and managed the classroom well.

During my first months, I came to realize the school was in transition. Previously, the school only accepted children of average and above-average intelligence. Furthermore, they did not serve children who presented serious emotional and behavioral problems. However, recently the school began serving more students who displayed high rates of inappropriate behavior in the classroom.

My office was located next to a secondary teacher's classroom. Mrs. Jones was extremely bright and had been teaching at the school for approximately 7 years. She was known as one of the strongest teachers and was particularly noted for working with the socially neglected or unpopular students. She developed and supervised several clubs that met after school. These clubs allowed secondary students who did not typically participate in teams, clubs, or organizations to become part of a group. Despite these strengths, I noticed the teacher was often screaming in her classroom. I could hear her through the walls.

Incident

One Friday, Mrs. Jones knocked on my office to express concern regarding three students in one of her classes. She wanted to know if I could help. As we began talking, Mrs. Jones began to express concern regarding other students. She complained the students were no longer motivated or intelligent and that they did not respect her authority. She felt they did not belong in this school. Although I tried to focus Mrs. Jones's attention on the current problem regarding the three students' misbehavior, she kept bringing the issue back to the changing school. Mrs. Jones also began expressing dissatisfaction with her career and even brought up problems with her spouse. As Mrs. Jones continued to talk, she often used the term *burnout*, but I could not help thinking the personal symptoms she was describing sounded like depression. As the meeting ended, I agreed to enter her classroom and record direct observational data.

After entering the classroom and beginning my data collection, it became obvious many students in the classroom were not following Mrs. Jones's instructions, demands, or requests. In fact, Mrs.

Jones spent 27 of the 40-minute class period addressing and often publicly berating students for their misbehavior. At one point she screamed to one student, "I keep telling you try harder, and you just don't get it! Why don't you just quit school."

Discussion

My job description includes consulting with faculty to address student issues. It is obvious to me this teacher may have some personal, professional, and mental health problems that may be interfering with her teaching. I had the impression she may be suffering from depression. Regardless, I think I can develop procedures designed to alter Mrs. Jones's behavior management procedures. In the past I have used some self-monitoring procedures with teachers to make them aware of how many negative interactions they have with students as opposed to positive interactions. For example, teachers have moved a nickel from one pocket to the other for every negative comment made and a dime for every positive comment made. In the past, teachers have used similar procedures and (a) decreased their negative interaction rates, (b) increased their rates of positive interactions, (c) improved student behaviors, (d) improved the general learning environment, and (e) made the classroom a more pleasant place for both teachers and students.

QUESTIONS

1. I am getting the impression Mrs. Jones may be experiencing some mental health problems that may be interfering with her work. What action should I take regarding these mental health concerns?
2. The content of Mrs. Jones yelling and screaming strikes me as psychological abuse at worse and poor motivational procedures at best. Should I inform the principal of this or would I be breaking confidence and confidentiality? I am scared that if I were to "turn her in," teachers would never speak with me again! What are the legal and ethical issues involved, and what could I have done before our meeting to help clarify my role or roles in these issues? How could I have avoided this mess?

3. If I use self-management or similar procedures to change the teacher's interactions with the students, I may be able to reduce inappropriate behaviors in the referred students and prevent problems from occurring with other students. However, I am concerned that merely addressing Mrs. Jones's classroom management style may only temporarily fix the problem and she will not be able to truly serve the students to the best of her ability until she deals with her personal and emotional issues. What should I do?

RESPONSES TO THE INCIDENT

Jackie M. Allen

Mrs. Jones is very stressed and appears to be responding irrationally to her students. The causes of stress may come from various sources: impatience as she grows older, "burnout" in her job, depression, lack of positive reinforcement for her many years of hard work, difficulty in adjusting to a growing population of at-risk students with increasingly severe personal problems that pose learning barriers, her own personal family or relationship problems, or as a result of a physical health problem. As a school counselor, I would keep open the lines of communication with her, creating a positive, safe atmosphere in which Mrs. Jones will be able to continue to come and talk about her school and personal problems.

It is obvious that the classroom atmosphere created by Mrs. Jones is not healthy and conducive to student growth, and her current teaching style is probably creating a barrier for student learning. Because Mrs. Jones permitted the school counselor to enter her classroom to observe student interaction and is seeking help, I would work with her to improve her communication with students. Validation of her concerns and her feelings is very important to establish rapport with her. Then I would actually share with Mrs. Jones my observations of the ratio of time she spent addressing students and time spent on the lesson. I would ask Mrs. Jones if she was willing to try some techniques that might improve her time devoted to the lesson. If Mrs. Jones was willing to work on her communication and teaching style, I would then share with her some of the comments she made to students during my observation and suggest some new methods for motivating students. Gardner's (1993) seven intelligences might be a framework for helping her to understand the learning styles of various students. Updated information on classroom techniques for working with students with attention deficit hyperactivity disorder and other types of learning disabilities along with specific methods for motivating at-risk students may help Mrs. Jones. I would also volunteer to come into her classroom regularly to bring guidance lessons and work separately in the counseling office with the most disruptive students. Mrs. Jones's classroom control problem should be discussed without being overly intrusive on her freedom to choose her personal teaching style. I might share with the principal that I was working with Mrs. Jones to improve her teaching and communication with her students. I would suggest to the principal that Mrs. Jones might benefit from an in-service on motivating at-risk students. It would not be appropriate or necessary to divulge other information to the principal at this time.

If Mrs. Jones was not willing to improve her communication with students, it might be necessary to share with the principal my concern that the school climate in her classroom was not enhancing student motivation to learn. I would suggest to the principal that an administrative observation be made to verify my observations and let the administrator proceed to work with Mrs. Jones on classroom control. Mrs. Jones's personal problems should be kept confidential. However, her behavior in the classroom that might be negatively affecting the welfare of the students is a school matter and should be brought to the attention of an administrator. I would personally work with the administrator to facilitate a nonpunative positive learning experience for Mrs. Jones.

In addition to any counseling provided on site by the school counselor, I might suggest that Mrs. Jones seek outside counseling to help her with any personal problems that she might have. Before making a formal referral, I would work with Mrs. Jones for a couple of counseling sessions to assist her in sorting out her possible personal problems from the school-related problems. I would reassure her that she has my support in working with her as well as with the students. I also would suggest that she might be able to receive counseling through an employee assistance program. Other suggestions would include in-service workshops to deal with burnout and motivating at-risk students, a physical checkup with her doctor, and family counseling, if appropriate.

Richard Pearson

While reading and reflecting on the several dilemmas posed by this critical incident, I found myself turning back to Shertzer and Stone's (1980) discussion of social role and role conflict for a perspective that would be useful in structuring a consideration of the issues the incident presents. Shertzer and Stone asserted that a social role consists of the behavior that is expected of a person occupying a status (or position) in a social structure (p. 118). In this case, the status is that of a counselor in a particular private school. They noted that the expectations of a variety of people (e.g., the status-holder himself or herself, as well as other persons who occupy other positions in the social structure in question) are typically involved in defining the role. They also pointed out that role conflict can occur when different people whose interests touch on the position have differing expectations of how the status-holder should function (p. 121).

It seems to me most of the counselor's questions center on the type of role conflict Shertzer and Stone (1980) identified as that caused by "mutually incompatible elements" (p. 121) of the role. In the present instance, that incompatibility revolves around the counselor's wondering if he should inform the principal about the classroom dysfunction of Mrs. Jones, a teacher for whom his job definition indicates he has consulting responsibility. With this background, let us examine the specific questions the counselor has posed.

It seems to me Question 2 (i.e., should the principal be informed of Mrs. Jones's classroom behavior management difficulties?) is the most problematic, therefore I address it first. The dilemma involves what Stone and Shertzer (1980, p. 121) identified as role conflict centered on mutually incompatible role elements, that is, consultation with teachers and reporting teacher deficiencies to administration. Apparently, such reporting is not a formal part of the existing job definition, but one which the counselor is considering taking on. I would note that, despite his concerns about the possibility of "psychological abuse" to students, calling such behavior to the principal's attention is not required by the counselor's ethical duty to warn. Thus, if the counselor does take such action, he would, in effect, be introducing an element of role conflict where it did not previously exist.

I agree with the counselor's hunch that to take the initiative of informing the principal of Mrs. Jones's classroom difficulties would create serious issues of role conflict and would, most likely, end her willingness (and that of other teachers) to bring professional and professionally relevant personal concerns to the counselor for assistance. Either the function of teacher consultation or that of monitoring teacher effectiveness must take precedence. My own view is that the counselor should not expand his existing role to include monitoring teachers' classroom behavior for administration unless he wants (at least functionally) to give up the teacher consultation element of his job description.

If the counselor has no clear sense of which of these elements should take precedence, then perhaps a conversation or series of conversations with relevant "role definers" (in this instance, teachers and the principal) would be helpful in clarifying and resolving the issue. A broadly understood, publicly articulated statement of this aspect of the counselor's role might result.

The recommendation that the counselor initiate exchange with role definers as a means of clarifying and defining his role can be expanded to address his query (in Question 2) about what could have been done to avoid "this mess." I believe that the current issue of role conflict could have been minimized if the counselor had previously examined his role in light of the differing expectations of the various stake holders, including himself. Such a consideration would increase the likelihood that the various types of role conflict identified by Shertzer and Stone (1980) could be identified enough in advance to allow preventive action. For example, the counselor might decide that consultation with teachers is not only required by his job definition but is also something he considers to be professionally fulfilling to him. In this case, the recognition that monitoring teacher effectiveness for administration is apt to cut off their willingness to discuss their classroom difficulties would dissuade him from taking this function on at his own initiative and to resist doing so at administration's request. Conversely, if (perhaps because he would eventually like to move into educational administration), he would like to gain experience with regard to supervising and evaluating teachers, then a clear sanctioning of that function by administration and a clear communication of his responsibilities to teachers would let all interested parties (teachers, administration, and the counselor himself) know exactly what the boundaries of his responsibilities are.

With regard to the issues raised in Question 1 (i.e., is Mrs. Jones depressed, and, if so, what should be done?), I would make a couple of observations. First, the counselor appears to be assuming Mrs. Jones's classroom difficulties are a matter of either burnout or depression. I am not sure what is gained by insisting on that dichotomy, especially with regard to appropriate counselor response. What we do know is that this person is a previously effective teacher who is now expressing dissatisfaction with the way things are going in her classroom and in her personal life. It appears the counselor believes he has the professional expertise needed to help Mrs. Jones deal with classroom management issues. He may also believe he has the competence to offer assistance with regard to personal and emotional matters she discussed (e.g., marital problems, career uncertainty).

If the counselor judges he has the time, expertise, and interest to embrace personal counseling for teachers as an element of his role, then perhaps a broadly focused intervention that examined the interplay between school and nonschool issues would be not only appropriate but reasonable. However, to return to a perspective offered in discussing Question 2, both consultation with regard to classroom management and consultation (or counseling) with regard to largely nonschool issues are, from the perspective of role conflict, incompatible with informing the principal of Mrs. Jones's classroom management difficulties.

Finally, the counselor asks: Is it therapeutically effective to address Mrs. Jones's classroom dysfunction without also dealing with her "personal and emotional issues"? It seems to me that in posing the question, the counselor is also giving us an indication of his theoretical orientation vis-à-vis attitudinal and behavioral change. That is, he puts forth the classical psychodynamic assumption that to "simply" change behavior without addressing the underlying causes will not really solve the problem. Although I am generally inclined to agree with that perspective, it seems to me there is an important interaction between underlying personal and emotional issues and Mrs. Jones's classroom functioning. This teacher has demonstrated sensitivity and effectiveness in the past. New behavior change seems to have occurred during the same period of time that the background, characteristics, and needs of her students also changed. In the absence of further information to the contrary, one could reasonably take the position that her difficulties center on problems in acquiring new behaviors that are effective with a changed clientele or on problems encountered in trying to modify and adapt existing behavioral repertoires to a changed context. In the latter case, what the counselor worries will be a temporary "fix" may, in reality, address the core of the problem.

Because it appears counselor consultation concerning classroom management issues is consistent with teachers' and administrators' expectations, perhaps a reasonable intervention strategy would be to focus initially on helping Mrs. Jones modify her dysfunctional interaction with students. If a behaviorally focused approach is not effective, the counselor can then appropriately offer the suggestion that counseling might be a useful resource in helping Mrs. Jones come to terms with her personal and professional malaise.

REFERENCES

Gardner, H. (1993). *Multiple intelligences: The theory in practice*. New York: HarperCollins.

Shertzer, B., & Stone, S. (1980). *Fundamentals of counseling (3rd ed.)*. Boston: Houghton Mifflin.

Faculty and Student Relations: "Am I Only a Student Advocate?"

CRITICAL INCIDENT

Background

This is my first job since getting my degree. It is in an alternative, behavioral school serving approximately 57 middle and high school students from 12 surrounding school districts (depending on who has run away, been put in lockup, or been terminated from the school for any number of reasons). The students present issues ranging from mild antisocial behaviors to one step short of jail, with some of them having already visited a variety of juvenile lockups. All are on individual education plans (IEPs). They come from foster homes, group homes, residential programs, fragmented families, and, for the lucky few, an intact two-parent home. They are Hispanic, African American, White, and mixes of all three. They are mostly young men with only seven young women.

The classrooms are small, with six to eight students, a teacher, and an assistant in each (there are seven teachers, with only one who is certified as a teacher and none of whom are certified in special education, although they are all working on it). There is also a reading teacher, two physical education teachers, and an art teacher who comes in once a week on a volunteer basis, as well as an on-site nurse and her assistant. The staff also includes two assistant principals, one each for the middle and high school, two on-campus therapists, and one per diem therapist who comes in 2.5 days a week. The therapists conduct therapy with all of the residential students and the more needy day students. There is also the director of education, two office staff, a residential case manager, and myself, a day case manager/school adjustment counselor. I am responsible for counseling 34 students on a weekly basis and managing their files. In addition, I chair all 57 IEP meetings and three additional quarterly case conferences, as well as crisis intervention, emergency meetings, impromptu meetings, monthly trainings, and scheduled support meetings with on- and off-site staff.

Incident

It takes a while to get settled into any new job. This one is no different, although it may be more challenging because of the students' behaviors. I think it is also challenging because of the staff posture toward the students. Because this is a behavior modification school, our primary responsibility is to implement a behavior modification system to better prepare these adolescents to interact more appropriately with society. However, at times I wonder if there is a clear understanding among the staff as to the importance of "walking our talk." We are trying to teach punctuality, yet our classes do not start or end on time. We are trying to teach responsibility, yet I have seen some of the staff shirk their own, with students being given very little. We are trying to teach better coping skills to daily stressors in their lives, yet there is a tone and a volume level from the staff directed at the students that contradict what we teach them. We try to teach them nonviolent measures of interacting with each other, yet there are physical restraints, physical escorting maneuvers, and, occasionally, some questionable physical contact between staff and students. We try to teach them about boundaries and the proper respect for people boundaries, yet the staff seem to constantly blur their relationships with these adolescents, sometimes being a teacher, sometimes a buddy, sometimes a disciplinarian, sometimes one of the guys (or gals), and sometimes all of them at once.

My office is in the high school building. When I am scheduled to see a middle school student, I will go over to the middle school (100 yards away) and bring the student back to my office. At the end of our half hour, I then bring him back (there is only one young woman in the middle school, and she is not in my caseload). Because of my schedule, I often see only parts of a complete interaction between staff and students, which I call vignettes. Most of the time I do not see what led up to them or how they are resolved. Sometimes I only see the beginning, the middle, or the end without knowing which until later. Therefore, I find it hard to assess what is actually happening in these interactions between the students and the staff. This issue is my dilemma.

Discussion

I am an advocate for the students. At this end of the educational system, it is clear to me that these students need all the advocating they can get. This is not to say they are mistreated angels. They are very adept at manipulating the system to their advantage. Still, I feel they are not treated with the kind of respect, consistency, and dignity that even the staff would like to be treated by their supervisors (this may be part of a more systemic issue!). In the 4 short months that I have been here, I have seen the following:

1. As I come for a student, teachers will say to me, in front of the whole class, "Please, take him and keep him. I don't want him" or "Oh, thank God! He really needs some help!"

2. A teacher's aide physically, with his whole body, pressed a student face-first in a corner of the shutdown room, literally screaming at him, "Come on! You want to take a swing at me? Come on!"

3. On another occasion, a different aide physically escorted a student down the hall to the shutdown room saying, "I'd love for you to try something right now!"

4. An adult teacher's aide in a doorway of a room with a female student laughed, joked, and touched her in a way that would best be described as two peers rather than that of a teacher and a female adolescent student.

5. Almost all of the male teachers at one time or another physically jabbed, joked, punched, or pushed the young male students in a way that, if the students did that to the staff or to each other, would get consequenced for their behavior.

6. The staff treat the young women differently than the young men, especially when it comes to consequences and time in the shutdown room. When there is a young woman in the shutdown room, it sounds as if there is a party going on in there, as opposed to when there is a young man in there and it sounds like a fight is happening.

7. The staff address students with looks and tones that one generally sees between two people arguing, fighting, or at least who do not like each other.

8. The staff putting down the students behind their backs when they think they are out of earshot (which they seem to model from the assistant principals, who, unfortunately, seem to model that from the director of education).

9. The students, in session with me, confide about their treatment by the staff, and consistently the same staff names come up with the same behaviors.

10. The list goes on, daily.

QUESTIONS

1. How does a new counselor balance the need to have teachers and staff as allies with the need to be an active advocate for the students?

2. As a new counselor, at what point do you speak out about the adult behaviors you are witnessing that interfere with your job and the purpose of the program?
3. How does a new counselor broach this subject without appearing as a crusader?
4. Is it possible to address these issues as they arise without alienating the teachers and empowering the students to act out even more?

RESPONSES TO THE INCIDENT

Greg Brigman

This example involves legal and ethical issues and is clearly a difficult situation. The first rule of thumb when faced with legal and ethical issues is to consult with other professionals. Some principles that apply include the following:

1. Keep in mind that if you separate yourself from the faculty you will not be effective in influencing their change or in working with them in the future. Without a working relationship with the staff, your ability to help the students will be greatly diminished.
2. This is not an either/or situation. As counselors, we are frequently in situations in which we need to align with the goals and speak from the perspective of our client. Whether with teachers, students, administrators, or parents, we need to reflect their concerns and offer assistance in helping them reach their goals. This may involve you, as counselor, helping them reframe their goals into something ethically comfortable to you. For teachers, two possible goals may be to reduce the stress of working with high-risk youths and to avoid lawsuits and being fired for losing control in heated situations. For students, the goal may be to get the aide or teacher off their back. For administrators, some goals may be to avoid lawsuits, improve staff morale, and improve student performance and behavior. For parents, one goal may be to figure out how to change the system to promote a safer and more humane learning environment for their child.

For example, with the aide who is pushing the student's face into the corner and taunting the student to hit him, you could say "I saw what a stressful situation you where in earlier today. Does that kind of thing happen often around here? I'm pretty new but I know it must be scary having to deal with those kind of explosive situations on a regular basis. Do you have much support for handling those kinds of incidents? I was wondering if you wanted to have an opportunity to discuss how to keep situations like that from escalating because I know you don't want a lawsuit on your hands and your job on the line every time one of these students lose it."

With the student, the offer would take on the student's perspective. You could say, "I saw what a tough situation you were in earlier today with the teacher aide. Does that kind of thing happen often around here? I'm pretty new but I know it must be scary having to deal with those situations on a regular basis. Does anyone teach you guys how to handle those kinds of situations so you keep the aides off your back? I was wondering if you wanted to have an opportunity to talk about how to keep situations like that from blowing up because I know you don't want that to happen again and you don't want your Department of Juvenile Justice counselor on your case either."

With the administrator, you might say, "Let me tell you about a situation that could be very serious." Give the details. Then say, "As you probably know, situations like this have resulted in successful lawsuits against schools. After you determine what needs to be done on this immediate situation, I would be happy to work with you and the School Advisory Committee on a staff development plan to avoid the same thing happening again. The best plans I have seen address the entire learning environment and not only avoid suits but also improve faculty morale and increase student performance. It would be a natural for our school improvement plan. I think, together, we could come up with a good plan. I could get some information to get things started if you like."

With the parent of the student who was pushed into the corner, you might say, "I would like to help you make sure your son is safe here. Can you tell me what you tried in the past to deal with teacher or teacher aide problems? How did that work out?" If the parent has not been successful, it may be because he or she does not understand how to use the system. You can be their coach. "Have you considered asking the principal to attend a teacher conference?" If the parent has tried to get administrative support and found it impossible, you might ask if he or she has ever considered going to the next level. "Have you ever contacted the district director? Do you need a phone number?"

3. Regarding the possible physical abuse and sexual harassment implied in this example, the counselor must be certain of the facts and then not be involved in unethical and illegal behavior of not reporting the abuse or harassment if reporting is warranted. Consultation with the administrator to voice concern of student welfare and concern of the possibility of lawsuits if appropriate action were not taken would be advised. If the administrator is reluctant to take appropriate action, the counselor should request that the school system attorney or a Department of Justice judge be consulted regarding the applicable law. There needs to be a clear paper trail that tracks the process. The administrator does not want to be on record of requesting that you not check out something that could be illegal. The counselor is bound by the American Counseling Association (1995) and the American School Counselor Association (1992) codes of ethics. They are the standards of practice in our field. Counselors cannot afford to let others intimidate them into jeopardizing all of their hard work to become a professional counselor.

As a new counselor, at what point do you speak out about the adult behaviors you are witnessing that interfere not only with your job but also with the purpose of the program? If the behavior is possibly illegal, then the counselor needs to take action immediately. If the behavior is not illegal, then some guiding principles apply:

A. To be effective as an advocate for students, you have to have credibility with the faculty and administration. The best way to build credibility is to provide direct services, such as individual and small-group counseling, classroom guidance, and consultation with parents and teachers, and to monitor student behavior and achievement and report on successes.

In this situation, it may be appropriate to work individually and in small groups with the students having difficulty controlling anger, dealing with authority, or handling conflicts. If the counselor were not up to this task yet, then coleading with a strong counselor from another school or an agency would be helpful. In this case, there are several resources within the school with which to team. Just coordinating this service will not build the credibility needed.

Working through the School Advisory Committee to develop a staff development series on conflict resolution may be very helpful. Collaborating with district staff or an outside consultant to provide the training to faculty would give the counselor some visibility without sole responsibility to provide the training. This faculty and staff seem to be a pretty difficult audience. Therefore, someone outside the school with high credibility would have a greater chance of changing attitudes and behaviors. The school counselor could volunteer to teach some of the lessons through classroom guidance, which could be seen as helping the teachers with a new task and providing another model for them. In order for the staff development training to have the best chance for success, it must be perceived as the project of the School Advisory Committee and the administrator versus just the counselor. The counselor needs to be seen as helping the school implement part of its school improvement plan.

Questions 3 and 4 seem to imply how not to look naive and be easily dismissed and how not to get caught in the middle of a power struggle and forced into taking sides. Many experienced counselors use the following strategies for difficult situations involving winning support from reluctant groups.

B. Don't take sides. The counselor is more in the role of conflict mediator, respectfully listening to both sides and helping each side determine prosocial ways to resolve the conflict.

C. Align with groups who have positive influence and act as a consultant in developing a collaborative problem-solving model. This is a team effort. No counselor working alone can hope to be successful in this type of situation. First, find a respected ally within each group. In this case, find a respected teacher. Every school has caring, professional, and respected teachers. They are one key to gaining and maintaining wide-based support. Another group from which to identify an ally is the parent/community group. Respected parents, community, and business leaders who are not timid about using positive power and the system to help the school and students are critical assets. The School Advisory Committee often has one or more parents as well as community and business leaders who serve on these committees because they want to contribute to making the school better. Recruiting students who have leadership potential and are respected among peers is key to winning student support. Some type of peer mediation program could be influential in changing the peer culture in this school. Finding an administrator within the school or at the next level can be a critical piece in the puzzle of changing a school culture. With all of these groups, their support is gained when they see joining the team as helping them reach their goals. Once the team is in place training in consensus building and collaborative problem solving can ensure a few power-hungry individuals do not take over the process.

4. Align with the "Best Practice" research and standards. Become knowledgeable about collaboration, consensus building, family and community involvement, and create safe and encouraging learning environments and "Best Practices"

for alternative schools. Provide the team with the latest research and standards related to your team's goals. This strategy is made easier by aligning with a university partner who can help provide the research summaries.

John B. Stewart

The counselor in this context has a number of concerns that implicate her or his professional practice. The counselor must have respect and dignity for professional colleagues while maintaining an advocacy perspective for students within this educational setting. Also, the counselor must be concerned about his or her professional relationships with colleagues so that together they can work to accomplish school program goals. Furthermore, the counselor must have staff and administrative support to provide a credible and meaningful counseling program that meets the short-term and long-term developmental needs of students.

From the description of the given context, it is quite possible that many of school staff may not know what is considered ethical behavior, because few of them have met the criteria for teacher certification. Thus, the counselor has an educative role to perform with coworkers. As a beginning step, ethical codes indicate that professionals work on an individual basis when dealing with what they considered to be unethical behavior. As individuals within a larger context, counselors ought always to conduct themselves in a manner that is exemplary for others. Such exemplary behavior acts as a social learning stimulus for both colleagues and students.

Counselors should consult with colleagues when situations arise that do not respect the rights and dignity of students. For example, when the teacher said, "Please, take him and keep him. I don't want him," the counselor could use this situation to teach how such words may influence the student's self-esteem as well as the student's willingness to work cooperatively with that teacher. Acting on the colleague-to-colleague level, the counselor has the chance to develop a working relationship with the teacher as well as instruct that person in positive ways to interact with students. With such open dialogue, the counselor will help the teacher through the frustration of dealing with inappropriate student behavior. In addition, the counselor's consultation with individual staff members, if done professionally, contributes to staff cohesion. If all personnel on staff behave consistently, then students are not prone to play one staff member off against another, which may empower them to act out even more.

Furthermore, I suggest that the counselor work with the senior administrator to address the behavioral and systemic concerns within the institution. The counselor should raise his or her concerns about specific behaviors and attitudes that are not conducive to the overall developmental and social needs of the student population. The counselor might suggest a staff-needs analysis in several areas, for example, staff knowledge about the characteristics of this student population and conflict resolution skills. On the basis of the needs analysis results, a professional in-service program could be planned that is designed to enhance the knowledge and skill level of teachers as they promote the short-term and long-term developmental needs of students. In addition, the counselor might recommend speakers and provide materials to address the issues raised by staff. Working with the administrator in a consultative role helps the counselor to advocate for students by having input into an in-service program that enhances the knowledge and skill level of other staff members. As a result of such an in-service program, students' needs will be better served. By working with an administrator, the counselor does not stand out as the "crusader" and positions himself or herself as a coparticipant in the program.

Another way that counselors can advocate for their students is to explain their role within the counseling program to fellow staff members and to suggest ways that they can promote the program. In this context, it is possible that staff members do not know the counseling program's goals and objectives, and thus educating them can heighten the staff's awareness of how their behavior may affect the program. Also, because the counselor is new to the staff, it is an excellent opportunity to explain his or her personal counseling orientation and program objectives. By educating other staff members, counselors not only provide them with program knowledge but also educate them about the counselors' expertise in meeting student needs. In addition, counselors help to promote their program by having others informed about its goals and objectives.

Counselors can advocate for students when they work with administrators to review and revise policies, particularly those that are outdated or do not respect the rights of students. Such advocacy could extend into the community by having community sponsors for student programs, such as work experience, working with seniors, and working in stores, hospitals, and so on. The counselor could form a committee with the approval of the senior school administration to review and determine how the total school programs meet the school's objectives of meeting the developmental needs of its students.

If all else fails, the counselor is obligated to bring ethical violations concerns to the governing professional group. Such procedures are spelled out and are specific to the local and state body. I suggest that this be a last resort, but a necessary one if all other methods are not fruitful. Also, if the counselor chooses to go this route, it is important to follow the prescribed procedures so that the concerns will be handled professionally.

REFERENCES

American Counseling Association. (1995). *Code of ethics and standards of practice*. Alexandria, VA: Author.

American School Counselor Association. (1992). *Ethical standards for school counselors*. Alexandria, VA: Author.

Group Counseling:
"The Counselor Blows Up"

CRITICAL INCIDENT

Background

I have been counseling groups for the past 6 years. The groups are conducted in a small book room used only by the person who grades papers for the English department. The room is furnished with a large table, chairs, and the grader's desk. The room lends itself to informality with no classroom atmosphere. I have used various criteria for determining which students should be members of the groups. However, membership is always voluntary. I meet with the students during their assigned study hall period.

This particular group met once a week over a 7-month period. The group consisted of four ninth-grade boys, two of whom were repeating the ninth grade. These boys were selected by their teachers, who identified them as having the "worst attitudes" of any of their students. Although the boys knew one another prior to the group sessions, they did not run in the same "gangs." All four of the boys had police records.

The boys were told they did not have to decide about group membership until the end of our first counseling session. If, at that time, they accepted membership, they were then committed to attend the remaining meetings. I told them there were only three restrictions I would place on the group:

1. No physical harm was to be done to anyone or any property in the room.

2. What was said in the group was not to be discussed outside of the room.

3. No one member could leave the group until we all decided to discontinue meeting as a group.

All four boys chose to continue. After explaining that I hoped the time would be spent in discussing their problems, I emphasized it was their group, and they could spend the time any way they saw fit.

I am still amazed at their ingenuity in finding so many ways of testing my commitments to them. I fought hard to keep from "correcting" their behavior as they attempted to challenge, ignore, annoy, and shock me. A workable group began to emerge from all the chaos, after many weeks of somehow living up to what I had promised. The boys slowly began to join me at the discussion table, one by one. The one exception was Danny.

Although none of the boys came from ideal home situations, only Danny lived in a fatherless home. Danny was an only child and lived with his obviously doting mother. His mother had a reputation for "covering" for Danny when the school had any occasion to check up on him. Unlike the other boys, Danny did not have to work in order to have money and clothes. In my judgment, Danny was "spoiled" but quite likable.

While it seemed the other boys were now ready to use the time to talk seriously, Danny was still instigating various distractions. The other boys never seemed to get upset with Danny and his constant shenanigans. I soon learned that their basic philosophy was "let and let live, don't bother anyone if he is not hurting you." In trying to live up to what I had said about each member spending his time as they wished, I began to ignore Danny's behavior, as he set about trying to lure other boys away from the table by engaging them in private conversations or diverting their attention in any way he could. It had been a long and frustrating wait to see the group come this far. I am afraid that my feelings were becoming rather hostile toward Danny, because he relentlessly tried to destroy what had taken so long to develop.

One day, Danny was sitting at a desk, opening the drawers and going through the contents while the rest of us were sitting at the table talking. I had asked him not to, explaining that the grader let us use the room and the desk belonged to her. When he chose to continue, my annoyance grew until I felt I could no longer keep still. Although he was not harming or taking anything from the desk, I felt I had some obligation to the grader to protect her privacy. I was unsure as to how the group would view my censure of Danny's behavior, because he was not really breaking a group rule.

I finally decided that if I were now accepted as a group member, then I, too, had a right to express my feelings, even if they were contrary to the feelings of the group. Although I spoke calmly, my choice of words showed I was upset. "This is a place to express feelings and right now I want to express mine. Danny is making me so damn mad right now that I can't even decide how to express my anger." Danny immediately jumped up, overturning his chair, and hollered, "All right, if that's the way you feel, I'll leave!" As he went toward the door, I yelled, "You can't! You can't leave the group because of our initial contract." I hoped the group had some meaning for Danny and that it would be strong enough to hold him, but my hopes were not high since he had displayed such total disinterest. Surely Danny knew as well as I did that I really was powerless to stop him from walking out the door, and I certainly could not force him to return again. On the basis of his past behavior, Danny's walking out would have been the predicted out-come. However, something held him there that day. He did not leave, and I have always wondered why he decided to stay.

Discussion

First, let me state that I do not recommend "blowing-up" as an acceptable technique for a counselor. I consider it my weakness and my inexperience that allowed me not only to lose control when the incident occurred, but also to cloud my vision to the circumstances leading up to it. Although I feel I was justified in being upset with Danny's efforts to sabotage the group, I know I was wrong in getting so involved with my own anger and tem-porarily ceasing in the process to care about or to understand Danny's feelings. I can see how Danny might have interpreted my permissiveness as rejection. By ignoring Danny's actions, I also ignored Danny. Perhaps it was only through this incident that I was able to show Danny that I did consider him a group mem-ber and that he was not insignificant. Nevertheless, my attack might have easily placed him in a position of feeling compelled to leave to "save face."

Another possible explanation for his failure to leave was his per-ception of me as an authority figure. He stayed because he felt he had to. However, I believe that I had already passed that test and was no longer a threat to any of the boys. Also, because Danny was not adverse to being absent from school, he could have easily arranged to be absent on group days.

I feel this incident is an example of the value of group coun-seling, indicating the power of the peer group. Danny was pos-sibly rejecting me as a group member and resented my feminine intrusion into this masculine group. Looking back at the type of distractions that Danny created, they were usually of a mascu-line nature, such a rough talk, "horsing around," and activities he felt would exclude me. I feel Danny had a strong need to belong and to identify with the masculine norms generated by his peers in the group. Perhaps he realized that to become a real member of the group, he would have to join with the others in their acceptance of me.

It appeared to me that Danny gained a great deal from his group experience. He looked up to Vik, a large well-built boy who emerged as leader of the group. I often watched Danny as Vik talked about such things as "love" and "fear," which I am certain Danny had viewed as effeminate. Danny's concept of what one must feel or do to be masculine was obviously altered.

I have offered several ideas that I feel were factors as to why the incident occurred and as to why I believe Danny would ultimately have chosen to remain in the group. But the question that is still in my mind is this one: Why did a boy with a history like Danny's choose to remain when I had put him on the spot in front of his peers at a time when he was obviously operating at an emotional level rather than a rational one? I would be interested in the opinion of others.

QUESTIONS

1. How active should a counselor be in a group? How emotionally involved should one become?
2. Was I really rejecting Danny, or was he rejecting me, or both?
3. How could I have better handled the situation?
4. Because Danny had not joined with the rest of us, was a clash of this type inevitable, or would he have found some other way to have joined us in time?
5. Why didn't Danny walk out?

RESPONSES TO THE INCIDENT

Rudolf Dreikurs

The counselor submitted this report for the purpose of understanding a crucial event in her work with a group. She tries to analyze the development of the group in a way that would perhaps be acceptable in a different frame of reference. From my point of view, her interpretations of the events are incorrect; I see them in a different light.

The cause of her difficulty seems to be evident on the first page. One may question the validity of an attitude merely from the words used to describe what happened. For me, the words this counselor used are highly significant. She says, "The boys *were told*," "they did not *have to decide*," "they *were then committed*," "no physical harm *was to be done*," "was *not* to be discussed," and "no one member *could* leave." It is obvious the counselor wanted to be democratic, but the choice of her words, along with her probable tone of voice, indicated a rather autocratic approach. All subsequent events show clearly that she got herself into a power conflict with the boys from the first moment.

Had she recognized her involvement, she would not have been so amazed at their "ingenuity" to fight her. Because she did not realize that the boys had involved her in a power conflict, she misinterpreted their behavior as "testing my commitments." It is her involvement in a power struggle that made it so difficult for her to keep from correcting them. She tried not to respond, but obviously she was annoyed and shocked. What made it difficult for her to "live up" to what she had promised was her pretense to be democratic, a pretense that the boys easily recognized and challenged. This is the reason it took her so many weeks to emerge from the chaos. When the boys realized they could not succeed in defeating her, they slowly gave up the fight, except for one boy.

The counselor recognized that Danny was spoiled. She refers to his status as an only child without a father, with a mother who tried to make up for that and who gave him the justification that he had a right to do what he wanted. This is how he behaved in the group. At no point did the counselor attempt to explain to Danny the significance of his own behavior; therefore, she failed to recognize his determination to defeat her at every turn. It was almost as if she was a sitting duck at whom the boy directed his potshots. When she tried to counteract his disturbance, he became worse, instigating the other boys to side with him against her. Naturally this behavior frustrated her because she did not know what to do with a boy in a power conflict, how to extricate herself, how to help him and the others to understand his goals, and how to lead him away from the power struggle. Under these circumstances, it is not surprising that by "waiting" she became hostile, not only because Danny tried to destroy the group but also because he continued to defeat her. That went on until finally she put the cards on the table, no longer pretending to be uninvolved.

The incident started off in the typical way such conflicts take place. She told Danny what not to do, and so he decided to do it until she could no longer stand it. When she blew her top, it was not because she tried to protect the privacy of the test reader but because she was helpless in view of Danny's power. In this moment, she came down from her throne and became human. But leave it to Danny to increase his pressure by jumping up, overturning his chair, and threatening to leave. She felt utterly helpless, and Danny, as well as she, knew she was powerless to stop him from walking out. Then why did he fail to leave? Why should he leave? She revealed her defeat, and he liked it. It was only his old game of defeating her. She was a good sparring partner, an easy target for his provocations. There was now no benefit for him to leave. This picture is how it looks to me. But the counselor gave a number of other possible reasons for his staying, which deserve closer scrutiny. The events look different from another point of view.

She considered it a consequence of her weakness and inexperience that she lost control. Actually, she gained control by admitting her defeat. Contrary to what she assumed, she was not "getting" involved with Danny when she got angry. In this moment, she extricated herself from the long-suffering involvement that she precipitated before the incident. She was right that her outburst gave Danny the realization that he was not insignificant.

In this light, the value of group counseling or the power of the peer group appears superfluous. The group actually played a limited role in the incident. Because the counselor did not identify the power conflict in which Danny involved her, she assumed, without any justification, that the boy was "rejecting" her. Once she began this kind of speculation, she even went so far afield as assuming that Danny resented her feminine intrusion into a masculine group. Naturally, Danny's destructions were aggressive, what else would one expect from such a boy? The need for masculine identification may be correct, but it does not explain the way he dealt with the counselor. His assumed fear of being effeminate reflects, rather, the counselor's preoccupation with masculinity and femininity and her own apprehension about being feminine in a group of tough boys.

Now let us consider the incident's questions:

1. The counselor of a group should always be an active partici-pant. Emotional involvement is not desirable. However, the counselor was deeply involved emotionally with the group long before the incident occurred.
2. I can see no evidence for either Danny rejecting her or she rejecting him. He provoked her; but this does not mean that he did not like her at the same time.
3. The effort of the counselor to keep Danny in the room was only the last step in her effort to control the group. What the counselor needed was not to handle "this situation" better, but to resolve the conflict long before it came to a showdown. Contrary to what she believed, losing her temper was con-structive. She admitted her defeat openly and he responded to that by not going much further.
4. The clash was inevitable when the counselor became more and more defeated in her attitude and transactions with Danny.

Don C. Locke

Obviously, the group had a history together and a relationship had developed among the boys and the leader (the counselor). If I assume that some 10–15 sessions had been held and Danny had not engaged in the process, I wonder if an earlier direct inter-vention, especially by an experienced counselor, might have been appropriate.

The ground rules for the group were only those that were "told" to them by the leader. Ground rules are most effective when group members can sense ownership of the rules by directly participating in their development. The leader can set rules like those she "told them" by asking the members to decide how they will relate to each other in the group. If the members do not express the desire to avoid physical contact, then the leader can suggest the rule, at least giving the appearance of mutuality in the establishment of ground rules. Leaders are responsible for telling group members that the rules will be reviewed periodically during the process to determine if they are still relevant or if new rules need to be introduced. Later in the process when Danny began going through the desk in the room, the leader used a new ground rule to restrict the behavior. The introduction of this rule suggests that the relationship between the leader and the members is indeed hierarchical and the leader could impose rules as she saw fit.

In most cases, school counselors should be participant observers in their groups. The exception would be the rare case of a therapy group. In most counseling groups, the counselors can use their participation as evidence of their humanity and involvement in situations similar to those experienced by group members. In doing so, the counselors can model appropriate behaviors rather than "explain how it should be done" or discuss situations in isolation. The role of participant observer provides the counselor an opportunity to become "emotionally involved" and to have group members use their skills in addressing concerns expressed by the counselor. For example, the counselor might ask group members how she or he might have handled a difficult situation. In this case, the counselor might have used the difficulties with Danny by saying something like, "I invited boys to participate in a group with me and I want all of them to be involved. I found that one member is not participating. In fact he is deliberately challenging my leadership of the group. How might I handle this situation?"

A number of possibilities exist on how the situation might have been handled differently. First, if all members had been involved in the development of the ground rules, there probably would have been a greater sense of ownership and willingness to abide by those rules. The counselor could have introduced a rule on member participation, requiring that all members participate at some level during each session or discuss reasons for their nonparticipation. Because the group met in a room used primarily by another professional, a ground rule regarding respect for this person's space could have also been introduced.

The counselor should have used ground rules to determine how well members would participate in her group. The group should have not advanced to a halfway point (or beyond) in a 28-session process before the confrontation occurred. Should the counselor have blown up? No. The counselor should have used general standards of practice to exercise leadership so that blowing up would be unnecessary.

HIV and AIDS: "What's Going to Be Done to Protect My Child?"

CRITICAL INCIDENT

Background

The public elementary school served fourth-, fifth-, and sixth-grade students. These students were bussed from different parts of the city, so there were a variety of racial and ethnic backgrounds as well as socioeconomic status (SES). Because it was a public school, all of the teachers were either certified or in the process of being certified (i.e., emergency certification). There was a mix of veteran teachers and fairly new teachers.

I had served as the school's only counselor for nearly 3 years. My caseload was about twice what it should be, about 750 students. I tried to incorporate classroom guidance lessons, small-group counseling, and individual counseling, in addition to much consultation with the teachers. I had a fairly good rapport with most of the teachers as well as administration.

Sam, one of the sixth-grade students, had recently returned to school after the death of his 19-year-old brother. It was a small town, and it was well-known that Sam's brother had died of complications acquired from AIDS. The family tended to be very private, so the method by which Sam's brother contracted AIDS was not known, although there was much speculation.

My office was located next to the teachers' lounge, and one day I overheard Sam and his family were the prime topic of conversation: "I heard his brother was gay," "I heard he was a junkie and so is the father," "I heard that some of the other family members have IT too," and so on. There had also been some incidents of rumors among the students as well as name-calling ("fag," "queer," etc.). I had already addressed the issue of HIV and AIDS—what it is, how you do and do not get it—in the classroom guidance lessons. I had dealt with the name-calling incidents on a small-group and individual basis, because the administration and teachers were uncomfortable with the issue of sexual orientation.

Incident

Sam's homeroom teacher, Mrs. Beck, came rushing into my office one day, along with the principal and assistant principal. Mrs. Beck was upset because Sam had fallen on the playground just a few minutes before and, as a result, had a bloody nose. The sight of the blood sent the children into an uproar because they were afraid of "getting AIDS" from Sam. After all, "he might be gay and he probably got it from his brother." Mrs. Beck also admitted her concern about possibly having an HIV-positive child in her classroom. The principal was already anticipating fallout from other teachers as well as parents.

There were only a few minutes left in the school day, and I asked to see Sam and also to address Mrs. Beck's class. I had talked with Sam privately before to express my sympathy about his brother and to offer a listening ear if Sam desired. Sam had been very polite but very quiet. I checked on Sam that afternoon to make sure he was physically and emotionally all right and told him that I would check on him first thing in the morning. I also told him I was going to contact his parents to let them know about the accident. I addressed the class and reminded them of the things we talked about in our lesson on HIV and AIDS.

Discussion

The principal was inundated with a barrage of phone calls and visits from parents and teachers that night and the next day. The majority were demanding to know the HIV status of Sam and to know what we were going to do to protect their children. The teachers were concerned about the safety of their students as well as themselves. The principal called me into her office and informed me of the calls and visits and of the pressure she was under. She wanted to know what I could do as far as talking to Sam and his parents and finding out what Sam's HIV status was— in a tactful way, of course. She reasoned that once we found out the HIV status, we could put the rumors to rest and take appropriate precautions.

QUESTIONS

1. Is it appropriate for me to inquire about Sam's HIV status or is that an invasion of the family's privacy?
2. If I already know Sam's HIV status, would I be justified in breaking that confidentiality; that is, is Sam a clear and imminent danger to other people in the school?
3. Do the parents of the other students in the school, the teachers, and administrators have a "right to know" what Sam's HIV status is?
4. What are the legal and ethical implications for proceeding as the principal wants to?
5. What is the best plan of action, legally and ethically, for me to take?
6. What steps should I take to help Sam?

RESPONSES TO THE INCIDENT
Linda Foster

Whether or not Sam has HIV is not the issue. The issue is whether or not the counselor is justified in inquiring as to Sam's HIV status. Sam's family has a right to privacy, and so does Sam. Even though a family member was infected with HIV, there is no reason to believe that Sam is infected, and certainly it is not appropriate for the counselor to ask.

The counselor would not be justified in breaking confidentiality regarding Sam and his HIV status. Sam is a minor, a sixth-grade student, who does not pose a clear and eminent danger to the other students. Students, including Sam, have been educated regarding transmission of AIDS and HIV, so consequently Sam should not pose a threat even if he is HIV positive. In addition, as Sam is a minor, his parents' permission would be necessary in order for the counselor to divulge any information.

Parents of other students and teachers do not have a "right to know." The administrator, the classroom teacher, the counselor, and the school nurse may need to be informed in the event an emergency arises, for which special precautions need to be taken with bodily fluids. However, this would be at the sole discretion of the parents. School officials do not have a right to insist that parents disclose medical information unless a child needs to receive medication during school hours.

Parents of a child with HIV could be encouraged to let school personnel know if a child has HIV; however, the parents should be assured that any information would be confidential. Of course, there are no guarantees the information would be secure, but the administration should do what is necessary to keep such information confidential.

It is not legal or ethical for the counselor to gather information for the purpose of disseminating to the community. The counselor could be held liable for harm suffered by Sam and his entire family. It also goes against the many professional counseling associations' code of ethics for a counselor to break confidentiality of a client, in this case, the student.

The best plan legally and ethically would be to advise administration of the counselor's unwillingness to obtain information regarding Sam's HIV status. A next step would be for the counselor to meet with Sam's family and discuss what is happening in the community with regard to Sam. By meeting with the family and discussing the situation, the counselor can formulate a plan to deal with the situation.

Sam needs a lot of support and acceptance regardless of his HIV status. The counselor can continue to help the other students and Sam be aware of HIV and AIDS, how it is contracted, its implications, and that no one can catch HIV by just being near or around someone with HIV. Community resources should be pulled together to heal the community and educate for the future generations regarding health, safety, and legal and ethical issues surrounding public education of children.

Rachelle Perusse

Although there exists professional ethical codes and legal rulings that serve as guidelines for school counselors, the issue of whether or when to disclose a client's HIV status is still under debate among counseling professionals. However, in this case study, the counselor's course of action seems clear. It is not ethically or legally appropriate to violate the student's or the family's privacy. Even if Sam were HIV positive, two necessary preconditions for disclosing confidential information as set forth by the American Counseling Association's (1995) Code of Ethics and the *Tarasoff* (Corey, Corey, & Callanan, 1984) ruling are not met: Sam is not engaging in high-risk behaviors, and there is no clearly identifiable third party at risk of contracting the infection from Sam. In the 1976 Tarasoff ruling, the California Supreme Court ruled in favor of the parents of the deceased, Tatiana Tarasoff, and held that a failure (by the psychologist) to warn Tarasoff of her boyfriend's plan to kill her was irresponsible. If the counselor chooses to breach confidentiality and proceeds as the principal suggests, he or she would not be acting in the best interest of the client. The student could suffer discrimination because of this disclosure, in which case the school counselor may be held legally liable. In any situation such as this, a school counselor would be wise to consult with other professionals in the field to ensure that the best course of action is followed.

There are many steps that the school counselor could take to help Sam. First, Sam may benefit from grief counseling to deal with the loss of his brother. More generally, I applaud the school counselor's use of classroom guidance, small groups, and individual counseling both to increase awareness about HIV/AIDS transmission and to deter name-calling. The counselor has at least disseminated information to students. However, I am concerned with the counselor's statement that the administration and teachers are "uncomfortable with the issue of sexual orientation" and that parents are worried about how the school will "protect their children." It seems that other members of the school population would also benefit from education about HIV/AIDS. To this end, the counselor could collaborate with the school nurse and persons from community organizations to provide in-service workshops for teachers and staff and provide an Information Night for parents. Given the comments and rumors circulating around the school, an essential element of these discussions should be that gay males are not the only population at risk of contracting HIV/AIDS. Because the school has students from a variety of racial and ethnic backgrounds, the school counselor might consider involving parents and school staff to develop culturally sensitive educational materials.

As the only school counselor at the school, this school counselor might benefit from collaborating with the middle school and high school counselors to develop a peer education program. Peer educators may be equally effective in disseminating information about HIV/AIDS to students in various formats, such as skits or plays.

Finally, it is essential for there to be in place a proactive plan for dealing with HIV/AIDS in school settings. In collaboration with school administrators, teachers, staff, parents, and students, this school district needs to develop guidelines and policies consistent with legal and ethical codes regarding the issue of HIV/AIDS in schools. At the very least, these guidelines could address education for the entire community about HIV/AIDS, information about preventing HIV/AIDS transmission, and how to respond when a student, teacher, or staff member has HIV/AIDS.

REFERENCES

American Counseling Association. (1995). *Code of ethics and standards of practice.* Alexandria, VA: Author.

Corey, G., Corey, M., & Callanan, P. (1984). *Issues and ethics in the helping professions (2nd ed.).* Monterey, CA: Brooks & Cole.

Parental Rights: "Hurt and Angry"

CRITICAL INCIDENT

Background

I have been a high school counselor for 7 years. Through my counseling position, I have had the opportunity to help students with their personal problems on several occasions. I am sure that most counselors have had many occasions to do personal counseling during the course of their work.

In my 5th year of counseling, there was a girl in my college prep group who suddenly seemed to throw in the towel as far as her schoolwork was concerned, even though she had been an honor student throughout the elementary grades. For the first few weeks, I simply commented that her work was certainly below her capacity, and I mentioned she should begin working harder. She finished the first marking period with a C-minus which should actually have been a D. On her report card, she also had two other C's and a D. Not expecting any real information, I asked her to remain after school one afternoon. I wanted to find out what was wrong, and I thought I would send a note home to her parents.

When I asked her what was wrong, she told me. She was the second oldest in a family of five children, and her family was quite poor. She had one older brother who had quit school in the eighth grade, gone to work, and then had been drafted. Her younger brothers and a sister did not like school and were doing poorly. During the summer her parents had told her that when she turned 16, in another year and a half, she would have to quit school and get a job. She told me that although she had put up a bit of a fuss, she believed she could never make them change their minds.

Upon hearing the story, I blurted out my opinion that they had no right to make this decision for her; it was unfair to deprive her of an education for the sake of some extra income that probably was not absolutely necessary. I said a few other things to her and left her with the idea that she should plead her case once more with her parents. She left me with the understanding that she would try, but it would not do much good. She said unless they would let her stay in school, she saw little reason for trying to get better grades.

When she went home that evening, she brought up the matter with her parents. In doing so, she apparently stated that her counselor had told her that "they didn't have the right to tell her what to do." She said something to the effect that they had no right to force her to go to work just so they could bring home a few more groceries and an extra case of beer. The very next day her father reported to the office, and my principal decided to let him settle the matter with me.

Incident

Her father, apparently feeling hurt and insulted, really lashed out at me. He told me I had no right to interfere because I did not really know what life was like, and he concluded by telling me I should have minded my own business. He insisted that I should tell his daughter I was sorry for what I had told her, and she should listen to her parents. The critical incident, as I see it now, took place in those few precious seconds before I replied to him. I could have refused to do so and faced possible disciplinary action on the part of the principal, although I doubt this would have happened. I could have answered the father angrily and probably insulted him more by telling him exactly what I thought of him. Lastly, I could have said nothing to him and walked out of the room, which was almost what I did.

Instead, I told him that I was sorry that I had apparently tried to overrule him in the eyes of his daughter. I said I would speak to his daughter again if he would just tell me why he and his wife had come to their decision. He told me that school was not really important for girls. Girls were supposed to get married and have children. Their place was in the home. I agreed that this was largely the case when he was growing up, but that today girls were thinking more and more of careers that they could pursue while also raising a family.

I asked him if his wife worked, and he replied that she worked in a local mill. I asked him to think of whether it would be different if his wife were working instead as a doctor, lawyer, or engineer. I told him that this was what his daughter had probably thought about many times. I hoped he saw my point. He did not reply to this, he merely nodded in the affirmative. I was polite to him and asked him to reconsider for himself and his daughter, and to speak with her when he got home. The next day, the girl told me her parents had told her she could stay in school. She went on that year maintaining an honor roll average, and she is planning to enter nursing school on graduation.

Discussion

I do not think my words influenced the father as much as my attitude did. My initial apology removed a great amount of his antagonism toward me and left him receptive to what I had to say.

Had I gotten into an argument with him, I do not think I would have achieved the same results.

This incident taught me that in dealing with parents I had to first respect their rights as parents, and, by doing so, I also learned the value of the expression, "You can catch more flies with honey than you can with vinegar."

QUESTIONS

1. Do parents have the right to determine their children's futures with respect to their education?
2. Should school counselors speak their mind, contradicting what parents say, when the counselor does not agree with them?
3. Should school counselors, upon finding out that they and the parents do not agree, try to call in the parents and deal with them directly when the counselors believes the parents are harming the child?
4. Could I have handled the whole issue better? I feel I mishandled it in the beginning but was able to extricate myself from a bad situation, which I should not have gotten into in the first place.

RESPONSES TO THE INCIDENT

Angelo V. Boy

Intervention in the life of a student is a time-honored tradition among counselors. Such interventions are often defended on the grounds that the counselor is justified in taking action because such actions are, after all, for the welfare of the student. Counselors glibly talk about the necessity of students becoming responsible for their own lives but contradict this dictum by engaging in certain acts of intervention.

It is tempting to intervene. When we see a person confronted with a difficult decision or situation, it is a natural inclination to want to help by doing something concrete. I often wonder whether intervention is actually helpful to the student or whether it is designed to appease our own consciences as school counselors. I wonder whether we are really helping the students to be responsible for themselves when we intervene, or whether we are making them more dependent on the need for intervention by others in similar situations throughout their life.

The school counselor in this case might have established a counseling relationship in which the girl was able to discuss the various aspects of her relationship with her parents, to bring a sense of how she could proceed to deal with her parents directly without anyone's intervention. That is, if the girl could begin to understand how she should deal with her parents, then this insight would enable her to communicate more effectively with them at other important decision points in her life. If she did not learn to do this now, then she would always need someone to intervene. She would always need an uncle, an aunt, a teacher, a counselor, or a social worker to be the intermediary between herself and her parents or her environment.

Counseling should enable clients to generate the courage to do something directly about circumstances in their life. If the counselor does something to and for the client, then how does the client ever learn to take responsibility for managing his or her own life? When does the client learn to confront and find solutions to his or her problems on their own, if the client becomes conditioned to the crutch furnished by an intervening person?

In the beginning of my own counseling experience, intervention was part of my modus operandi until I began to realize that my interventions were fulfilling my own psychological needs rather than being truly helpful to my clients. At the end of each day, I could close my office door with the comfortable feeling that I had done something. But what had I really done? In my evolution as a counselor, I came to the clinical realization that behavior modification—if it were going to be internalized, operational, and long lasting for a client—had to be produced by the client. I became aware that counseling was viable and effective only when I was able to create a relationship in which the client could reach a point at which he or she could make personally relevant decisions about his or her life.

The fact that this girl stayed in school and planned to enter a school of nursing is, indeed, noble. It fits our American concept of a success story. The counselor can take satisfaction in the fact that he did the right thing in the incident depicted. He earned his keep. But I wonder if today this girl is a freely functioning person who is able to manage her own life? Or does she scurry to find someone to intervene whenever she is faced with a difficult situation.

Don C. Dinkmeyer

This incident shows a way of developing more effective relationships. It relates closely to the democratic approach to solving problems that Dreikurs (see Corsini, 1979, chap. 2) developed. The counselor basically refused to have a poor relationship with the father. He did not fight him, nor did he give in. Instead he listened and established mutual respect by showing his willingness to consider all opinions. Then he suggested that he and the father attempt to solve the problem together. This is an example of the fact that we can only change ourselves, not others. It seems that as soon as the counselor demonstrated willingness to reconsider his position, the father felt free to participate in a reconsideration of his own position. It is true that an argument would not have accomplished much. However, I think the counselor feels that he was using a ploy by "catching more flies with honey than vinegar" and perhaps does not realize that he was simply using a democratic approach to problem solving.

Certainly, parents do not have the right to determine their children's future with respect to their education. On the other hand, if parents are financially responsible for that education, their attitudes and wishes certainly must be taken into consideration. I believe the school counselor should be prepared to offer a child other alternatives in such a situation, especially when the child desires to go on academically and is at a loss to find ways to finance his or her education. It would probably have been better if the counselor had first listened to what the child had to say and then dealt directly with the parents to determine how they felt about the educational future of their child. It is true that the matter was mishandled in the beginning and could have been avoided by a well-structured parent interview.

REFERENCES

Corsini, R. (Ed.). (1979). *Current psychotherapies (2nd ed.).* Chicago: F. E. Peacock.

Parenting:
"The Incorrigible Parents"

CRITICAL INCIDENT

Background

I was in my 5th year as guidance counselor in a junior high school. During the 5 years of my tenure, there have been many disciplinary cases similar to the one I am about to describe. What distinguished this case from the others was the extreme manifestation of a student's behavior that was so obviously indicative of a problem. The fact that his actions were so aggressive and his attitude so contemptuous should have alerted us to the likelihood of worse things to come.

The problem in this case should have been easily identified before it neared the critical stage.

Ken, a ninth-grade student, had been in our school since the middle of his seventh grade. He had come from a parochial school. He had a twin sister and two older brothers in high school. Both Ken and his twin sister were above average in academic ability and performance. The sister was an aggressive and disruptive child in the seventh grade. In the eighth grade she calmed down. Ken's behavior suddenly changed at the beginning of the ninth grade. His grades dropped off sharply. He created incidents in the classroom that brought the teachers down on him. On occasion, he struck other students for no apparent reason.

In one such incident, he struck a seventh-grade student, causing the boy to spend 5 weeks in a hospital with a badly broken jaw. School personnel were fearful a similar incident would occur again. The parents were talking of having Ken committed to the state youth correctional institution. He had been suspended on three occasions and was currently on probation. Ken seemed outwardly defiant toward guidance personnel. If I would even approach him, he seemed to get upset. Despite such periodic troublemaking, Ken still impressed me as being a likable and capable boy.

Just prior to the incident, Ken left home and had, as a consequence, been suspended from school again. He kept in touch with his twin sister, who kept us informed of his whereabouts and activities. He relied on her to get clothes to him from home and to report conditions at home and at school. The father was out of town working. The mother refused to concern herself with him and his disappearance. She simply listed him with the police as a runaway.

Incident

On the third day of his disappearance, I was on my way home from school when I passed Ken riding on a bicycle with a friend. I felt sure that Ken would run and hide before I could stop him, so I drove on home and exchanged my car for one he had never seen before. I drove back to the vicinity of his appearance. As I drove around the block I saw Ken walking alone in an alley. I stopped near the exit to the alley and waited. I noted that he had no shoes on. I jumped out of the car as he came out of the alley and approached him saying that I wanted to talk to him. His first impulse seemed to want to run. Surprisingly, he decided to stay and listen; perhaps it was simply because he did not have his shoes on and could not have run very effectively.

I asked Ken to get into my car and he complied. I explained his status as far as the authorities were concerned. If caught while a runaway, he would probably be charged as such and be committed to a juvenile detention home. If he returned voluntarily, he might avoid the charge and the commitment to a juvenile home. We talked for about an hour. During this talk, Ken opened up and told me about his problems and the reason for changes in his behavior at school. He was fighting the attitude of his parents, who were constantly downgrading him by comparing him with his older brothers. He was convinced that he could not compete with his brothers in athletics. He noted that his teachers were always comparing him with his brothers. He was completely fed up with it all.

I did not offer to take Ken home or to the police station. I wanted him to know that the decision of what to do would have to be his own. However, I hoped our talk would influence his decision. He said he had to do some more thinking first. I dropped him off where I had picked him up as he requested and went home.

That evening I got a phone call from Ken. He said, "I am home now, and I want to thank you for taking the time to talk to me. No one has ever done that before." I said, "Fine, Ken, I'm glad that you decided to go home. I would like to have you and your mother come to my office in the morning and we'll discuss how to get you back into school."

Discussion

Ken and his mother came in the next morning. They had discussed his problems at great length the night before. There was a different attitude on both sides, and there seemed to be more understanding in the family. We arranged with the court to have

Ken's custody handled through the guidance office during school hours. Ken's grades improved; he had no more clashes with his teachers, and he was a much improved student during the remainder of the year.

Ken and his family moved to Tacoma as soon as school was out that spring. I was in Tacoma during the latter part of the same summer and called Ken to see how he was getting along. His father answered the phone. I explained to him who I was and that I was curious as to how Ken was behaving. His father said, "Let's not talk about him; did you hear that our oldest son is at a baseball summer camp now? He's trying our for the BlueJays baseball team," and so on. He never again mentioned Ken during the conservation. Things did not work out well for Ken. I received a request for his school records from a state and county detention and correction home for boys a short time later.

QUESTIONS

1. Frequently we cannot understand unusual behavior on the part of children. Do such behavior changes often have to do with home conditions?
2. When I related the incident to several others, they felt that I had made a mistake in not taking Ken home or driving him to the detention home. The idea did not even occur to me. Does anyone think I should have done other than what I did in this case?
3. We certainly did not do much real or lasting good for Ken in view of his father's unchanging attitude and Ken's later trouble. I wonder in retrospect what I could have done that would have been more helpful. Any ideas?

RESPONSES TO THE INCIDENT

Rudolf Dreikurs

This example is significant because it shows how far a "good" counselor can succeed and where she will fail if she is not sufficiently trained to understand faulty behavior and motivation and how to correct them. The counselor described the aggressive and disturbing behavior of Ken well. Her lack of psychological training made her assume that he hit other students "for no apparent reason." There is always a "reason" for whatever a child does, but there is no indication of the counselor trying to understand and help him.

In a direct confrontation, she acted well. She did not criticize, condemn, or preach but helped the boy to decide to do what would be best in the situation. She listened to his complaints, although she did not understand their meaning. She did not understand Ken's own overambition when he could not live up to the demands of his parents and teachers who compared him with his apparently successful older brothers. The fact that she listened to him seemed to be the turning point, and the boy improved.

Now comes the crucial question: What had been achieved by the guidance office? The student obviously received much help because he improved for a whole year. But why did he relapse after he moved away? One can only guess that the counselor was encouraging and appreciative. This fact accounts for the improvement. But did she change the basic pattern on which the boy operated? Apparently not. This issue can be seen by the counselor's reaction to the boy's father. She sided with the boy and felt sorry for him to the extent that she spoke about "incorrigible parents."

There is a basic fallacy. The less the mother knows what to do with a child, the better she knows what the father should do. The less the teacher or counselor knows what to do, the better they know what the parents do wrong. The father's remarks indicate the tremendous overambition that probably characterized all members of this family. Ken was just like the others, and the counselor probably never recognized to what degree she played into his hands by treating him as someone special during the year he worked with her. He switched from a good to horrible and then back to a good boy, which reveals his overambition. If he cannot be the best, he becomes the worst. Had the counselor understood these dynamics, she could have helped him change his pattern. As it was, Ken reverted to a "bad boy" role (in a less favorable and supportive environment).

The following thoughts are what I consider key points to this incident:

1. Unusual behavior must and can be understood by a trained counselor. The personality of the child is greatly influenced by home situations, but the trained counselor can undo the harm that family and environment have done in the past.

2. There are definite reasons for Ken to change his behavior from good or bad, and they may or may not have any connection with domestic problems. The improvement in the sister's behavior may have been a factor, because the competition between brothers and sisters usually leads each in the opposite direction. But this does not explain why Ken suddenly became so violent and aggressive. A counselor should have investigated the situation and recognized the factors instead of blaming the parents for having rejected him. In many instances, the "rejecting" or critical attitude of the parents is provoked by a child who gets his status and significance through disturbance and defiance.

3. It was the sensitive and sensible reaction of the counselor to a boy in trouble that brought about the improvement. It is interesting to note that other professionals expressed their doubt, when actually the counselor's behavior was correct.

4. Here is the crucial point: One must agree that the counselor "did not do much real or lasting good for Ken." But, instead of realizing where she failed, she blamed the "father's unchanging attitude" for Ken's later trouble.

T. Antoinette Ryan

Counseling should be directed toward helping individuals develop behavior repertories and implement decisions to ensure that they play productive roles in the social environment. The counselor's task is to provide services needed to help students acquire a total education, to become fully functioning members of society. In accomplishing this goal, the counselor directs his or her resources and efforts to help each student meet the developmental tasks of their age successfully and realistically. The problem of identity is a central one during the adolescent years. Coming to grips with oneself is one of the primary tasks to be achieved by youths like Ken in the early high school grades. By performing in a supportive role and providing carefully selected cues to guide cognitive and affective behaviors of the boy, the counselor in this instance was able to help Ken develop a more realistic understanding of himself. The counselor provided information relevant to the decision at hand and reinforced the boy's decision-making capacities. The outcomes to be expected from this approach to counseling can be seen in the behavior changes that took place in Ken during the remainder of the school year.

The importance of looking at any problem situation in the context of its environment cannot be overemphasized. What this means to the counselor is that efforts to understand or modify a client's behavior should take into account factors in the environment that may impinge on the person. It may be that the desired change in a client's behavior can only be achieved through changing the reward system of the person's environment. In this case, there apparently was little, if any, reinforcement being provided from the home to encourage the kind of school-oriented, adjustive behavior that would characterize a fully functioning adolescent. The counselor's decision to have Ken and his mother come to the office to discuss the problem is an implicit recognition on the part of the counselor of the need to consider the home environment. Because the father, as well as the mother, functioned as a critical variable in the boy's environment, it seems most unfortunate that the counselor confined her efforts to working with the boy and his mother. The apparent lack of long-term success in achieving counseling goals in this case may have been related more to what was not accomplished, rather that what was done.

Whether the counselor should have taken Ken to the detention home could be answered only by looking at the counselor's goal in relation to Ken and the ethical considerations involved in the case. In this instance, it appears that the counselor was concerned mainly with helping Ken to develop a better understanding of himself and to make the decision himself. As long as the counselor could satisfy herself that she was not ethically bound to perform in the capacity of truant officer, then she need have no compunctions about not turning the boy in to the authorities.

The counselor raises the question about the apparent lack of long-term effects in this case and points to the father's unchanging attitude to the boy. This suggests that perhaps what was missing was the commitment of the father to the plan that was worked out by the counselor, Ken, and his mother. The father apparently was a key factor in the situation from the start, and to avoid involving him in the plan to help Ken probably was a serious error of omission. The opportunity for success in helping Ken realize his full potential was indicated by the short-term changes in the boy's behavior. Perhaps long-term effects might have been attained had a plan of family counseling been instituted at the time of Ken's return to school.

Peer Pressure: "She's My Best Friend, No She's Mine"

CRITICAL INCIDENT

Background

I was hired to provide counseling services for the second half of the school year to sixth-grade students in a middle school environment following the retirement of the previous counselor. The previous counselor had been ill for quite some time but nonetheless had maintained a very close relationship with the students she served. She had worked in the school district for 24 years, so many of the students' parents knew her and regularly called on her to assist them with problems their young adolescent children were experiencing.

The school serves sixth-, seventh-, and eighth-grade students who are economically, racially, and culturally diverse. As one of three middle schools in the district, the school serves children who have attended seven local elementary schools. The socioeconomic status of the residents within the school boundaries is broad. There is one private school that serves fewer than 100 children located in the area; all other children attend public school. There are several large corporate headquarters in the city, and children of the executives attend the local schools. Children of the local university faculty, staff, and employees also attend the public school (many of these families have come from abroad). In addition, the school is located next to government-subsidized housing. The school district also services a racially diverse population. White, African American, and Hispanic children are approximately equal in representation, with other cultures also represented.

Children attend seven class periods daily. Students are divided into three groups to accommodate extracurricular activities and limited lunchroom facilities. Students in Group 1 eat lunch before fourth period, Group 2 students eat halfway through fourth period, and Group 3 students eat after fourth period. Home room is held before fifth period for half an hour. During this time, students participate in club activities, assemblies, and other structured school activities. No study halls are available to the students. Generally, owing to schedule constraints, students attend many of the same classes throughout the day with other students who are members of their group, but they rarely see students outside their group except before or after school or on weekends.

A large number of students have regularly visited the previous counselor for help with typical adolescent difficulties (e.g., difficulty with a teacher or assignment, trouble with a boyfriend or girlfriend, lost lunch money, decisions to quit band). Similarly, students continue to visit my office. In the past, parents have supported and encouraged this activity. I have been told the previous counselor was valued for her ability to counsel children. However, the counselors for the seventh- and eighth-grade students have told me that the principal only tolerated that behavior and that it is more important for me to complete the necessary paperwork and next year's fall schedule. They reported that they are tired of doing the scheduling for the sixth-grade students and that they expected me to "pull my weight" in the counseling office. They offered to show me effective strategies they had developed over the years.

Incident

One Friday, three sixth-grade girls were sent to my office by the vice principal for arguing in the lunchroom. It appears that there has been an increase in these types of altercations. I remembered that the previous day four girls were suspended for fighting in the hall. The vice principal reminded me that during the incident, one of the girls had been slightly injured. He informed me that her parents had called the school to complain that several cliques appeared to have developed and their daughter was caught between two groups of girls who were pressuring her to choose sides.

I talked individually with each of the girls. In general, each of the three girls reported that the argument began as a result of one girl trying to exclude another and threatening to exclude both girls if her wishes were not honored. Although this issue was problematic for these three girls, I found out the same issue had also started the fight the day before. Also, I was disturbed to find out this was occurring not only between small groups of girls but also between the larger groups that the school had artificially created with their grouping system. By the end of the next week, I found that at least 21 girls were involved in this behavior and that what was considered a clique one day was no longer a clique the next day. Whereas one girl was excluded one day, the next day she was the one to do the excluding. The girls were becoming increasingly distracted by the changing composition of their friendship groups and parents were regularly contacting each other to smooth over what had once been long-term friendships built across families.

After further investigation, I was able to determine that no single individual was the source of the difficulties and that on any given day any student might be a target of this relational aggression by other students. Parents, teachers, and staff were concerned that this pattern of behavior might result in more serious difficulties (e.g., depression, lasting peer difficulties, and escalation of aggression).

Discussion

I wish to establish a working relationship with the other counselors as well as relationships with parents. Furthermore, I know that I must complete the necessary paperwork requirements that the school has assigned me. Although I have not been asked to directly resolve this issue and, in general the vice principals handle behavior problems, I believe that this is more the responsibility or domain of the school counselor than the vice principal. I believe that someone with expertise in counseling children and youth should help the students learn to resolve their difficulties. I wish to assist these students with a minimum expenditure of school time in the most effective way possible. Regardless, as a new counselor when I started my job, I also had intended to address other issues faced by young adolescents in a diverse school in a middle-sized city. I am worried that I will only have an opportunity to do one or the other and that anything I do may be viewed by my colleagues as neglecting the paperwork they have had to do for the previous counselor.

QUESTIONS

1. I am getting the impression that the role the previous counselor served in the school was an essential one, although it was resented by her colleagues. Should I attempt to develop a counseling program, to address either the girls' behavior or other issues, despite the message that it was not valued by the school?
2. If I do decide to address the girls' behavior, how should I go about doing so? How can I be sure that I do not expend an inordinate amount of time on the problem?
3. Can I bring in some of the other issues that adolescents often experience in a middle school setting? If so, how and when can this be done?

4. Do I involve any of the other school personnel (e.g., the other counselors, vice principal) in the program?

RESPONSES TO THE INCIDENT
Susan B. Wilkie

Where school counseling programs have existed in the past, school boards, school administrators, and teachers have perceived the primary tasks of on-site counselors to be virtually administrative (i.e., curriculum planning, scheduling, and discipline). In addition, students have perceived counseling services to be restricted to students in trouble, placing counselors in a reactive role. Despite former perceptions, however, informed and progressive state departments of education have gradually begun to ascribe to conclusive developmental research affirmed by counselor educators and professional counseling organizations. This counseling literature recognizes the importance of continuous developmental programming, not only to prevent conflict among middle school students but also to help students anticipate developmental stages, tasks, and crises and to enhance individual growth.

In this scenario, the counselor should immediately address the girls' behavior by speaking to the entire sixth grade about the problem and its ramifications. More importantly, the counselor should attempt to develop a comprehensive developmental counseling program that calls for the other counselors to work cooperatively across the grade levels to provide systematic direct and indirect prevention and intervention for all middle school students. An inclusive team effort dedicated to completing paperwork, scheduling, and programming will help to soften the competitive edge between the counselors. Specifically, a balanced program should be designed to deliver programs in curricular fashion that address prevention goals in a proactive role and intervention goals in a reactive role. Therefore, continuing education for the counselors and regular in-service staff development to activate the support of the entire faculty will be a first step forward.

An inordinate amount of time is already being spent on intervention because behavioral conflict has not been addressed by the entire school. School standards and consequences for students' present actions must be uniformly established and specifically designed programs put into action to assist students in learning new behaviors and skills for negotiation and creative problem solving, including conflict management and resolution programs, peer mediation programs, relationship training, assertiveness training, and contracting. When students enter middle school with limited experience, changing circumstances challenge their already existing values and attitudes and cause them to feel confused and vulnerable. Helping adolescents to become more aware of their feelings as well as rehearsing appropriate choices clearly builds coping skills and greater confidence in their ability to resist peer pressure. Consequently, less time will be needed in remedial and crisis counseling.

With the cooperative help of all faculty and parents, sequential curricular programs should focus on developmental information that directly address the central process of peer pressure during the adolescent stage. Subsequently, the positive or unsuccessful resolution of coping with peer pressure will ultimately determine the outcome of students' psychosocial crises of group identity versus alienation. In fact, according to research, peer pressure can be so daunting that "friends" is the category listed most frequently as children's greatest daily stressor. Therefore, middle school students should be taught what to expect so they can at least anticipate the challenges of adolescent physical maturation, emotional development, and problems and conflicts associated with sexuality and peer pressure. More importantly, learning a diverse repertoire of knowledge and skills will enhance adolescents' self-esteem and prepare them for effective personal, social, and educational decision making.

Robert Milstead

The situation described is one all too common in today's schools. Counselors at all levels often feel torn in trying to satisfy the wishes of administrators, parents, and peers. Only rarely do these three groups agree on the priorities for the school counselor. Uncertain in the scenario given is whether or not the school has any type of comprehensive program in place. Gysbers and Henderson (1997) suggested a shift away from the heavily reactive services described toward an integrated guidance curriculum coupled with individual planning.

The counselor's statement "I wish to assist these students with a minimum expenditure of school time in the most effective way possible" should be the guiding philosophy. In an effort to enlist the support of the other two counselors, this counselor could discuss a plan to bring a series of discussions throughout the grades covering such topics as communication skills, anger management, cooperation, and decision-making skills. If presented by the entire counseling staff, the relationship with the faculty might be improved. In taking a more proactive approach, the counseling staff might reduce future student conflicts. Enlisting the support and cooperation of the faculty and administration sets the stage for the creation of a schoolwide program rather than a guidance service.

Recognizing that some paperwork is a normal component of a school counselor's duties, the counseling staff can establish a comprehensive guidance program that allows time for paperwork to be completed while focusing primarily on a guidance curriculum appropriate for this school and its students. In the implementation of such a program, in-service training may be necessary for all or part of the school faculty. By completing their training together, the faculty and counseling staff can improve their peer relations, just as the student–teacher and student–student relations should improve as a result of the lessons to be taught as part of the comprehensive program.

REFERENCES

Gysbers, N., & Henderson, P. (1997). *Comprehensive guidance programs that work II.* Greensboro, NC: ERIC CASS.

Pregnancy: "To Whom Am I Responsible?"

CRITICAL INCIDENT

Background

I had been a guidance counselor for 8 years in a public senior high school. Before joining the staff, I was a counselor for 4 years at a local Catholic high school. I was raised a devout Catholic and still found myself drawn to its ceremony and tradition; however, I was forced to resign from my previous job because of a "difference of opinion" regarding the Catholic Church's position on sexual issues. I fear it was my own self-doubt and inner conflict that allowed this incident to get so far out of hand. Our school had recently seen an influx in the number of teenage girls becoming pregnant. While the problem seemed to be increasing, I had not been assigned to counsel any of the students involved. Most of the girls had withdrawn from school or their parents had arranged special classes for them.

Renee, a 14-year-old freshman, had always been an honor student. She had perfect attendance through junior high school and never received any disciplinary action. Renee had four siblings (two step, two biological), all of whom were younger. She and her stepfather had a strained relationship and she was not close to any of her siblings. Renee's mother had been recently diagnosed with cancer and was in and out of the hospital most of the time. Renee's behavior changed abruptly in February of her freshman year. Teachers reported she was skipping her early morning classes, she was absent frequently because of "illness," and her grades were falling drastically. The physical education teacher referred Renee to me out of fear that Renee was pregnant and possibly suicidal.

Incident

Renee came to my office on Monday afternoon. She looked pale, dehydrated, and was not the vibrant cheerleader I remembered seeing during football season. Her persona was different. She was withdrawn, almost fearful. During our session she admitted she was pregnant, perhaps 6 or 7 weeks; she was not really sure. She said severe morning sickness and abdominal cramps made attending class difficult, if not impossible. Renee told me that over Christmas break she had been raped by an upper classman. She had not told anyone. He was a varsity football player and had convinced her it was her fault and that no one would believe otherwise. Adamantly, she insisted I not report the incident to anyone. She went on to say that since then she had become quite promiscuous, even having intercourse with multiple partners in one evening. Her embarrassment and pain echoed with each spoken word. I told Renee she needed to seek medical attention and her parents must be told immediately. Tears welled in her eyes as she insisted she could not share this information with her family. Again I told her she needed to tell her mother, but she said she did not want to burden her mother with another crisis. She also did not want to tell her parents until after her first trimester out of fear her stepfather would force her to have an abortion. After much contemplation, Renee agreed to tell her parents by Friday. She scheduled an appointment with me on Monday of the following week to discuss the outcome. I gave her referrals to Planned Parenthood and Sav-a-Life, as well as handouts on pregnancy options for unwed mothers.

Renee missed her appointment on Monday. I checked with her teachers and they advised me that she had not been at school for several days. Later that week I received a call from Renee's mother. On Tuesday, the day after her missed appointment, Renee began hemorrhaging and collapsed in the floor of her bedroom. She was rushed by ambulance to a local hospital where it was discovered that she had an ectopic pregnancy. Emergency surgery was required and Renee will never be able to have children. She still had not told her mother about the pregnancy.

Discussion

Renee's mother found the information I had given Renee and confronted her about it. Renee explained what I had advised her to do and that she had chosen to wait a little longer, at least until her mother had finished her chemotherapy. Renee's mother was livid and said she felt "betrayed and let down" by the school system that was supposed to be protecting and educating her daughter. She also blamed me for Renee's infertility, claiming that if I had told her the day I found out Renee could have received appropriate medical care sooner. Renee transferred schools the next year and her mother contacted a lawyer about the incident; however, her cancer relapsed and she stated she simply did not have the energy to pursue the issue. Last I heard Renee had attempted suicide twice and was considering dropping out of school.

QUESTIONS

1. After the fact, I consulted with several peers about this case. Most felt that I had erred in my judgment not to inform

Renee's mother immediately. How should I have handled this situation differently?

2. In retrospect, Renee's depression seemed to have been basically "lost in the shuffle." Should I have assessed her level of depression and addressed the possible posttraumatic stress in our initial session?

3. Renee's fear that her stepfather would make her abort the baby was also a concern for me. I feel that maybe I let my values cloud my decision-making process and affect my actions. What were my choices?

4. What are the possible ethical and legal issues in this case?

RESPONSES TO THE INCIDENT

Pamela Sanders

As a junior high school counselor, when dealing with extremely important issues such as pregnancy, it is a good idea to encourage the student to inform her parents. This way the counselor is viewed as a confidant, a friend, and an adult to turn to in times of trouble. However, the counselor should have given Renee until Thursday to tell her parents and scheduled a follow-up conference Friday morning. At that time, if Renee failed to show up for the conference or call to inform the counselor of the results of the conference with her parents, Renee's parents should have been notified immediately.

The case study indicates that after the missed appointment, no intervention or contact was made. By giving Renee until Friday and scheduling the follow-up meeting on Monday, the counselor allowed an entire weekend to pass that was more critical because these are days during which a student may have less supervision than during a school week. If handled differently, Renee's mother may not have blamed the counselor for her daughter's infertility. Renee probably would have had the ectopic pregnancy regardless of the counselor's response, but at least the parents would have been notified earlier of their daughter's condition.

Posttraumatic stress should not have been addressed in the initial session. Renee has been through, and is living, through stressful events. Her immediate crisis is the fact that she is sick and pregnant. Therefore, medical cares for nausea and prenatal care are her immediate needs. Also, because of prior incidents, Renee needs to be tested for the HIV virus and other sexually transmitted diseases.

When someone is in a crisis situation, depression is natural. Without addressing the immediate need or needs, a student may not even be aware of his or her depression. After immediate needs have been met, secondary issues such as depression need to be addressed in the counseling sessions.

It is clear that the counselor was empathetic toward Renee's fear of her stepfather wanting her to have an abortion. A girl has to be 18 years or older to have an abortion without parental consent. However, there are no laws regarding age restriction with parental consent. Abortion is a surgical procedure and there are health risks. Renee's stepfather may not be aware of health risks that are common to this type of surgery. If the counselor had taken Renee to a home for unwed, pregnant girls wishing to have their babies, this would have been a clear indication of values interfering with the counseling process. If the counselor's background and views on pregnancy were not shared, I do not believe this issue would have surfaced. Therefore, I do not feel that the counselor's personal values interfered with the counselor's decisions in the counseling process.

Legally, Renee is a minor and her parents should be contacted with any issue regarding her health. The counselor was making efforts to notify the parents but did not follow through or react in a timely manner. Ethically, the welfare of the student is the primary concern. Even though this situation could have been handled more efficiently, the counselor appears to have the welfare of the student at the forefront of his or her decision.

Lawrence E. Tyson

The issues of confidentiality and counselor responsibility are central to this incident. The first issue the counselor must address is Renee's statement regarding her rape by an upper-class varsity football player. Renee is successful in manipulating the counselor into not taking action regarding her accusation. Renee has stated that a crime (rape) has been committed. The school counselor is ethically and, most importantly, legally responsible for reporting this accusation to the appropriate law enforcement agency. It is my belief that, after entering in a counseling session with Renee, the counselor was negligent and may be held legally responsible for Renee's physical and emotional condition.

As soon as the rape incident was described to the counselor, a series of steps should have been taken. First, the counselor should never have agreed, or led Renee to believe, that such information could be kept in confidence. Whether Renee was telling the truth or not is a nonissue and is not for the school counselor or administration to decide. Second, the counselor should explain to Renee why this information is of particular importance and who should be notified. Because of Renee's physical and emotional state, I would expect that Renee would not be thinking of what is correct and proper, let alone the legality of what she has shared. Third, Renee should be told that she would not be allowed to go home until the proper authorities were notified and had the opportunity to talk with her. The proper authorities in this incident may include the school principal, the appropriate law enforcement agency, and her parents. It is my belief the school counselor should consult with other counselors (if available) and the school principal. Few, if any, school principals like to hear about serious issues pertaining to their school and students second hand. Fourth, because a law has possibly been broken (rape), it is my belief that law enforcement should be notified to come to the school. Certainly, this decision has ramifications for the school counselor, students, faculty, and administration. By taking this action, the school counselor has suspended his or her role as confidant and has moved into the area of responsible adult school counselor. As in most cases in which student confidentiality has been forfeited, the counselor has decided against the wishes of the student. Many times school counselors do not like to be placed in this position, wanting to be perceived as an adult who does not wish to jeopardize the "trust factor" in a student–counselor relationship. The argument presented is the belief that the student will no longer trust the counselor and will be reluctant or even resistant to seeing the counselor again. This is the trap that many school counselors fall. In this incident, the counselor must resist the personal feelings related to abandonment or violation of confidentiality and assume the role of "rational adult school counselor." The issue is not how Renee feels toward the counselor regarding the disclosure of information; the issue is that a possible crime has been committed against Renee. The decision to disclose such information and to keep Renee at school until law enforcement and her parents can speak to her has ramifications for the student body and faculty. All precautions must be made in ensure Renee's privacy. The principal and school counselor need to do all they can to ensure that the arrival at the school of the parents and law enforcement be done in the most private manner. The decision to disclose to others what has happened must be given to Renee. The students and faculty are not considered on "need-to-know" status, and therefore precautions must be taken to inhibit rumors and innuendoes, which could result from witnessing police and distraught parents in the guidance or principal's office.

In this incident, Renee's "depression" is not the most important issue. While in truth Renee may be depressed, she also may be acting normally given her age and situation (during her session with the school counselor). However, as noted in the incident, Renee had attempted suicide twice since leaving the school. It is obvious that Renee needs psychotherapy; what kind, how long, and with whom is up for discussion as not enough information has been provided. However, Renee's depression should not have been the counselor's first area of concern.

In incidents like this, the values of the school counselor often surface (though whether they should or not is up for debate). School counselors and other helping professionals are encouraged to evaluate their personal values and beliefs regarding such issues (i.e., abortion, pregnancy, right of privacy, right to die, the death penalty). However, the counselors' values and beliefs should not cloud their ability to make responsible, ethical, and, most importantly, legal decisions.

Professionalism: "The Antipathetic Boy"

CRITICAL INCIDENT

Background

My high school is located in an upper-middle-class neighborhood in a suburb close to a very large city. The parents of the school children who attend this school are highly competitive in these respects: socially, financially, athletically, and academically. It is not unusual for me to have at least one parent ask me daily why John or Seymour "isn't doing better?" or "Do you think Sandra will make it at Smith?" or "What does a Scholastic Aptitude Test score of 980 mean?" and so on. I spend a lot of my time trying to reassure parents, telling them that getting into Harvard is not the only important thing in the world. I explain to them that it will not automatically raise their child's IQ if he or she takes a speed reading test. In this school, everyone aspires to become a doctor or lawyer—provided they have rejected the idea of becoming bankers or investment advisers. I hope I have given the reader a sense of the kind of school it is.

When Mr. Meyer came in to see me and when he began his story about his lazy son Philip, it seemed to me I had heard this story before. I looked over Philip's chart, and it was quite evident the boy was average for the population he was in but not the genius his father wanted him to be. The father had this one theme: His son did not do what he was capable of, and I had to motivate him. To motivate the boy, I should call him in and tell him he was breaking his mother's heart, hurting his father's reputation in the community, affecting the school image, disappointing his relatives, and irretrievably harming himself by not studying harder and getting better grades.

I reviewed all the objective evidence with the father carefully—grades achieved in elementary school, grades in high school, and psychological tests. But Mr. Meyer dismissed the importance of the data, telling me about his life, how he had pushed ahead, how he had conquered obstacles, how easy young kids have it these days, and how Philip would someday be appreciative of his father's efforts. Mr. Meyer, who started his own business, was a man of extraordinary vitality and conviction and, under his sway, I began to wonder whether it were not possible he might be right. In any event, I promised to see Philip and to have another meeting with the father.

Incident

There was a suicide attempt in this case, and I feel it was the consequence of the incident. I feel sure about that. I believe my betrayal of Philip was the last straw. But let me try to explain my part in this tragedy and where it became a critical incident for me.

I called in Philip, and I was first struck by the fact that he was singularly unattractive. He had buck teeth, protruding lips, sallow skin, and an unpleasant voice. He had the look of a hounded boy. He was definitely quite fearful, and his language was replete with "I don't know ..." and other noncommittal statements. He was obviously uncomfortable and wanted no part of me. I found myself behaving differently with him than I do with other children. I disliked him instantly, and I could empathize with the father who had put up with this reluctant, defiant, negative youth of 15. I tried to control myself and behave in accordance with the dictates of a professional relationship, but I was keenly aware of my feeling toward this boy whose behavior and appearance repulsed me. I could understand very well how he could drive his father to distraction.

Nevertheless, for some time I tried to make contact and be reasonable and friendly, even though I was constantly aware I was not being genuine with him but was playing a role. I wanted to say something like, "I can see why your father hates you; you are so ugly both in your appearance and your behavior. I want to be of some help but your manner is so antagonistic and even insulting that I too feel hate toward you." When I became aware of this feeling of antagonism, we were looking at each other, and I think we knew just how I felt and what I was thinking. I went to my files and pretended to look up something and I was angry with myself for this almost uncontrollable feeling. When I felt calmer, I went back and made my speech.

"Look, Phillip, you just seem to have a lousy attitude, and I think your fairly poor academic performance is due to that as much as anything. I have just been with you for 5 minutes, and you have already antagonized me. I have the feeling you are operating on the revenge motive and have it in for everybody. I suppose that you don't study just to get your father mad. Well, my friend, you are going to be unhappy in life unless you learn to cooperate." I felt my anger toward him increasing as I spoke and realized I had gone too far. I had no right to talk to this boy in this manner, especially since I hardly knew him. His eyes became small, his lips pursed to a point, and he just glared at me. I lost my temper. "I think you are just ungrateful. I don't blame your father for being so damn disappointed in you. Here I want to help you and you just do nothing: Stare and glare at me as though I were your enemy. Get out! Come back to see me when you have a better attitude." I pointed to the door, and he got up sullenly and left the room.

Discussion

I heard several days later that Philip had attempted suicide. His mother heard a crash in his room, ran in, and discovered him with a noose around his neck in his closet. Apparently, he had tied the other end of the rope to a hook in the wall of the closet to jump off of a chair, but the hook had not held. He had not left any suicide note.

By the time that Philip had left me, I realized I had made a very serious mistake in venting my own hostile feelings toward this unattractive, shy, and awkward boy, and I had become the father's ally without any information at all, without really knowing Philip. I do not know if the suicide attempt was genuine or whether it was a sham to punish the father and perhaps me. I wonder if it was another aspect of his hostility toward the world or whether it was a manifestation of his desperation. He did not return to school. I subsequently learned he had been put into a private mental hospital for a while and later transferred to a residential school elsewhere. I never saw the father again, and I have no idea whether the father knew of my encounter with Philip. I just know that years after this event I still feel badly about my own behavior.

QUESTIONS

1. I showed my real feelings, but I think I should not have. This boy struck me the wrong way at the wrong time, and I empathized with the father and blasted the son. Do you ever have irrationally strong attitudes toward counselees? Positive or negative feelings? What do you do about them? Every once in a while I go overboard one way or another, positively or negatively, toward students.
2. Do you think my behavior might have contributed to the suicide attempt?

3. How does one deal with these sullen, negative, "I dunno nothing" types? You want to help them, but all they want to do is get your goat.

4. Sometimes I think that misfits like Philip are better off dead anyway and that treating them kindly no matter how they treat others is a mistake. I know I sound hostile, but there is a lot of hostility in the world, and some of it is very blatant and open in this school. Are we always to nurture the sick egos of repulsive students?

RESPONSES TO THE INCIDENT
Edward S. Bordin

Too much of the literature on counseling and psychotherapy conveys the impression that all people are likable. Sometimes, the emphasis on acceptance has carried that implication. It is certainly true that the role of counselor or psychotherapist is epitomized by a dedication to helping persons overcome personal obstacles toward fuller development and toward living productive and satisfying lives. The persons who seek out such professional responsibilities should and usually do have an interest in other people that transcends class, status, and personal appearance. Yet clients, as do all persons, differ in physical attractiveness, the richness of their personal resources, the prickliness of their reactions to others, and, generally, in the attractiveness of their personalities. If we assume, as many do, that a client's problems inevitably reflect interpersonal difficulties, some degree of strain in counselor–client relationships are the expected norm.

The successful counselor–client relationships are those in which, despite strains and momentary frustrations, there are basic gratifications to be obtained by both parties. Initially, it involves their interest in each other. On the client's side, he or she initially experiences the counselor's understanding and commitment to be helpful and later the gratification of seeing desired changes occurring. On the counselor's side, there is the pride in doing one's job well, the satisfying of curiosity, the desire for a limited kind of intimacy, and an interest in influencing significantly the development of another.

The counselor's account suggests there was virtually no basis for mutual satisfaction in this relationship. The counselor initiated the contact and did not seek to establish a positive motivation for counseling. In the counselor's words, "He was ... uncomfortable with me and wanted no part of me." Even before meeting Philip, the counselor seemed more committed to the father's views than Philip's. Thus, we must ask how this counselor views his task. Does he see himself as an agent of parents and school in exerting a socializing influence on his clients? Or does he see himself as a special agent delegated to aid his clients in their struggle to attain self-integrity and integration despite external pressures?

If the counselor chooses the latter orientation, which is the representative one, then he must establish a base for operation in the client's desire for his help. He needs to learn how his client is willing and able to use his help. Such efforts often carry a counselor beyond initial feelings of dislike or aversion. The experience of intimate collaboration tends to increase one's responsiveness to positive characteristics in the other and to decrease one's sensitivity to less attractive characteristics, especially those of a surface variety. Nothing could be more destructive of a relationship than feelings of irritation and dislike, masked by a thin veneer of acceptance and benevolence. A genuine dedication to helping another coupled with basic interest can make honest expressions of momentary feelings of anger or dislike tolerable, even constructive. In this instance, the counselor gave honest expression to his adverse feelings toward the client but without having established any commitment to the client.

The counselor seems so estranged from his clientele that one wonders why he stays in the school. It is clear that he sees both the parents and students served by this school as spoiled, privileged persons undeserving of his efforts. Perhaps he could better tolerate the neurotic foibles of an underprivileged person. But one wonders whether he has made a proper choice of vocation. Counselors must be able to respond to the underlying plight of persons which, because of their need for a corrective relationship, drives them into excessive destruction of the very relationships they seek. If the counselor is to interrupt that destructive cycle, his or her sense of the underlying confusion and pain must be strong enough to enable him or her to endure an uncomfortable period so he or she can respond appropriately.

Philip, whose father appeared to have no interest in his son except as his own status was enhanced or undermined, must have been an extremely unhappy boy. His apparent defense against becoming a despised pawn was stubborn inaction coupled with an effort to exaggerate his appearance and manner, which others found painfully repulsive. He would express his anger at this rejection by using these qualities as weapons. The counselor was surely another in a line of such relationships. We are not told enough to be able to decide whether it was a genuine try at suicide and whether the encounter with the counselor was a decisive factor, but clearly this boy needed to give expression to his anger and despair. Most importantly, he needed the experience of another's understanding interest to be able to search for the useful parts of himself.

Allen E. Ivey

This case represents an almost classic example of what the New Left might call the failure of the establishment. We see a "hounded" boy abandoned by a counselor in a moment of need. We see the father who sees the son as an object rather than a person. We see a guidance counselor hounded by an achievement-oriented society and school to the extent that he is not sure of his own self. And, finally, all too common, we see a school whose prime aim is to train students to fit into a tight mold, a school that is responding to a society that demands excellence at the price of personal and human development.

Who is the villain? The son repressed by his father? The father repressed by his job and society? The counselor repressed by the school? The school administrators who must meet the demands of the college and the upper-middle-class neighborhood?

There is no villain. This situation, while dramatic, is not unusual. There are very few counselors who do not have a case in their files in which they have failed a person in need. Too many parents see their children as extensions of themselves rather than as independent entities. Too many schools are more concerned about college admission over personal growth.

What can be done by a counselor to prevent such instances from reoccurring not only in this setting but in others as well? Counselors must have a deep understanding of their own needs and feelings in addition to counseling skills and knowledge. Therapy and personal growth training for counselors is becoming more available as part of the standard counselor education program. Until counselors can understand themselves and have a sense of personal freedom, their chances of significantly aiding students in need is greatly reduced.

The role of the counselor in relation to the school must be considered. No matter how personally integrated a counselor is, if the school within which he works has inadequate objectives and methods, he cannot be fully effective. Individual or group counseling even at the highest professional levels in a school such as that described here will be remedial at best. Counselors must take an active part in humanizing their school settings. It has been a habit of the counseling profession to complain about the settings in which they work but to do nothing about it. Models of developmental psychology, community mental health, and educational innovation all point to the need of a new counselor role—that of community consultant to the student developmental process in the schools.

Although counseling is a useful technique, it can no longer be considered the only behavior-change method of the school counselor. Counselors have a responsibility to work to make their schools more fully human through helping teachers with their classroom instructional procedures, administrators to sometimes sacrifice humanity for expedience, and parents to learn new ways of helping their children grow. The counselor can no longer accept a role as passive facilitator to the goals of society. Minority students and student militants have aptly pointed out that school counselors have been a major force in maintaining "the system." Instead of merely parroting a school's rules and goals, counselors must step out and take an active role in helping a school examine its purposes and relations with students and also serve as an active force for positive change.

The school needs to examine its role in relationship to its middle-class neighborhood. The academically striving school discussed here has been fostered by a community and society concerned with objective material gain at the expense of subjective human values. By responding to this press with emphasis on academic, as opposed to personal, excellence, the school has done the community a major disservice. Recent school upheavals at all levels clearly illustrate the need for the school to reexamine its values and relationship to the community. Are schools to lead society or to follow?

Speaking more directly to the questions of the counselor, all counselors experience irrational feelings toward their counselees. Therapy and counseling are often recommended for those who are to become counselors, so they will understand their biases and work with them more effectively. If a counselor cannot live with his or her feelings constructively when he or she feels negatively toward a student, this student must be referred elsewhere.

The counselor's values and opinions are clear. He apparently sees such students as anxious to get his goat rather than as frightened individuals needing help. The statement, "how does one deal with these ..." reveals the counselor's tendency to objectify his students. The counselor admits this, yet he still goes "overboard" with students. A counselor with attitudes such as these should honestly admit them and resign his position. As an alternative, intensive therapy seems necessary if the counselor is to remain in his position.

Yet, it is not wise to completely discount the counselor in this case. He had openly and honestly discussed a deep, personal concern. He seems angry and frustrated, but he seems also to be honestly asking for help. Let us not prejudge him but encourage him toward future growth. With the statement of this case, he has made an important beginning.

To the question of one should "deal" with sullen, negative students, the answer is simple. One does not prejudge but waits to see the beauty emerging from within the beast. Unless one has patience and trust in human nature, they will never see the true nature of the beast. One who does not see potential beauty in even the most ugly is perhaps the one most in need of aid.

Purposeful Behavior: "Mother F——"

CRITICAL INCIDENT

Background

I was appointed as a counselor in an integrated school where the student population was about 80% White and 20% African American. The teacher population was the other way around, 20% White and 80% African American. Because this statistic may be important in the incident that follows, I should report that I, myself, am African American.

One of the kids I received reports about was Kenneth, and the reports were all the same: filthy language! Never did he use this language with teachers, but rather in the yard, in the playground, in the auditorium, and in the classes with other children. His favorite term was "mother f———."

Incident

I called Kenneth in to find out what I could. He was just 9 years old, very dark, quite small. He seemed cowed, and when I began asking him about his language, he showed resignation, as though saying, "Oh, this again." I tried to be neutral, but he did not want to discuss the matter. He expected me to warn him not to use such language or to give him a lecture on its impropriety. All I did was ask him if he could tell my why he used such language. I could not get a satisfactory reply, so I made it quite clear that I did not think his language represented acceptable behavior. I assumed he probably heard such language in his neighborhood, but so did all the kids in that school.

I also knew he had been warned repeatedly. He had been seen on this matter several times, and I could well imagine that he had been advised many times to stop using such language. I also assumed that his foul language provided him with a secondary gain, namely, attracting the attentions of others in this useless manner. After all, he had gotten to see me because of his language. Using such language obviously conferred some status on him. At the same time, being a little fellow, he probably felt he could not be outstanding in any useful way.

Several weeks later, the vice principal, the school psychologist, and I met to discuss a number of problem referrals and, sure enough, one of these was Kenneth, our foul-mouthed boy. We reviewed his problem and discussed various solutions. We agreed that all the usual methods of dealing with him were likely to fail. Then the psychologist made an extraordinary suggestion. "Look," she said, "this can be the beginning of a very bad pattern. I think that something has to be done. I have a suggestion. It comes from a theoretical position that I have. Instead of trying to stop him, which hasn't worked so far, let us encourage him to use such language." "How is that?" asked the vice principal. She and the psychologist were friends. "I suggest that we call him in and encourage him to use this kind of language with us. I think he will resist and that we should urge him to use it, and the more we insist the more he will resist. This could do it." We discussed this unusual suggestion, and after a while, we agreed to act on it. Moreover, we also agreed on how to do it, by the procedure being described in the incident.

Discussion

The next day, Kenneth came in for a conference with us, and I can still see his big, black eyes looking at us over the table. The vice principal started off by saying that we wanted to have a nice talk, and in the second sentence she used the word "shit," one of Kenneth's favorite words. Then the psychologist began to talk sweetly to him, and she used the word "nigger," another of his favorite words. And when it was my turn, I used "mother f——," his favorite-of-favorite words. His eyes looked as if they might pop out. He got up and backed away from us toward the door, putting his hand on the knob. At this point, the psychologist used all three of his favorite words in one sentence, which ended in a question mark. The vice principal, using several more expletives, asked him to come back to the table, which he did, slowly, with his mouth open. Then we began to discuss him and his language among ourselves, freely using his own terminology. Our sentences went somewhat like this: "Can you figure out why this little p——, this f—— Black uses such mother f—— language?" "I just think the little s—— doesn't know any f—— better, that's all."

The session lasted no longer than 3 minutes because the psychologist had warned us that Kenneth might not get the shock of the intended session if we overplayed our hand. We finally told him to get his "f—— Black a——" out of the room, and he left, not having said a single word during the entire session. The consequences were dramatic indeed, in a behavioral sense. The boy's verbal misbehavior stopped immediately and completely. I checked with his teacher, who reported that his foul talk had totally stopped.

QUESTIONS

1. A number of teachers, counselors, and administrators with whom I have discussed this incident have stated that the ends do not justify the means, and it was wrong in every sense, regardless of the results, to do wrong things to get good results. What do you think of the propriety of what we did?
2. If someone, say Kenneth's mother and father, preferred charges against us on the grounds that we used unacceptable language in front of a young child, and if we had admitted doing so, would you think that some sort of reprimand would have been justified?
3. How far can a counselor go on doing what is ordinarily unacceptable behavior? In one instance, a counselor in a therapy group actually pulled out his penis to show it to his group. He was immediately dismissed. I believe this event would be an example of completely unacceptable behavior. He argued that in his judgment what he did was proper at the time and in the circumstances. What guides, besides common sense, can one have in such matters?
4. Do you think we harmed Kenneth in any way? Or, if the other students had heard about the incident (they had not), would it have affected them adversely in any way?

RESPONSES TO THE INCIDENT

Rudolf Dreikurs

The technique suggested by the psychologist is not as unusual and "extraordinary" as the counselor assumes. I have described a similar approach many years ago as *antisuggestion*, and Viktor Frankl uses *paradoxical intention* as a major part of his therapeutic procedures (Frankl, 1984). When one asks a person to deliberately increase his symptoms or misconduct, the person will stop it. A stutterer cannot continue his stutter if he deliberately tries to produce it.

However, the application of this method, as described here, is not quite acceptable. One could get the same results by inviting the boy to several counseling sessions, asking him to repeat all the dirty words he knows, and encouraging him to find new and stronger ones. That, too, would stop him cold, but without the necessity for the adults using these words.

It is interesting to speculate as to why this particular tactic was so effective. In a sense, it goes beyond the application of paradoxical intention. It is usually quite effective when a mother of a thumb-sucking child puts her thumb in her own mouth as soon as the child does it. Usually, the child get furious. Why? The child had the right to suck the thumb, but the mother does not. The child feels justified in stealing but would object violently if somebody takes what belongs to him or her. In other words, imitating the child's misconduct gives the child a new perspective of what he or she is doing. It is an invasion into the child's domain.

However, one wonders why the counselor did not discuss with Kenneth the reason for his misconduct, helping him to become aware of his goals. This question is particularly justifiable, because the counselor, who apparently has been trained in other approaches, assumes he is probably right about Kenneth using his language to get special attention and to gain status among his friends as a compensation for his being small for his age. It might have given him a feeling of masculinity, particularly among his peers because it is primarily with them he felt compelled to use his language.

Of course, the counselor was ill-advised to ask the boy to tell him why he used such language. Children never know why they do something wrong. The trained counselor or teacher has to help them to understand it, so they can see alternative forms of behavior for feeling important and significant. Therefore, the counselor should not have been surprised when he got "no satisfactory reply" to his question. Instead of dismissing Kenneth, telling him that his language did not represent "acceptable behavior," the counselor should have discussed goals with him. The counselor succeeded in changing the child's behavior without uncovering his goals and intentions.

These are the questions that this incident raises and that the counselor does not take into consideration. To repeat, applying this particular form of paradoxical intention or antisuggestion is quite improper and unnecessary. As to the "propriety" of such action, one can expect to find angry reactions. On the other hand, one can use "unacceptable behavior" if it is understood to be part of a game. When a child lies, one can make an agreement with the child that everyone in the family can do the same so that the child realizes the futility of his or her conduct. Obviously, the limits to which one can go in changing behavior might be defined by common sense and propriety. It is precisely common sense that provides some guidelines for how far one can go. Exposing one's penis, for example, certainly goes far beyond acceptable behavior. Whether thumb-sucking, lying, swearing, and dirty words go beyond the limits depends on circumstances. At any rate, one can be sure Kenneth was not harmed by this procedure, but neither was he helped to understand his behavior and change his motivation. Failure to do so is the prevalent deficiency of our counseling services.

E. G. Williamson

What a honey of a suggestion the psychologist made! How risky in that it might very well have traumatized Kenneth in a way that could have been damaging. Although it seems a desirable technique, one must be very careful in using it. The shock of hearing his own language in the mouths of those he has put up on Mount Olympus or consigned to the other side of the River Styx must indeed have been a dramatic shock to Kenneth. In my opinion, the technique was not wrong at all. It worked. It produced the kind of results that may have shocked Kenneth into maturity and into a more realistic perception of his own behavior, which he either lacked or at least did not seem to be affected by.

I think it would have been preferable for the counselor to follow up on this matter by arranging a conference with Kenneth's parents, being very careful about what was said, certainly not reporting on the youngster's traumatic experience. I suppose that some parents might prefer charges against the school personnel because they used unacceptable language, but I think the conference team could have justified the technique and gently have brought the parents around to see that the intention of the procedure was good and that the results were desirable. Possibly Kenneth was imitating his parents, and I would at least explore that possibility.

I do not think Kenneth was harmed. I think he was helped. However, the people in the incident had to run the chance that word would get around to the other students and that they might misinterpret what happened. They were lucky to get away with it. Counselors once in a while have to take chances. Their bosses should be tolerant. Professional people frequently are unable to inform their superiors about the strategies they use ahead of time because of the desperation of the moment and the availability of limited alternatives. Such shock techniques can be devastating, but they can also startle people into becoming alive. Kenneth is a case in point.

REFERENCES

Frankl, V. (1984). *Man's search for meaning.* New York: Washington Square Press.

Role and Function: "Counselors Caught Up in Other Responsibilities"

CRITICAL INCIDENT

Background

As a 2nd-year high school counselor, I am distressed by the nature and function of my job as determined by the principal of my school. It was my intention, indeed it was my training, to be a counselor who would be instrumental in helping students with career and educational plans. However, I am caught up in administrative tasks that have little to do with my role as supporter of students' academic achievement.

My school, Brandon High, is one of 22 high schools located in a large urban school district. This school has many superlatives attached to it, and unfortunately they are these negative superlatives: the highest dropout rate (22%), the largest percentage of students on free or reduced lunch (85%), the smallest number of students pursuing a higher education (12%), and the least percentage of enrollees in higher level mathematics and science (8%).

I see no effort in the way of programs or services to give the students of this school knowledge about higher education. The majority of these students' parents do not have a higher education, and a recurring theme is being voiced by parents, teachers, and administration: "a high school education is as far as anyone needs to go." It is my observation that the students of Brandon High wear their "we don't have time for the prissy airs of higher education" label rather proudly. Dead-end jobs and dead-end courses seem to be a rite of passage in this community.

It is precisely because of the limited experience this community has had with postsecondary education that I feel the students of this school need a counselor to aggressively seek to supply them with information that will increase their knowledge and understanding of how the curriculum can widen their options. They need to know how higher education can raise their standard of living. It is unacceptable to me that the demographics and backgrounds for these students should limit their motivation to seek higher education. I contend that, if made aware of the salary scales that correspond to postsecondary training, many of Brandon's students will develop a commitment to achieve beyond General Mathematics II and anatomy and physiology.

Unfortunately, this guidance program will not be fostering conditions that ensure Brandon's 1,956 students are prepared to choose from a wide range of postsecondary options, including college. My colleagues and I can continually try to wrestle ourselves free of many of the administrative duties we have been assigned. In addition to doing all we can for the 1,956 students in our charge, the principal has assigned our counseling staff of three the following duties: all the standardized testing for this school; the patrolling of halls in the morning, afternoon, and during class changes; lunch duty for each counselor once a week; crowd control during all assemblies, pep rallies, and events that happen during the school day; many administrative tasks that require report writing such as the special education incident report, which took a week of data gathering; and the wearing of a two-way radio so that one of us is on duty each day for emergencies, such as reporting to the scene of a fight or intercepting an intruder on campus. Some days we do little beyond patrolling halls, responding to fights, and monitoring assemblies.

My two colleagues are not nearly as distressed by these assignments as I am. They maintain that it is all part of the job, will not change, and is not worth getting worked up over. They point out that the students do not want the services I want to put into place anyway. Because I talked incessantly about the need for change, my colleagues grew weary and decided to appoint me department chairman so that I would become the spokesperson for the counseling department. They told me to go ahead and make whatever changes I wanted, and they will try to support me if it does not require any after-school work.

They told me they like me as a person, but I am terribly naive. They good-naturedly harass me about my inability to recognize how deeply rooted the beliefs of this community are and how resistant these beliefs are to change. They assure me over and over that I am expending a great deal of emotional energy for naught, as I am fighting a losing battle. However, they are quick to tell me that if I insist on pursuing this crazy notion of changing things, they will lend their signature or voice to most of my idealistic notions.

Incident

Having secured the endorsement of my colleagues, albeit an unenthusiastic endorsement, I used this first year to seize every opportunity to try to win the administration over to my point of view and to gradually be relieved of many of our administrative obligations. I started the campaign by designing a program aimed at helping our ninth graders understand the impact financial aid could have on their future.

I developed a program in which I would train volunteers to walk each ninth grader through the financial aid process for

higher education. My thoughts were that if these students understood that higher education was a financial possibility, it may
increase their commitment to achievement and more students
would enroll in the higher level classes. I mapped out the time it
would take to train the volunteers and put the program into place
and explained that we could do this program in the same amount
of time it takes us to monitor halls each day. My administrator's
reply was, "We are short-handed in administration. We all have to
be team players and be willing to pitch in to do our part. This is
not really a needed service as these kids aren't interested in college." I then asked him if we could negotiate shifting something
else out of guidance so that we could put this program into place.
His reply was, "I don't know what that could be." I asked him to
consider a workable plan for hall monitoring that did not use the
counselors. He appeared exasperated with me and said, "Why do
you have to push so hard?" and turned and walked away. Several
similar incidents followed during the first year.

At the close of the first year, the guidance staff did not have a
single new program in place and ended the year with as many
administrative duties as they had at the beginning of the year. I
decided I needed to present my case in writing. During the summer I carefully outlined the activities the guidance office would like
implemented during the year. The activities involved many broad-
based programs designed to develop in the students a commitment
to achievement and an understanding of career and educational
opportunities beyond high school. I listed programs, activities, and
tasks and included a detailed time line of when and how to accomplish each. The report, signed by all three counselors, was submitted to the principal with a cover letter requesting a meeting to discuss the goals of the guidance program and expressing our desire
to problem solve with him about how the administrative duties
could be handled. Two weeks passed and we heard nothing.

Discussion

After 2 weeks and still no word from the principal on our proposal to transform Brandon's guidance program, I decided to drop

by his office and try to get him to discuss the proposal. He said he had not had an opportunity to even take the report out of the envelope as he was busy revamping the physical education/athletic program. "You know we had a miserable football season last year, and I can't see standing by and letting that happen this year," he said. I was able to shift his attention to the guidance program (after 20 minutes of hearing about the problems of the athletic department). I explained that because school was starting in 3 weeks, we needed him to read and react to our plan, so we could agree on changes and have time to implement the approved programs. His reply was, "Things are just fine like they are." He went on to express that this low-socioeconomic community embraced their future in menial, low-paying jobs and that I should "respect the rights of these parents to guide their children and quit imposing your values on these children." He went on to say, "By harping on higher education you are making these people feel lesser than those who have college degrees." It was obvious he had no intention of discussing or listening to our proposal for change and that his basic beliefs about the students in this community would prohibit any changes in the near future.

I was angry at the inconsequential way he was disregarding my views and my proposal, which had taken hours to put together. My reaction shocked even myself. I asked him if he would help me get a transfer to another school where I could do the job for which I was trained. He curtly replied it was past the transfer request deadline but that I was welcome to find another job in another district and angrily added, "As a matter of fact it would be best for you to find another job, as you have snubbed your nose at the people of this community and their values since you got here. You think you know what is best for them and you haven't tried to understand why they don't want what you want for their children."

QUESTIONS

1. What steps should I have taken to present the proposal so that it would be considered by the principal?
2. Was I insensitive to the community standards, and should I

have been more accepting of the status quo for these students and their future?

3. What strategies could I have used to better identify with the community and eliminate the impression that I did not respect and value the parents' rights to guide their children?

4. Should I have tried to make changes more slowly? Should I have started my campaign with someone other than the principal?

5. Should I abandon this fight and seek a job elsewhere?

RESPONSES TO THE INCIDENT

Jim Whitledge

The counselor at Brandon High School is to be commended for having the desire to do the job for which he or she was trained and educated. There are other factors that must be considered, however, in the above scenario. Prior to his or her interview, for example, the counselor had an obligation to find out what the position was all about. Finding out what he or she knows now may have determined whether to take the position in the first place.

Once in the counseling position, the counselor perceived him- or herself to be proactive in providing a positive counseling program for students and attempted to work with the principal and colleagues toward that end. According to Section D.1.a of the American Counseling Association (ACA) Code of Ethics in reference to role definition, "Counselors define and describe for their employers and employees the parameters and levels of their professional roles" (American Counseling Association, 1995). Sections C and D of the American School Counselor Association's (ASCA) Ethical Standards for School Counselors also support this premise in referencing the school counselor's responsibility to colleagues and professional associates as well as to school and community (American School Counselor Association, 1992).

The counselor must consider that there is some conflict with the above and Section D.1.l of the ACA Code, which states that "The acceptance of employment in an agency or institution implies that counselors are in agreement with its general policies and principles." This same section indicates that counselors work with employers toward professional standards and bringing about institutional policy changes that are conducive to students' developmental growth (American Counseling Association, 1995).

Another factor to consider is that the counselor appeared to impose his or her values on the students (and community) in terms of emphasizing solely the need for a college education and suggesting a guidance program that would bring this to fruition. The ACA Code of Ethics, Section A.5.b (supported in Section A of the ASCA Standards) provides that "Counselors are aware of their own values, attitudes, beliefs, and behaviors and how these apply in a diverse society and avoid imposing their values on clients" (American Counseling Association, 1995).

The counselor may have used a slightly different approach in working with the principal. The counselor could have enlisted the principal's support to provide a counseling program that would better meet the developmental needs of the students in the school. There are many resources the counselor could use in working with the principal. The state may have a comprehensive guidance and counseling model that would call for implementing a developmental counseling program in all schools. The National Career Development Association (1999) guidelines and ASCA's national standards for school counseling programs could be referenced and used in working with the principal, colleagues, and community members. Consulting with professional counseling associations, such as ASCA and ACA, and their codes of ethics, could also prove helpful.

The counseling colleagues did not appear to be that supportive of change, so the counselor really had to work to get their support as well as the principal's support. In addition, the counselor could work to form a guidance advisory group that might consist of teachers, parents, administrators, community members, counselors, and others who may have a vested interest in the students of the school. The advisory group could work to conduct a needs assessment and implement a comprehensive guidance and counseling program.

Overall, perhaps it would have been in the counselor's best interest to emphasize the importance of a comprehensive guidance program for students as opposed to how the counselor's values being reached might provide a better future for the students. This approach may have prevented the counselor from being viewed as attempting to impose his or her values on the community and the school.

Change is something that can take some time to occur. People in the school may have been reluctant to change if they felt comfortable in what they were doing and did not see the benefits that would result from change. The counselor in this scenario does have the option to seek employment elsewhere if he or she feels that students' needs are not being met and the school district, through its employees, is unwilling to work to bring about needed change.

Lawrence E. Tyson

One of the most important tools to obtain support and ownership of a school counseling program is through the creation of a guidance committee. Guidance committees are often overlooked by counselors who see the creation, approval, and delivery of services as a territorial issue. That is, they see ideas for programs, services, and maintenance of those services as the responsibility of those working as counselors. This mentality could not be further from the truth. Guidance committees, when properly created and functioning, can be the best way for discussing and initiating ideas regarding the delivery of services. Guidance committees operate on the premise that the school counseling program is comprehensive in the sense that it is interdisciplinary. Therefore, because the counseling program permeates across and through disciplines, the leaders in those disciplines also have a stake in the quality and delivery of guidance and counseling services. The counselor in this scenario should have created and nurtured a committee comprising essential personnel who would be supportive of his or her efforts, contribute new ideas, and act as a "sounding board" regarding future plans. A guidance committee should comprise leaders within the school community. These members might include representatives from the faculty, administration, as well as parents, possible business leaders, and students. In response to Question 3, the inclusion of parent leaders on the guidance committee would allow the counselor to "get a feel" for the community's feelings and thoughts about some of the initiatives being considered. The counselor would have had a much easier time "selling" his or her ideas if the counselor were not alone in his or her efforts. A guidance committee would be able to give support and offer suggestions for program initiatives and implementation. However, most of all, the committee would feel a sense of ownership that would transfer to the remaining faculty members and administration. A school's counseling and guidance program should be a shared ownership by the entire faculty and administration. The development of a guidance committee is a good start to achieving that goal.

School counselors, especially counselors new to their jobs, should always be sensitive to community standards, morals, and values. It is imperative that school counselors who are new to their school become acquainted with their parent and community population. Community profiles are essential to understanding the "climate" within which the counselor will be working. School counselors should always ethically advocate for positive growth and the attainment of healthy goals of their students. However, in this case, it appears this counselor does not understand the community within which he or she is working. One's values can become very much the issue in being accepted in the school and home community. It is imperative for school counselors to examine their rationale for actions being considered. Our personal values always play a role in our personal decision-making process.

Often, one of the necessary ingredients for successful employment is often ambiguous. This ingredient is "a good fit." This is sometimes hard to define, as the parts of "a good fit" are hard to quantify. However, some tangible ingredients regarding relationships may be how one observes interactions between them and others, or the quality of conversations between colleagues (i.e., other counselors, faculty members, administration). Some questions asked might be, "How do I think I'm perceived by others?" "Do I feel like I have the support of my principal?" "Do I feel like I have the support of my coworkers?" "Do I seem to be running into walls at every turn?" and "Am I valued in my opinion and as a professional?" In this scenario, the counselor does not seem to be in a situation that is a "good fit." This might be an opportunity to reflect on mistakes made that would contribute to future success and look for another placement.

REFERENCES

American Counseling Association. (1995). *Code of ethics and standards of practice.* Alexandria, VA: Author.

American School Counselor Association. (1992). *Ethical standards for school counselors.* Alexandria, VA: Author.

National Career Development Association. (1999). *National Career Development Association ethical standards* (Revised) [Online]. Available: http://ncda.org/polethic.html [1999, July 17].

Rural Schools:
"What My Daughter Does
Is None of Your Business!"

CRITICAL INCIDENT

Background

This incident occurred in an area that has resisted consolidation. It is located in a geographic area that had, in earlier generations, been dominated by dairy farms and lumbering operations. Its residents worked primarily as skilled tradespeople, in small factories (e.g., furniture factories, paper mill) and in the service trades (e.g., restaurants, stores, tourist-oriented motels), and the nearest "city" (population 10,000) was 20 miles away. The following incident provides an example of the challenges of counseling in a rural setting.

I had finished my master's in counseling at a nearby branch of the state university the spring before and was hired during the summer. I had lived in the area only a few years, having grown up, gone to college, married, and worked for several years in the Boston area. When my husband took a job in the North Country, I decided to go back to school to prepare myself for a new profession that involved working with kids.

Although I had done my practicum in a rural school not too far away, I realized that I still had much to learn about the physical and social setting in which my clients-to-be lived their lives. In addition to all of the usual intentions that new, idealistic counselors have, I made a specific commitment to getting to know my students, their individual characteristics and needs, and their families as soon as possible. I will also say that I came to my first year in the district with a firm belief that, as a school counselor, I could play an important role in opening my students to the opportunities and options that existed for them in the larger world beyond the district. My practicum experience had taught me that it was possible for people to build a satisfying, productive lifestyle in a rural setting. However, I also saw many bright students who either were not aware of their own possibilities or withdrew from those possibilities because of lack of confidence, lack of interest, or the discouragement of significant others in their lives. True to the admonitions of my professors, I know that the decisions about what they would do with their lives were theirs to make; however, I wanted to make sure that they made those decisions with access to good information about the full range of possibilities that were available to them.

Incident

After the uproar of beginning-of-the-year schedule adjustments had subsided, one of the first programmatic, intentional things I did that first year was to call in all 24 seniors for individual conferences to discuss post–high school plans. I gave a high priority to talking with them because I believed that, by intention or default, they would be making decisions in the next few months that they would live with for the rest of their lives. I assumed I would have more time to get to know and work with the younger students.

My general format for these individual sessions was to introduce myself if I had not spoken directly to the student before. I told the student a bit about aspects of myself that I judged to be pertinent to establishing rapport with the student (e.g., that I had recently finished my graduate work, that I was married and had a son, that though I had grown up in a very different setting I was glad to be working here and looked forward to getting to know the people). As I had expected, few of the students planned to further their education beyond high school. Common objectives were getting a job "somewhere," going to work in a setting that they already had some connections to (e.g., the military), getting married, and finally "I'm not sure." Of the four students who voiced intentions to go on to further education, one (the son of a college-educated local businessman) planned to go to a small private liberal arts college in the state, two voiced the intention to attend a 2-year state technical school, and one said she thought she might go to a branch of the state university but was not sure yet.

One of those meetings raised issues that I, probably naively, had not anticipated. I knew Annie by reputation to be an active, well-respected member of her class. An examination of her records before I met with her revealed that she was a good student with a solid record of A's and B's. During the initial "let's get to know each other" portion of our exchange, she presented as an alert, vivacious young woman who was enthusiastic about her school experience and excited about the future. When I asked her to tell me about her plans after graduation, she said that she planned to go to work in the office of a local trucking firm. Her father was a driver for the company and had been able to use that connection to get her a part-time clerical job there during the past summer. She said that the people there seemed to like her work and had encouraged her to believe that there would be a position there when she finished high school. She said that she liked working in a business setting because doing so allowed her to interact with people. She also said that she liked the way the order and structure of the work allowed her to know how she was doing. She said that she liked being able to look back on her day's activities and know that she had done a good job and had accomplished something concrete. Annie said that she felt she was lucky because, unlike some of her classmates, she had the security of knowing there was an interesting, rewarding job waiting for her when she graduated.

Annie also related that she planned to continue living with her parents for a year or two while she and her boyfriend, Ronnie, got ready for marriage (i.e., saved some money, found suitable and affordable housing, and made wedding plans). I had met earlier with Ronnie, an attractive, athletic young man whose postgraduation plans revolved around going into his uncle's plumbing business. Thinking it over, I could see what a well-matched couple they were. Both were attractive, popular with their peers, work-oriented, playful, and optimistic. Although I saw Annie's plans as apparently realistic and appropriate, I also asked her if she had thought at all about getting some college-level work in business. Such course work, I pointed out, might open up other employment options for her. When she said that she really wanted to begin a real job, in the real world, I pointed out that the nearby branch of the state university had business courses that could be taken on a part-time basis, and that some employers even paid for business courses that were relevant to an employee's job. I noted that such a strategy would capitalize on her proven interests in business while also opening up some broader options for her—higher levels of clerical work, accounting, or even some aspects of management.

Annie seemed somewhat puzzled by my suggestions. She wanted to know if I was suggesting that's what she *should* do. I said no, but just that I felt it was useful for people to examine all their options so that later in life they do not look back and wonder why they had never thought of doing something else. Annie expressed doubt that she could afford to go to school. I pointed out the possibility of loans and part-time study as strategies for covering the relatively low costs of courses at the technical school. She said that although a couple of her classmates were going to a nearby (35 miles) branch of the state university or regional technical school, she really did not know much about what was involved in college-level courses, that neither of her parents or two older siblings have gone to college. Our time was running out, so I told her to think about it, talk to her parents, and if she wanted to discuss it some more I would be glad to. After the interview, I remember thinking what a pleasant young woman Annie was and how much I had enjoyed talking with her.

My satisfaction was short-lived. The next morning I received an irate phone call from Annie's father. In brief, he told me to mind my own business, that Annie *would* go to work for the trucking company, that she *would not* go away to any damn college, that she and Ronnie *would* get married, live in town, and raise his grandchildren where he and his wife could see them every day! I struggled to get in a few words, explaining that I had never questioned the validity of Annie's plans but simply wanted to make a few suggestions that might be useful. He thundered back that it was none of my business what his family did and that he did not want me talking with his daughter again, and that he would have my job if I did. With that he hung up.

Discussion

I was dumbfounded by the father's reaction. In my own mind, it was obvious that it was not my intent to meddle in family matters, that I had only made some well-intentioned suggestions that Annie, her family, and her boyfriend were welcome to reject if they wanted. My first reaction was to call Annie down again, to explain my position and to assure her that, of course, it was her business to decide what she would or would not do after she graduated. Further consideration, and recollection of the unveiled threat Annie's father had made to my job security, led me to reconsider that plan.

I will also admit that for the remainder of the year I dealt with Annie only with regard to specific, structured, largely obligatory activities that were a part of my responsibilities. Beyond that, I was very careful in all of my interactions with other students to avoid any suggestions that might be interpreted as "meddling" in family matters. Finally, the incident led me to examine my own assumptions about what constitutes the "good life," to think about my own cultural embeddedness and the implications of my assumptions for how I presented myself to my clients, their families, and the community at large.

QUESTIONS

1. I believe I was taking a path with Annie that appropriately balanced a respect for her established plans and my need to broaden students' perspectives. Annie's father obviously did not see it that way. I still think my actions were appropriate, but I wonder if I could have done something that would have softened the "us versus them" situation that quickly developed.

2. Although Annie's father reflected it in a more extreme fashion, I came to see his apparent distrust of outsiders, a preference for the local tradition, and an assumption that it is appropriate to treat children as extensions of one's self as deeply embedded in the culture of this rural area. I wish I could have understood the culture more quickly. How might a new school counselor obtain a quicker insight on the important dimensions of that culture?

3. I took a "let sleeping dogs lie" stance with Annie and her family. I think that in doing so I did a disservice to them and weakened my own sense of professional integrity. What are some of the things I could have done to open communication with Annie's family, to let them know that they had misread my intentions? Should I have informed anyone about Annie's father's phone call or threat?

4. Did Annie's father misread my intentions?

5. I later came to realize that one of the issues that was feeding into Annie's father reaction was the community's experience with my predecessor. By all reports, she was a flamboyant, progressive, independent woman who had quickly gotten the reputation (probably undeserved) of being a radical feminist. My appearance as a mid-life, child-bearing person, I subsequently found out, was a major factor in my obtaining the job.

I wonder how the community's perception of me (or my predecessor) and my role influenced my ability to effectively perform my job as school counselor?

6. Who might be the key informants with regard to such information?

7. What practical, unobtrusive strategies could be used to put one in a position of anticipating negative stereotypes?

RESPONSES TO THE INCIDENT

L. C. Hand

Counselors in any field, school, agency, or rehabilitation will be faced with similar situations such as this. The need for balancing the counselor's agenda versus that of the client's is of utmost importance. School counselors are often referred to as the guidance counselor. Guidance may take many forms; however, in this case, the counselor may have overstepped her bounds. A fine line exists in the control of who leads a client session, whether the client is a child or an adult.

The counselor in this incident felt strongly that her job entailed making the student aware of possibilities for future education and employment. A concern in this incident is that the background and past cultural experiences of the counselor had an undue influence on her effectiveness. Recognition on the part of the counselor of imposing her personal values is an ethical standard that all counselors must be aware. The counselor in this case was exerting unjustified authority on Annie that was a direct result of the counselor's value system.

In addition, the counselor must work within the cultural values of the community. The community in which this counselor was employed did not see the importance of a college education. The counselor stated she needed to understand the culture of the rural area quicker. One possible avenue of exploration for the counselor could have been more listening to the community by holding parent meetings and student meetings to understand the value system of the community before making suggestions and giving advice. By listening to the community, making observations, and gathering data, the counselor could have build rapport with the community to try alleviating the stigma of being an "outsider."

The counselor's feeling regarding weakened professional integrity is a valid concern; however, the counselor needed to recognize that clients' perceptions may not always match the counselor's intention. In the case of Annie and her parents, the counselor could have opened communication by asking for a conference with them. In a small rural community, either a home visit or conference at school would have been the best way to schedule a time to interact with Annie and her parents. A conference could have assured the parents that the intent of the counselor was only to be helpful. The school administrator should always be made aware of any potential problems that arise in a school counseling situation. Annie's father may have misread the intentions of the counselor, but the counselor must be aware of her own personal values and appropriateness of sharing one's values with a client. Certainly taking into account prior history of the community and the previous counselor is necessary to form a good working relationship without past experiences being a hindrance. Overcoming past judgments and perceptions of the community regarding outsiders and previous counselors would be a challenge for a new counselor.

Formation of a communitywide school guidance steering committee would serve to assess the needs of the school in relation to the community and its value system. Teachers, students, parents, community leaders, school administration, and school district officials could be included in such a committee to brainstorm and find valuable, desirable ways for the school counseling department to serve the school and community.

This counselor had great expectations for helping her students see the larger world and its opportunities. In order for a counselor to help a client or student, the counselor must first understand the world of the client or student. The eagerness of the counselor in this incident is desirable, but once again, walking the fine line between balancing counselor values and client values is paramount to forming a successful counseling relationship.

Harry Steven

Even for an experienced school counselor, moving into a new, geographical area can be filled with obstacles that may impede one's transition into a school and the development of a successful school counseling program. Underestimating or not recognizing community norms and standards of a school population can cause the school counselor to question personal abilities, perceptions, and values. The school counselor cannot afford to misread or ignore the influences these norms have on the expectations of people in the community (parental and school). Paul Pedersen of the University of Alabama at Birmingham maintains that to understand the meaning of an individual's behavior, attitude, and values, one must understand the behavior, attitude, and values in the cultural context of that individual (Pedersen, 1997). The counselor obviously did not take into consideration these pieces of the puzzle. To understand the cultural context referred to in this incident, the counselor did not seem to be able to integrate into the community. This was a mistake. For all school counselors who are in a new school setting (school and community), the ability to integrate into that community is of utmost importance. The question often asked in such instances is "You're not from around here are you?" This question is often like a sign attached to a person, signaling to others that "You are not one of us, you are a stranger, and you cannot be trusted."

A new counselor should attempt to acclimate and integrate him- or herself into the community as soon as possible. This is necessary if the counselor wishes to be seen as part of the community. In this case, the counselor could have attended local events such as little league baseball games, local church functions, Rotary or Chamber of Commerce events, and parent–teacher association meetings. Another way to integrate into the community is for the counselor to spend some time with teachers who live in the community. These individuals have insight from which the counselor could learn. This would also help build support from within the school community, between faculty and the counselor. The counselor should remember that teachers are employees of the school system but, most importantly, they are probably active members of the community and are likely parents themselves. This seems to be a valuable resource this school counselor did not take time to acknowledge or utilize.

I do not believe that school counselors should entertain the practice of making home visits. However, I agree with the first respondent that making a home visit in this instance is most appropriate. In terms of answering Question 3, a home visit might show the parents the school counselor's sincere interest in Annie. However, I would use extreme caution. The intent of the home visit would not be to change the minds of the parents. Instead, I would only use the visit to acquaint myself with the "cultural context" of my student and parents. I must remember that I would be seen as an "outsider" and understand how they would view me from their perspectives. Believing that I wanted what was best for their child would be a view that I would have to earn.

Question 4 is an interesting question. While it could be argued Annie's father was protecting her, he also could be protecting what he believed to be his family (from his value system) and his way of life. Losing a family member can be threatening to anyone. The threat of Annie going to college in another town and perhaps moving away is a loss issue with the father (and perhaps other family members). However, the school counselor did not entertain this as a possibility and therefore did not take the time to understand the father's issues. This knowledge would have helped the counselor immensely in the effort to move Annie and her father to the next step of seeing other possibilities.

It is necessary for every school counselor to understand how their predecessor was viewed by administration, faculty, students, and the community. Whether one likes it or not, there are always comparisons made. The knowledge of how the previous counselor was perceived was important information that was neglected, or at least not given its due appreciation. Armed with this knowledge, a new counselor can "level the playing field" with respect to expectations and concerns. The logical place to find this type of information would be the administration and faculty. However, the student body, especially those students who worked closely with the former counselor, would be obvious individuals with whom to talk. It should be noted that these conversations should not be seen as obtrusive or invasive toward the previous counselor, nor should they be seen or allowed to be gossip sessions. The conversations should be undertaken in a professional manner, focusing on initiatives and ideas that the previous counselor promoted and "hurdles" that caused implementing such strategies difficult or impossible.

REFERENCES

Pedersen, P. (1997). *Culture-centered counseling interventions.* Thousand Oaks, CA: Sage.

School Counseling Program: "We Know Exactly What Our Students Need"

CRITICAL INCIDENT

Background

I work on a team with three other counselors in a middle school in an urban area. We have worked together to build a counseling program for the past 6 years and believe that we are doing a good job, within the limits of our resources. Recently, there has been a change in administration, and although we remain, a new principal and assistant principal were assigned to the school. Our shared goal over the past 6 years has been to develop a comprehensive guidance program for the benefit of all of the

2,200 students in our school. We have collaborated with teachers to develop and deliver classroom guidance units at each grade level. We have a guidance committee, consisting primarily of faculty representation from each grade, a couple of parents and students, and the assistant principal. We meet as a committee two to three times a year to assess our school's guidance program and to identify program areas that need strengthening. The informal feedback we receive from teachers and parents is mostly positive. However, we want something more formal to demonstrate to our new administrators that we have a strong program that deserves continued support.

Because we had our classroom guidance schedules in place, we realized that we could, without much extra time and effort, survey every student and teacher in the building by simply following our prearranged classroom visitation schedule and collect our surveys. One of the counselors on our team brought in a copy of what seemed to us to be a pretty thorough evaluation of a school guidance program and also a student needs assessment. We combined the two surveys so that respondents would be asked first to reflect on and evaluate the previous year's program and then to identify current needs. We used parallel forms for teachers, parents, and students. In all, each survey was only three pages long, and we felt it could be completed by students in class in 10 to 15 minutes. The parent version was shortened and was published in our school's monthly newsletter, thereby not requiring extra time to mail.

Incident

We were excited as the returned surveys began to pile up. Initially, we used a shelf in the guidance office to store all the surveys and keep various categories separate (students by grade level, teachers, and parents). Within 3 weeks, we had collected approximately 2,200 student surveys, 73 teacher surveys, and 340 parent surveys. However, the gigantic task of collating the information from the surveys never happened. During the first week of November, test booklets for the eighth-grade state assessment program arrived. We needed space to organize test booklets, so we put the surveys in cardboard boxes and labeled them carefully, thinking that we would spend a few days right before the winter break to look at them. Naturally, the week before winter break was much more hectic than anticipated, so we postponed tallying the results until spring semester, and then, until the end of the term. We were much busier than ever that spring, and the four huge boxes of surveys were put in a closet so they would not be in the way.

Discussion

We never truly forgot about the boxes, but we were just too busy meeting the demands of individual students for counseling, maintaining our schedule of small- and large-group counseling, keeping up with our peer facilitators, and providing STEP groups for parents and in-service to our teachers to ever collate the data from our nearly 3,000 surveys. Our four large (and dusty) boxes haunt us every time we open the closet door. The surveys are 2 years old now, and if we ever do a formal evaluation of our program we probably would need more recent data. But why should we attempt another survey, if it might also end up in a closet?

QUESTIONS

1. We have a student–counselor ratio that is over 1:500 students. How are school counselors supposed to operate a comprehensive program and do all of the public relations work that seems to be required to maintain it?
2. Is it really necessary to evaluate a school counseling program every year? It is so time consuming that it seems a waste of time to conduct one every year.
3. We thought we were behaving in a professionally responsible way that would make our administrators appreciate our hard work and the strength of our program. However, we would have had to sacrifice time from direct work with students to compile a report of our program evaluation. I wonder if it's worth it.

RESPONSES TO THE INCIDENT

Nancy Nishimura

Clearly the four school counselors in this scenario have worked hard to provide a comprehensive guidance program for their students. However, it was evident to this reader that the tone in the description of the background information underscores a "them versus us" perspective in terms of how the school counselors viewed their relationship with the building administration. This came out in their statement that "we wanted something more formal (the survey) to demonstrate to our new administrators that we have a strong program that deserves continued support." They may do well to consider using an approach that emphasized the fact that administrators and school counselors are all members of one team whose common goal is to serve the comprehensive educational needs of the students that would focus on the need for everyone to support both administrative and guidance-related activities. Such an approach would foster a collaborative atmosphere rather than a defensive stance. Operationalizing this philosophy would entail working closely with the principal and the vice principal to dovetail administrative and guidance priorities and goals with each other. As these priorities and goals overlap, the rationale for administrative support for guidance activities is then built into the process. The structure of the guidance committee has already begun to formulate the basis of the "team" mentality. The assistant principal is currently a contributing member of that committee. The next step would be to involve the "future" guidance coordinator in administrative meetings (with the principal and vice principal) so that the counselors have an opportunity to contribute to important decisions being made about how the needs of the students are to be addressed.

The impact of fostering a collaborative relationship with the building administration will directly affect the counselors' dilemma in regards to program evaluation. Assessing the effectiveness of a guidance program is crucial in terms of future program planning. It provides accountability—a key word in administrative circles—which may well influence future budget and staffing considerations.

That being the case, by obtaining the principal's support on the front end, it would seem reasonable that the principal would approve clerical support to help process survey data. While program evaluation is critical, it requires the coordinated efforts of more than just the school counselors.

The first step for the counselors in the case study to begin formal program evaluation would be to use the data that they have already collected as a foundational information base. A sample of 25% of the respondents in each of the three groups (students, parents, and teachers) would provide the counselors with a sense of how the guidance program is currently perceived. They could then use these main points as a format organizer for the guidance committee to establish program objectives and goals for the upcoming academic year. Similarly, Special Education programs routinely develop individual educational plans (IEPs) to demonstrate accountability in meeting the individual needs of their students.

Designate one of the counselors as the guidance coordinator. It should be someone who is comfortable in the role of liaison between administration, teachers, and parents. The guidance coordinator will handle the public relations aspects for the guidance program. However, it is impossible for the guidance coordinator to "do it all." It is imperative that duties be distributed among the counseling staff.

It is necessary to conduct an annual program evaluation. Sampling (25%) each of the three groups would provide adequate data. Its purpose is twofold: (a) to assess the effectiveness of current guidance activities and (b) to identify areas that need to be strengthened in the future. Thus, the guidance committee will be able to adjust next year's goals and objectives to reflect the evaluation's results. The first year will be the hardest. It takes time to fine-tune any process, but after that, it will be much easier. The basic report format will have been established, and everyone will be familiar with the roles that they must play.

The objectives and goals established by the guidance committee should be the basic outline that will determine how the time and energy of the counselors will be spent. Reality is an important perspective to maintain here and may need to be periodically checked as to what is humanly possible under current conditions. Also, it is imperative that program evaluation be written in as a priority as opposed to an activity that is labeled "to do when free time is available."

Delegating responsibilities and coordinating activities with other building personnel are key concepts here. The recommendation was made that a guidance coordinator should be selected to conduct public relations activities. However, each counselor should be assigned an area or task to oversee, for example, teacher involvement, guidance program newsletter for parents, annual evaluation data assessment, and annual evaluation final report compilation. If each counselor is responsible for a portion, the whole will seem less insurmountable.

Kathleen Doherty

The above scenario of a large student population (2,200) to a counselor caseload of four counselors and time management concerns is very reflective of the frustrations experienced by overloaded counselors. Besides providing the direct services of counseling young people in their academic, personal, and social development, counselors are expected to do their own public relations work and related administrative duties, including filling out reports, preparing for and organizing testing and special projects such as college planning, consulting with teachers and administrators, and meeting with parents. In the 1997 National Standards publication, the American School Counselor Association (ASCA) recommends a ratio of 1:100 to 1:300 as a manageable caseload for school counselors to effectively implement a comprehensive school program. ASCA further recommends that 70% to 80% of school counselors' time be spent in contact with students. These goals would make it more possible for counselors to be effective and perhaps lessen the frustration school counselors experience.

Given a large student-to-counselor ratio, such as the school situation mentioned above, school counselors must come up with creative solutions in dealing with their challenges. There are a few different routes they can take. School counselors need to work closely with support or classified personnel and sometimes train them in some of the administrative duties that they are expected to do. In other words, counselors must find ways to more effectively use paraprofessionals, provided they are employed and accessible, in their day-to-day operations. This can potentially strengthen public relations, because it creates a more cohesive and collaborative work environment among educators. A second option is to commit a period of time to working outside of contracted time in order to complete a special project such as program evaluation. If counselors want to do more than their expected responsibilities such as program evaluation, unfortunately, the work must be done beyond contracted hours (for example, the majority of this response was written on my lunch hour). Although this can be difficult, it helps the image of counselors because it shows their dedication and commitment to the profession.

If counselors work within their contracted hours, there simply is not enough time to do all that is expected of them by their school district administrators and to fulfill the demands they place on themselves and do it well. Including the paraprofessional in some of the regularly scheduled counselor meetings can be a beginning. They can do some of the work for counselors with close monitoring. In time, they can be a positive support system. Getting involved with the parent–teacher–student association is a great avenue, too. School counselors can volunteer their time at their parent night meetings. Many times parents do all the "work" for counselors by setting up events and by highlighting school counselors and their projects in their parent newsletters.

Evaluating a program every 3 to 5 years is more rational than every year. In my experience, it takes about 2 years to realistically learn the job. By the 3rd year, one can reasonably begin to make evaluations of what works in a counseling program and what does not. Then it takes another year or so to come up with strategies for change. By the 4th and 5th year, a staff would be making changes and then reassessing their effectiveness. It also is more realistic to make little changes along the way rather than to look at the complete list of tasks counselors undertake.

Evaluating an entire counseling program is an overwhelming task, especially considering the amount of surveys this group of four counselors had collected. Using small, cross-sectional samples of student responses is a more time-efficient way of gathering information. Also having a simple questionnaire available for students and parents to fill out in the office as they wait for school counseling appointments is another creative method of collecting information. School counselors can use the school newspaper and student leaders as other helpful resources. Many infrastructures are already in place for counselors to utilize, they just have to brainstorm and be willing to ask others for help in places they may not have looked before.

REFERENCES

American School Counselor Association. (1997). *Sharing the vision: The national standards for school counseling programs.* Alexandria, VA: Author.

School Violence:
"I Thought It Was a Toy"

CRITICAL INCIDENT

Background

I am one of three counselors at a middle school that is 8 years old and serves about 1,200 students. This middle school is one of four middle schools in a county that is both rural and urban. We have a significant mixture of students from 30 different nationalities. Cliques, groups, and some gangs are prevalent at this school, regardless of the efforts of the administration to dissuade such activity. Every day there seems to be a fight between students from different groups. We have a tolerant dress code but do not allow students to wear obvious gang colors and dress. It has become apparent, however, that students who want to be identified with a particular group find ways to advertise their allegiances (i.e., same shirts, pants, coats, rings, hairstyles). We have employed a police officer from the city to serve as a police liaison. Her job is to be seen around campus in a public relations effort and to assist the administration in certain situations that require police investigation. It should be noted the school is located in one of the urban areas of the county and is in close vicinity to several apartment complexes. The school has a security fence around it, with a gate and attendant whose job is to direct visitors to proper parking areas. Most of our students are bused, but many come from the surrounding apartment complexes. The faculty is somewhat tolerant of the student unrest, citing it as normal middle school behavior. However, at a recent faculty meeting, some have voiced their concern about their personal safety, citing the incidents of violence at other schools in the state. Some have said that they no longer feel safe staying after school and working alone in their rooms or walking to their cars. Several students have been caught after school hours hanging around in certain hallways. The administration has repeatedly acknowledged the concern of these faculty members and has tried to keep students off campus before and after school. They have also suggested that teachers who work in their rooms should lock their doors or try not to work alone. This thinking has done little to ease the rising tension among the faculty. Since the rise in violence on school sites in our state, there has been some discussion by the administration about the need for planning in case of a school crisis or emergency. The principal has spoken to one of the other counselors about helping out with a schoolwide crisis plan. Quite frankly, in 8 years we have never found the time, or had the energy, to develop such a plan.

One afternoon, toward the end of the school day, I received a note from a student. The note said another student, Mike, had come to school that day with what looked like a toy gun. Mike had kept it in his locker and had showed it to some students. I called the student who sent me the note and met her inside my office. She said she had seen the gun and though it looked real, it was a toy. She said she knew that bringing such devices to school was against school rules and that is why she sent me the note. I questioned her more about why she thought the gun was a toy and felt satisfied she knew what she was talking about. As we finished out conversation, the final bell rang ending the school day and students started filing out of their rooms toward the school buses. I decided to wait until the next day to talk with Mike. I would see Mike first thing in the morning and discuss the situation with him.

Incident

That same afternoon, several teachers and students were holding a student government meeting in the media center while students in the band practiced in their room. All the buses had left, as had the parking attendant. The administrators were in the main office holding their customary Monday afternoon meeting. Teachers were checking their mail boxes and copying materials for the next day's lessons. It appeared to be a typical afternoon at our school.

We were in the guidance office conference room holding a counselor's meeting when we heard the sounds. At first we did not know what the sound was or where it was coming from. Was someone shooting fire crackers or was that a car backfiring? The sound was sporadic and seemed to be coming from the school's inner court yard. Suddenly, something flew through one of our windows, breaking and scattering glass all over us and the office. We ran outside our conference room, down the hallway, and into the inner courtyard. What we saw scared us beyond belief. Two students were holding guns and shooting at each other. One of them was Mike. The two students were yelling, cursing, and seemingly crying at the same time. As our police woman came running out of the office, I noticed her gun was drawn. Students began running out of the media center, not sure where the shots were coming from, but seemingly scared and trying to run as far away as possible. The first student who ran from the media center fell instantly, screaming and holding his leg. As soon as the other gunman turned his attention to the students running from the media center, the police officer shot him and he fell to the ground. Mike dropped his gun and stood still.

When the shooting stopped, there was an eerie silence and nobody moved for what seemed like a long time. I noticed that everyone around me was crying and teachers who were in the office, along with the police officer, ran to the wounded. I heard police and ambulance sirens as vehicles of all descriptions arrived at the school and uniformed officers and paramedics began shouting instructions and attending to the wounded. I have never been so scared in all my life and I will never be the same again.

Discussion

Mike was immediately handcuffed. The paramedics attended to the other gunman and the student who ran from the media center. Suddenly I remembered the student who had brought me the note. I remembered that Mike had been the student who had allegedly brought a toy gun to school that same day. As paramedics attended to everyone, I noticed how badly I was shaking.

QUESTIONS

1. What is the counselor's role in linking law enforcement, administration, and faculty in the institution of policies and procedures designed to deal with the concerns this faculty expressed?
2. What is the counselor's role in determining who the key students are to avoid such an event as portrayed in this incident?
3. What is the counselor's role in trying to help students resolve personal issues within and without the school system?
4. What is the counselor's responsibility regarding responding to the note?
5. What should the counselor's involvement be in developing a schoolwide crisis plan?

RESPONSES TO THE INCIDENT

L. Edwin

I believe school counselors have a direct role in serving as an agent of change in a school, especially when the change involves students, faculty, and parents. In this incident, the faculty's mood and issues of concern affected their emotional state and ability to perform their duties as educators. The school counselor, being the on-site mental health professional, should take the lead in discussions with the administration concerning the faculty's "state of mind." The counselors did not exhibit proactive behavior in this regard. School counselors should primarily be student advocates. In this scenario, the faculty's concern for their safety and the administration's seemingly nonchalant attitude toward these concerns directly affect student learning. By being an advocate for the faculty, the school counselors are also advocating for the student body.

This incident portrays students in fights and being caught in areas where they do not belong (e.g., hallways). Again, the issue of proactivity surfaces. Nowhere in the incident does it say these counselors were involved in diffusing, mediating, or intervening in any way the apparent continual student disturbances (fights) that were happening daily. The incident paints a picture of the school counselors as being reactionary and not preventative on how they see their role. The school counselors could have been much more involved with the faculty issues by intervening directly. Direct intervention might include meeting with faculty members directly to discuss their concerns; seeing students who are referred by faculty as potentially violent; holding conferences with parents, teachers, the police liaison, and identified students; meeting with administration and the police liaison to discuss current concerns; holding teacher in-services (using community resources); and advocating for the implementation of conflict management programs.

I believe the counselors should be very involved in the resolution of personal issues, especially those that might lead to violence (as this incident demonstrates). As stated in the previous paragraph, I believe the counselors should have been more proactive in advocating and initiating conflict management programs (e.g., peer mediation) in their school. Again this stance describes counselors who see themselves as student advocates and as prevention specialists. Some school counselors do not see their involvement being outside the school. They may see that involvement being provided by a school social worker or the police. In this case, there are too many clues that describe this school as a "powder keg" waiting to explode. As there is no indication of the existence of a school social worker, the school counselors should have taken a more active approach to meet with parents outside the school setting. Students were primarily bused into the school, with a significant number walking in from apartment complexes that seemingly surrounded the school. Holding parent meetings in the community (i.e., apartment meeting rooms, community clubhouses) would have been a way to proactively try to address concerns students and parents had and also elicit the support and help of the parent community.

It is obvious the counselor was negligent in not notifying school officials about the note immediately and by not stopping Mike before he got on the bus or went home. The counselor should not have taken so much time talking with the student who wrote the note. As soon as it was discovered that a gun or a toy gun might be on campus, all attention should have been directed toward Mike. The police liaison officer should have been consulted. This now becomes a police matter. If Mike had already left the school on a bus, the police liaison officer should intervene (as she would know the best way to handle this situation). If Mike was walking home, he should be stopped for questioning by the police. The police are obviously aware of the procedure for questioning an individual who might be carrying a concealed weapon.

I have always believed that school counselors should be involved in the development of their school's crisis plan. However, in many cases the development of such a plan comes only after a crisis has happened. Many school systems are now developing systemwide plans and mandating individual schools to follow their example. As horrifying as this incident is, a school that is ill prepared to deal with any crisis will undoubtedly be in much worse shape the days following such an incident. Crisis plans should not only be developed but also updated and changed accordingly each new school year (as personnel change). The fact that this school had talked about developing a plan and had delayed in doing so is inexcusable. No plan can prevent such an occurrence, but the aftermath is almost as frightening as the event.

H. S. Lawrence

School counselors have the skills and training to recognize, respond, and intervene when there are early signs of alienation and anger in children. Nothing is mentioned in this incident regarding the prevention efforts of the existing school counselors. I would assume that these counselors had the necessary skills and training to respond to these issues before they become "out of control." However, there is an implied belief that these counselors were not very involved in prevention efforts as indicated by the lack of follow-through regarding the crisis plan assignment. If these counselors are like many across the country, their job is made difficult and challenging because of the number of hours hired. I believe such an effort requires the counselors to be there enough hours to work with the students (in an ongoing relationship) and with the parents in a supportive role. In addition, if more than the school counselors' services are warranted, they can then make appropriate referrals and follow up as needed. Some school counseling programs operate on a differentiated time schedule. One middle school I worked in had three full-time counselors and one social worker. This staff decided to differentiate their workdays to allow them to start and end their work day at different times. Everybody had different starting and ending times. For example, one counselor really wanted to work with families. To see families, she had to stay later in the afternoon and into the early evening. Therefore, her work day began at 11:00 a.m. and ended at 6:30 p.m. She was responsible for her assignments during the school day and was responsible for seeing parents (i.e., individual, group, parenting classes) until 6:30 p.m. The bottom line was that we were all working our regular contract hours, but we worked at trying to meet the needs of our school community. This system allowed us to see more students, parents, and families; make better referrals; and operate as a true counseling center. And we still fulfilled our other school counseling responsibilities!

Counselors tout themselves as prevention specialists. I believe the counselor must be a life-skills educator in the areas of conflict resolution, anger management, interpersonal relationships, values clarification, tolerating differences education, human relations training, civility training, ethics, and moral education. Many of my colleagues may disagree with these responsibilities. However, I believe they are not seeing the reality of how and where students are living and are being raised. I become very annoyed when I hear school counselors say, "It's not my job to raise this child!" I disagree, and it seems that this mentality is very much like the ostrich which hides its head in the sand, thinking that the lion doesn't see him. My question is, Isn't that what we are about? Are we not the knowledgeable professionals who have the skills and tools to help others with their responsibilities?

It is obvious the counselor was negligent regarding not acting on the note in a more timely fashion. I got the impression that the time of day when the note was delivered was just an excuse not to proceed with an investigation. I also got the impression that this counselor approached the job with a "laid back" attitude. The counselor not wanting to pursue Mike, regardless of what time it was, seemed to be representative of how this counselor and perhaps the counseling department (the lack of follow-through regarding the crisis plan) approached their jobs.

We know that school is a microcosm that reflects society. It is hard to understand this culture, but counselors who do work in schools understand this. If they are still hiding under the college admissions paperwork, the special education paperwork, and any other paperwork, they need to find a way to define the role as is now necessary, as we approach the new millenium.

Sexual Harassment: "I Never Thought It Would Go That Far"

CRITICAL INCIDENT

Background

Christa is a senior at B. A. Beckum High School and has been a member of the volleyball team for 2 years. She is a talented athlete, well-liked among others, and regarded as an excellent student among her teachers. Christa is expected to earn a full athletic scholarship to a well-respected college where she wants to pursue a finance degree. Christa's coach, Mrs. Sandlewood, has worked diligently with Christa as someone who also has the potential to participate in the next Olympics. Coach Sandlewood has spent a great deal of time with Christa and her family and is considered a close friend.

Colletta, a senior recently transferred to the school, is the newest member of the team after only 3 months. During this time, Colletta has established herself as the "jokester" of the team, continuously saying and doing things to make the others laugh both on and off the court. Christa has been one of Colletta's favorite targets because she seems to take the jokes in stride or at least does not attempt to retaliate. Coach Sandlewood is aware of the joking among players and considers it harmless fun and probably a sign of cohesiveness.

Incident

About a month ago, Colletta discovered that creating sexual innuendoes involving Christa and Coach Sandlewood resulted in the greatest laughter and is best received among the team members. When seeing Christa and the coach together, especially after practice, Colletta makes comments among team members such as, "There they are, Mr. & Mrs. Sandlewood, aren't they lovely together?" "I bet Christa is the one who spikes the ball in that game!" and "Hey, Darla (another team member), how about you go over there and ask if you can join them, I hear that Coach loves Conte Christa Sandwiches for lunch!" Christa was aware of such comments as disclosed through a friend on the team. She was usually embarrassed about Colletta's comments, although she continued to work very hard and focus on her game. Still, Christa could tell she was not able to train to her potential because of such distractions. After talking with the Coach about this, the Coach told Christa, "Look, Christa, they're just stupid words! How could you let their childish behaviors distract you? You know, if I were to make a big deal about this it could get worse! Colletta and the others could do this stuff more, be even more secretive about it. You should just focus on your game and keep your eye on the prize—you're going to get a scholarship and go to the Olympics one day. Won't they be jealous then!"

During lunch that day, Coach Sandlewood talked about the situation during casual conversation with teachers and the school counselor. Some at the table laughed in amusement and others acted surprised. Others dismissed such behavior as characteristic adolescent antics. The school counselor considered the situation to be detrimental to personal and academic success and in need of special attention. However, upon initial response, the counselor decided that the situation was best addressed within the "jurisdiction" of athletics. The situation, the counselor thought, was not one in which she was invited to intervene and would probably best be handled by the Coach anyway. Also, by approaching Christa, the counselor may be intruding on the Coach's current handle on the situation.

One week later, Christa heard from her locker a loud and peculiar vibrating noise. Somewhat frightened, she yelled for Coach Sandlewood, who immediately told everyone to get back while she opened the locker. She found the sound was emanating from a vibrating dildo, which had a gift label attached to it which read, "Christa, you're my number one, Coach." The Coach was initially both shocked and amused as evidenced by her wide eyes and hint of a grin. Afterward there was a wave of laughter and talking as the news of the incident quickly spread throughout the room and then throughout the school. Those on the team assumed this was a result of Colletta's work and chalked it up as her most hilarious gag ever. Students who had heard about the incident and were not aware of the details simply assumed that Coach Sandlewood and Christa were involved in some sort of relationship.

Rumors of the incident were passed along the study body, changing slightly along the way to accommodate increasing sensationalism. After only several hours, some students in the school believed that Christa and the Coach were caught having sexual relations in the office. Others heard, and erroneously believed, that Christa was only on the girls' volleyball team so she could be with the other girls on the team, especially in locker room situations. The Coach immediately reported the incident to the principal and to the Dean, who then prompted an investigation without delay. At this time, the Coach started to become angry at the thought of how the incident might affect the team's status and upcoming competition.

Discussion

It had been 4 school days since the incident and Christa was not in attendance. The perpetrator of the incident was still not officially known, and the investigation continued. The school counselor called Christa's home to express concern and offer help to Christa and her family. Christa's father answered and sounded angry after learning it was someone from his daughter's school. After calming down, he disclosed he was actually a bit glad that the counselor called. He told the counselor that he needed help to coordinate meetings with several others: the family attorney, Christa, and relevant others as needed for a lawsuit against the school and individual personnel. "The suit," he said, "was for sexual harassment. It would include damages of $2 million for loss of potential scholarship and Olympic participation, pain and suffering, and possible violation of Title IX." The school counselor told the father that it would not be appropriate for her to handle such a task and that she could refer him to the principal. The counselor was also quick to add that, "Instead, it is my primary concern that I help Christa, you, and the family to recover from this situation as best as possible so that she could effectively continue with her studies and athletics." Although the counselor did not tell Christa's father, she was also interested in challenging other students about sexual harassment, gossiping, and disrespect. Christa's father simply responded, "In that case, I'll see you later—in court."

Without access to Christa and her family, the counselor decided to then focus her efforts on working with the student body in regard to the incident. She would engage students in large group guidance for learning knowledge, skills, attitudes, and behaviors that foster protective factors against sexual harassment. The counselor consulted the literature and gathered relevant materials and activities. The principal and school board worked with the family, attorneys, and the media to manage the incident and come up with a mutually agreeable reconciliation. Meanwhile, Christa transferred to a private school with a comparable volleyball team.

QUESTIONS

1. Does the scenario constitute sexual harassment? Who is/are the victim(s)?
2. What is the school's responsibility in dealing with this incident and to what extent are individual liable?
3. How would you evaluate the actions of the counselor?
4. What are other possible implications of this incident?

RESPONSES TO THE INCIDENT

Paul Pedersen

It is much less expensive—emotionally and financially—to prevent problems than to remediate problems once they have occurred. The coach was not being a close friend to Christa when she allowed or even forced Christa to deal with false accusations about sexually inappropriate behavior by herself. It seems the coach was more concerned, even after the affair became public (!), by the effect this situation might have on the team's status and upcoming competition.

The counselor, who apparently knew about the false accusations earlier and did nothing, was also to blame for not preventing this conflict from escalating by confronting the parties in conflict. The counselor would have been in an ideal role as mediator of the conflict at an early stage, pointing out the dangerous consequences of continued harassment for everybody involved and finding some more constructive way to manage the conflict.

The public humiliation of planting a dildo in Christa's locker was the moral equivalent of planting a bomb or other explosive device and does not qualify as a practical joke. The tolerance of this high level of harassment by the coach, the counselor, the students, and presumably other faculty relates to the tolerance of high levels of violence in public schools recently resulting in death and physical injury. It seems apparent that the "school culture" was seen as allowing harassment as acceptable and even funny as indicated by the coach's and other's reactions. The school made itself very vulnerable to victims such as Christa and others of the violence resulting from this permissive attitude who are seeking legal recourse.

Having failed to prevent—or even try to prevent—the harassment at an earlier stage it is understandable that Christa's parents did not want help from the counselor at this late stage, except possibly to testify against the school. The resulting disaster was completely preventable and, in retrospect, all parties can probably identify what should have been done earlier to avoid the escalation of hurtful behavior. Disasters such as this do not require the involvement of evil or bad people. All that is required is the apathy or reluctance of counselors, teachers, students, parents, and others who fail to prevent the harassment from escalating. Many if not all the people in this incident may be well-intentioned, but nonetheless dangerous through their perhaps unintentional encouragement of hurtful behavior in the school among students.

Katherine Niebuhr

Consider the two primary criteria for assessing if sexual harassment is occurring. First, quid pro quo, giving something to get something, does not seem to be evident. However, the second criteria, a hostile environment, certainly is. Another female student athlete had subjected Christa to several sexual innuendoes. She reported the problem to her coach, who dismissed it. The coach eventually told the counselor (though in an unprofessional, unconfidential manner), who also chose not to respond, feeling that to do so would infringe on the athletic department. Although traditionally the cases have involved male-to-female harassment (or behavior), recently some same-sex cases are being heard in the courts. Whether or not this particular situation involves legal sexual harassment will depend on current judicial decisions in the Federal district of the school system.

The school has dual responsibilities in this case. Before the possibility of a problem, the school administrators and counselors should have developed a comprehensive, preventative program. For example, a school climate survey could be administered anonymously to all students. Do they see detrimental behavior, such as telling dirty jokes, inappropriate touching, or seeing pictures or comments about female students in the locker rooms? Reactive responses to sexual harassment should be in place so that all faculty know the process so that any complaints will be documented immediately.

Any adult in the school who does not take action to prevent a student from having to endure a hostile environment is at risk for legal action. The school counselor was negligent in not advocating for a student in need. Just because Christa was an athlete, she was first and foremost a student. Would the counselor ignore a similar situation for band members, art students, or the yearbook staff? Certainly not.

This incident suggests implications regarding other issues in schools. How are threats of violence handled? Would certain students be allowed to intimidate others? Is gang graffiti ignored? Can racist remarks be made without the faculty's intervention? In fact, the school counselor, with specialized graduate training, can be the key person to promote a safe and accepting school for all students.

Sexual Identity: "I Don't Know"

CRITICAL INCIDENT

Background

I am a male school counselor in a high school of 2,000 students that is located in an urban setting. I am part of a guidance department with three other counselors, one of whom is female. We are a close department, often consulting with each other regarding particular students, parents, and teachers with whom we are working. We are about the same age, are energetic, and consider our program to be one of the more effective guidance and counseling programs in our school system. I did not realize how an incident like this could divide us so quickly and decisively. I am still not sure if I made the right decision, and frankly am waiting for the repercussions of my actions. However, I consider myself a student advocate first and, fundamentally, an advocate for human individuality and believe that my decision was the most appropriate.

Incident

One day during class change, one of our physical education teachers asked if she could speak to me. She stated that our meeting might take some time and she would appreciate if we could be alone and our discussion be in the strictest confidence. I asked her if the problem dealt with any type of physical or sexual harm or potential harm to our faculty or students. She told me she believed this was not about anything physical, but it very much might be sexual. Then she added, "but not in an abusive manner." The first bell to class rang, stopping our conversation. Because I did not have any appointments scheduled after school, I told her I would be happy to see her and assured her our conversation would remain confidential.

About 3:15 p.m., the teacher knocked on my door. She sat down and reminded me about the confidentiality of our conversation. As she began, it became apparent that what she was talking about was that she did not want her name connected in any way with what she was going to tell me. I told her that was a reasonable request and I would do my best to honor it. She then proceeded to tell me about two junior boys (both of whom were in my "alpha") she had in her class, one of whom was a fairly new student to our school. Apparently over the course of about a month, she had noticed they had become friends. I responded I had been a little concerned about the adjustment of the new student and was glad he had found a friend. The teacher then stated that was not the problem. The problem was the two boys were too friendly. When I asked her what she meant, this is what she said:

I began noticing them always standing together, talking, and laughing. At first I didn't think anything about it, espe-

cially since one of them was new to the school. Then one day I noticed they seemed to be looking and laughing at and with each other in a way that was different—in fact it looked like the behavior one would see between a boy and girl who liked each other. It was sort of flirtatious. One day I was walking by a group of students and overheard one of them make a reference toward the boys. I heard the words "gay" and "faggot." I immediately stopped and questioned the boys about who they were talking about. They acted as if I was the last person on the earth to hear about any of this. They said it was common knowledge around school that both boys were "faggots." They had even been seen walking together after school with their arms around each other and dancing together at weekend parties.

As the teacher finished her story, I started to get a queasy feeling in the pit of my stomach. I thought I knew where she was going with this and what she was going to ask me. However, I was wrong. She launched into how this type of behavior was unacceptable, immoral, and sinful. She stated that young people have enough to worry about (growing up) without being subjected to this type of indecent behavior. She wanted me to call in the two boys and find out if they were indeed gay, then she suggested I call the parents and tell them what was going on. Then she added again that she did not want her name brought into this.

Discussion

After she left, I sat in my office and stared out the window. I felt hollow inside. I began to think about the issue of homosexuality, my personal feelings, morals and values, the rights of individuals, and what my responsibility was to the students in question, their parents, and the students of our school. I decided to think about the teacher's request overnight, but I was leaning toward calling both boys into my office.

The next morning I decided to speak to both boys. I sent for them and they arrived about 5 minutes later. It was the most difficult conversation I have ever had with anyone. I told them there were rumors going around school that they were "a couple." They said they had heard the rumors but had decided to try and not pay attention to them. Their response surprised me, so I asked them pointedly if they were a couple, to which they replied yes! At that point I knew that I was about to "get in over my head." I asked them did their parents know of their relationship. They stated they did not think their parents knew, but they thought they would find out sooner or later. I told them their behaviors were being noticed around school by both students and faculty. They agreed, but felt it was not their (the faculty and students') problem and they could "weather the storm." I cautioned them on acting inappropriately because of the trouble they could get into. One of the boys looked at me and said, "What do you mean acting inappropriate? Would you be warning us if one of us were a girl? Or are you calling our behavior inappropriate because we're gay?" As I sat there listening to the question, I realized I did not have an appropriate answer. So I answered the best way I could. I replied, "I don't know." The two boys got up and left my office.

After a few moments, I asked for a meeting with two of the other counselors and explained what had happened with the teacher and the students. The general consensus from my colleagues was that I needed to inform the parents of the two boys. In their opinion, this was information the parents needed to know. To my surprise, one of the counselors talked about the "unnaturalness" of the relationship and if one of the boys were his son, he would want to know. The other counselor cited health issues (sexually transmitted diseases, AIDS) that mandate the parents to be notified. In addition, she stated I should tell the principal immediately so that he could deal with any repercussions from parents. I was confused as to why the principal should be informed. She explained that eventually word will get out and parents will call wanting to know what he is going to do about it. As I listened, I found myself becoming more and more angry. Trying to remain calm, I thanked them for their suggestions.

I decided not to call the boys' parents, nor did I inform the principal. I met with the teacher the following day and told her that I had met with both boys and had cautioned them about their behavior. I also told her that I probably would be seeing them again in a professional manner, though that would be up to the boys. She said she thought I was acting unprofessionally. She said she thought I would "take care of this." She also had thought about it over night and believed her religious convictions mandated that she report this entire situation to the principal. She turned and walked away, leaving me to wonder what was going to happen.

QUESTIONS

1. Was I correct in speaking to the two boys?
2. Should I have contacted the boys' parents?
3. Should I have reported this to the principal?
4. Were my colleagues correct in their rationale?
5. I stated that I would probably see the boys "in a professional manner." Can I ethically do this? Do I want to?

RESPONSES TO THE INCIDENT

Lawrence E. Tyson

The counselor in this incident promotes himself as a "a student advocate first and, fundamentally, an advocate for human individuality." This counselor allows his emotions and overt pressure from others to taint his approach and ethically compromise his behavior. It appears that his behavior is not congruent with his philosophy.

The counselor is approached by a teacher who is concerned about the personal interaction between two junior boys. According to this incident, the teacher is concerned that "the two boys were too friendly" and that "they seemed to be looking and laughing at and with each other in a way that was different...like the behavior one would see between a boy and girl who liked each other; sort of flirtatious." At no time did the teacher state that the boys' behavior was causing any type of disruption in her classroom. This is where the counselor made his first mistake. The teacher disclosed her personal agenda regarding the boys "allegedly inappropriate behavior." This had nothing to do with her classroom management style or the students' behavior that might be contributing to her teaching other students.

First, the discussion with the counselor would not have taken place if the students in questions were male and female. It would be a mute point. Second, it is apparent the teacher had her agenda to promote and was approaching this as a discipline issue. The counselor allowed himself to be manipulated into the role of disciplinarian by not defining his role to the teacher either during the initial conversation or later in his office. By inferring he would and then deciding to talk to the students, the counselor changed his role and reinforced the teacher's perception of that role. If the teacher had a concern about the students' behavior (in terms of class disruption), she should follow the required preliminary steps as stated in the school's discipline code, which would be consistent with action taken for any student. This is not a counseling issue unless the two students wish to discuss concerns with a professional counselor.

The counselor should not have arranged an appointment with the two students unless they wished to speak to him. The question should be, "Would the counselor call a female and male student in for the same behavior as described by the teacher?" The answer is no. Again, it is a nonissue unless the behavior is disrupting the normal operation of the school day.

In addition, the counselor should not contact the boys' parents or the principal. The teacher has described flirtatious behavior (not disruptive) and second-hand information overheard from other students regarding student behavior that allegedly occurred off-campus. There is nothing to discuss with parents. This is not the role of the school counselor. It is also not the role of the school counselor to discuss this issue with the principal. This should have been made clear to the teacher during their initial conversations. The teacher always has the option of reporting anything to the principal herself. If she felt this was worthy of such an option, she should do so—but without the initial involvement of the counselor.

In this case, I would have suggested the counselor consult with his colleagues before making any decision. We have the luxury of knowing their views, which are ethically and professionally incorrect. However, it is important for counselors to consult with their colleagues, while protecting student confidentiality, before critical action is taken. If the counselor in this incident was troubled by the information provided by the teacher, then consultation was in order. In this incident, his colleagues were incorrect in their assessment. And it should have been clear to the counselor that there really wasn't any issue here to contemplate. He apparently was overwhelmed with the issue, and perhaps had personal, unresolved value issues that contributed to his improper action.

It is my belief this counselor has acted unethically. In addition, there is no indication in the incident that this counselor is professionally competent "to see the boys in a profession manner." The counselor has overstepped his professional boundaries and has given the indication to the teacher and the boys that he can provide a service I seriously doubt he is competent enough to deliver.

Harry Steven

I believe the counselor was correct in speaking to the students in question. Their alleged behavior was causing some disruption in the school given the fact that other students were already talking about them and calling them names. The teacher, though obviously promoting her personal agenda, seemed to be coming to the counselor because she initially did not want to involve the principal. The fact that groups of students were already discussing the boys' behavior could escalate into a volatile situation given the attacks on gay men and lesbians in other parts of the United States. Therefore, this was proper behavior on the teacher's part to ask the counselor to talk to the boys and for the counselor to call them in to discuss their alleged actions.

I do feel the parents should he notified, but only after the boys admitted they were in a personal relationship. There are other issues here beyond that of two same-sex individuals in a relationship. It is insinuated in this incident that the school, located in an urban area, is perhaps in a more liberal area than if the school was located in an rural environment. However, because of the developmental age of other students in the school, it is very probable that issues of concern (e.g., emotional and physical abuse) may develop; the students in question may be in potential harm. Of course this could happen in a city or in the country.

The principal should also be notified. Because students are already talking about the students in question, it will be just a matter of time before more students and parents will become informed. The principal needs to know because of the potential of parents and others outside the school commenting and questioning school policy and wanting to know what the principal is going to do about this. We may not like this course of action, but this is the reality of our culture and we must be prepared to deal with the "real world."

Student Motivation: "Motivated for the Wrong Reasons"

CRITICAL INCIDENT

Background

I was in my 2nd year as a guidance counselor at a small-town junior high school. Overall, this school was a quiet one where there were no real discipline problems. The most I really had to handle was mischievous teenagers. Matthew was a seventh-grade student who had moved to the town when he was 3 years old. He attended a private, Christian school beginning in kindergarten and went into the public school system at the beginning of the fourth grade. He had a younger sister, Emily, who was 14 months younger than he. Matthew also had an older brother who was 19 and an older sister who was 21. The oldest brother had also gone through the middle school and high school. He was labeled as very intelligent but an extremely mischievous child who stayed in constant trouble. Emily was in the same school in the sixth grade. Emily was a successful student and a high achiever, much like the oldest sister. Matthew and Emily lived at home with both parents. Matthew had excellent grades throughout elementary school but seemed to run into difficulties when he reached seventh grade.

Incident

From the very beginning of the year, Matthew appeared to be rebelling against his family. There were several incidents during which he would sneak T-shirts to school that had crude and vulgar sayings on them. He would leave his home dressed normally and then change into these at school. His grades were rapidly declining because he simply refused to do the work. His parents were called about the situation, and it was reported they attempted to handle it. Still, nothing seemed to resolve his behavior and grades. I attempted to talk with Matthew about improving his grades and getting him to do the work. He informed me that he was bored in class and that he already knew how to do everything.

This story may very well have been true because he placed first for his grade level in the advanced math and science tests. I began to work from his standpoint to see what we as a school could do to keep him motivated. All of his teachers said they would be happy to let him work ahead at his own pace. I also talked with his parents about exploring the possibility of getting him enrolled in the school of Math and Science to help him achieve even more. From what I was seeing and being told by him, I felt this would resolve the situation, and the grades would begin to increase. By the end of the third 6 weeks, his grades were worse than ever. His parents were seeing the grades but doing nothing to resolve the situation. I decided to call them in for a session to get to the root of this problem.

Matthew's mother and father came in for the talk. I explained that Matthew's grades were really getting out of hand and if something was not done soon, he would be forced to repeat seventh grade. His mother said this was the first time she had heard anything about any of this. As the discussion progressed and the report cards were shown, we discovered that Matthew had been pulling stunts on all of us. He had created a report card with all B's instead of D's for his parents to view, and he had forged his mother's signature on the copy to be returned to the school. He was motivated in every aspect to create an elaborate cover-up for his problems.

Discussion

I asked his parents to allow me to speak with Matthew alone before they did anything. I felt there had to be more to this problem for such a smart child to go to all this effort just to get out of doing some school work. I brought Matthew in and explained we had discovered all that he had done to keep his grades hidden. I told him I felt the clothing incidents and the sneaky acts to cover up his grades did not add up to what I had known of him as a student in sixth grade. I explained that he was brilliant and should be trying to fulfill his potential. He said he had heard it all before, and he was getting sick of hearing it again. As I pressed further, he became angry and stated that no one ever considered his feelings or cared about his life, only what his potential was. He became indignant about how he saw his role in his family and what it was like following an older brother through school. I began to gather that Matthew had been his brother's shadow up until the point he left for college.

I realized that his brother had also been very intelligent but had began doing many of the sneaky things in middle school that Matthew had done. In fact, Matthew began to describe specific situations in which many of the teachers he now had would frequently discuss the things his older brother had done. They often told Matthew he was following in his brother's footsteps.

QUESTIONS

1. Adolescents are often trying to begin to create an identity in the seventh grade. Was this an example of the beginning

development of identity foreclosure where one solves the problem of creating an identity by accepting family ideals?

2. I labeled the issue with Matthew as an issue in which a child was bored in class because he was not being pushed to work to his fill potential. Was I wrong to assume this from the situation at hand?

3. Should I have discussed with Matthew more the idea of separating himself from his brother to develop his own pathway in school? Are there any other things I could have suggested to help him deal with missing his brother besides staying in close contact and visiting him?

4. What is my role as Matthew's school counselor in helping him achieve a separate identity from his brother? Should I refer Matthew for therapy, or is this something that I can help Matthew with?

RESPONSES TO THE INCIDENT

Robert Milstead

Matthew is displaying many of the characteristics of bright, middle/junior high school students. Apparent boredom, attention-seeking behaviors, and putting a lot of energy into avoiding good grades are but some of Matthew's behaviors. As preteens, many students struggle with establishing their identity. Whether through imitating someone else or by reacting in an opposite manner from another person, adolescents often find the path to self-identity strewn with obstacles and experimentation. Matthew is no exception.

Being frequently compared with his brother will almost certainly eventually lead to rebellion. It appears that at the present, Matthew is enjoying the comparison with his brother. On the other hand, one can reasonably expect that it is just a matter of time until Matthew decides to outdo his brother's activities. His two sisters made good grades, so it is very likely that Matthew is deciding to seek his identity through misbehavior because he feels he cannot compete academically.

His in-class behavior is likely to be partly a result of boredom with the current assignments. Just about every school counselor has dealt with students who are capable but who earn poor grades. The counselor's challenge is to work with the teachers to offer Matthew additional or alternative assignments while working with Matthew to change his behavior and to develop a plan to complete the missing work. Matthew's challenge is to make and follow through on a commitment to get back on track academically.

The counselor might want to consider seeing Matthew on a regular basis to work on self-concept and follow-through in addition to academic motivation. This could start with determining Matthew's areas of interests and potential career areas. If the school has career exploration software or interest inventories, Matthew could be encouraged to begin using these resources. As he learns how his skills and interests relate to career possibilities, he should be encouraged to determine how his choices in school courses and activities also can affect career options. His test scores indicate he should do well in a math- or science-related area. This would make an excellent starting point.

The counselor apparently already enjoys a good relationship with Matthew. That relationship should be used to begin the process of helping Matthew refocus his energies in a more positive direction. By aiming for small but steady changes in a positive direction, the counselor can help Matthew achieve academic success while becoming better prepared for his personal future.

Lawrence E. Tyson

Middle school is often the place where a child's search for an independent identity manifests. During this age, children struggle to integrate with others, while at the same time begin their search for independence. On the surface, Matthew seems to be struggling with the same issues most other middle school children struggle with—the need to be accepted and liked while being perceived as "having it together." In this scenario, however, there are obviously other serious issues dealing with trust, family values (personal and parental), and personal identity. There is more to this family's areas of concern other than making poor grades, wearing inappropriate clothing, and forging report cards. It is a miscalculation for the school counselor to believe these are the problems, when in fact they are only the symptoms. Mathew has displayed these behavior choices over a period of time, and these must therefore be taken more seriously than just seen as adjustment issues. Mathew's behaviors warrant a referral for family therapy.

Mathew's behavior are cries for help through attention. His behavior represents those ideals that mean the most to his parents and teachers. Often times children in middle school realize they actually are in control of more of their life than they thought or believed. One of the control items are grades. No matter how many times a parent has a teacher conference or how long the child is placed on restrictions, the child is still in the power seat when it comes to grades. Another issue of control are the clothes the student wears to school or, in this case, changes into before arriving at school. This is a realization the parents have yet to discover (until the conference regarding his grades). The last area described in this scenario is the issue of trust, or dishonesty. The counselor decided to look down the path marked "You're too smart for this behavior." This path was actually a deception by Mathew. His intelligence has nothing to do with his behavior choices. The counselor trivializes Mathew's behaviors and does not look below the surface for the real issues.

Substance Abuse (Drinking): "How Involved Should I Be?"

CRITICAL INCIDENT

Background

John is a 17-year-old senior who is not very interested in school but continues because of the insistence and support of his teachers and peers. He comes from a small rural farming community and attends a middle-senior high school of about 500 students. His parents operate a farm and work hard to make ends meet. They attend church regularly, but John does not, something which has been a contentious issue between him and his parents. John had difficulty with teachers during his middle school years, often being sent to the office for inappropriate behaviors such as talking back to teachers or refusing to cooperate with teachers when asked to do tasks appropriate to classroom learning. During his years in high school, he has been more cooperative in the classroom but does not always have his homework completed to his teachers' satisfaction.

During his 12th grade, his average in the university preparatory program was about 65%. He has a car he affords by holding down a part-time job. He comes from a family of five children, three older sisters and one younger brother. He has difficulty getting along with his father, whom he says is a lot like himself—he likes to do things his way.

Incident

One of the activities I did with seniors was to interview them to discuss their plans after high school. In April of his senior year, John came willingly to the office and openly discussed his desire to finish school and get a job. He was anxious to be on his own. He had considered community college and a course in electrical wiring but said he had "enough of school" and was "trying his luck" by making it this far without any real catastrophes. During the course of our conversation, John indicated he used alcohol every day and kept a bottle in his locker. We discussed the extent of his habit and how long he had been dependent on alcohol. His current pattern of use has been in place for the past 6 months. He freely offered information even after I explained the limits of confidentiality. I explained to him the seriousness and possible lifestyle implications of his habit and that he should get help.

I strongly suggested to John that he do these three things: immediately remove the alcohol from his locker and put it in his car, get help at the local hospital that runs an addiction program for alcohol abusers, and not drive while drinking. In addition, I reviewed the school rules concerning students using alcohol while on school property and about having illegal substances on school premises. John acknowledged he was aware of consequences of his behavior but felt he had been lucky and would not likely be found out in the month of school left. I told him I would not report this information to the principal or to his parents unless I was questioned, in which case I would have to break confidentiality.

He said he would take his chances.

Discussion

The school rules indicated that any student using alcohol in school would be automatically suspended for the rest of the school year. In addition, it was school policy to report such illegal student acts to their parents. I decided I could do neither. If I reported this information to the principal, John would be suspended from school. If I reported this information to his parents, a confrontation would likely develop, and he might leave home. With either outcome, he would not complete his senior year and would not graduate from high school. I felt some obligation to respond to his purchase of alcohol, which is illegal owing to his age. I wondered if I should alert the local police, as I suspected someone of legal age must be purchasing the alcohol for him and possibly other students under the legal drinking age.

QUESTIONS

1. What responsibility does the school counselor have to school rules? Should counselors respect the welfare of their clients above all else?
2. What responsibility does the school counselor have to protect society from individuals who might do others harm? While I acknowledge I do not have to prove John drinks and drives, or that someone of legal drinking age is buying him alcohol, should I have reported the information to the police?
3. What responsibility does the school counselor have to the parents of students? If John's parents had been notified, they may have been successful in getting him help, such as admitting him to a hospital or an alcohol abuse program.
4. Is it possible I am aiding and abetting his illegal behavior? Because I did not report the information to the principal or to his parents, is it possible John may have construed my lack of reporting as condoning his behavior?

5. What are the possible consequences of not complying with school rules and policies?

RESPONSES TO THE INCIDENT
Paul Pedersen

The "road to hell" is indeed often paved with "good intentions." It is apparent the counselor likes John and wants to help him succeed. John is a pretty independent person who likes to do things his way, an attitude that is quite facilitative on the farm and probably quite characteristic in the small rural farming community where John lives. John must also like the counselor to share his behaviors openly, knowing they are against the law and subject to disciplinary action by the school as well. This trusting relationship was probably difficult to establish and the counselor is unwilling to risk destroying the relationship. Breaking the law and rules does not seem to bother John, and the consequences of these illegal behaviors do not seem to get in the way of John's plans for the future. John is not willing to modify his behaviors and believes himself lucky enough or clever enough to get by without getting caught.

The counselor needs to find a way to keep the relationship with John, without either John or the counselor breaking the law in the process. This may involve confronting John with the reality that the authorities will be notified when laws are being broken. The counselor's decision not to disclose the illegal activity until or unless asked a direct question is likely to get John and the counselor in serious trouble and offers little potential toward any long-term positive outcome for John. Causing trouble in a "small, rural farming community" is a big problem, and the counselor is right in assuming that disclosure will cause many people in the community to get angry, whatever might be right or wrong in this situation. Disclosure will bring in "outsiders" when the local community might rather want to solve its own problems.

The counselor assumes that disclosure will prevent John from graduating, which is probably not true given alternative schooling programs that are available. It is likely that disclosure will involve conflict with John's parents and with the supplier of illegal alcohol.

The consequences of disclosure, however painful, are much less severe than the consequences of nondisclosure. The counselor, by protecting John's drinking habit, displays a classic style of facilitating John's alcoholism in the future if not already in the present by "protecting" him.

The counselor's caring attitude and unconditional positive regard for John would, in this instance, be better applied toward helping John deal with the conflict in his life than by helping John avoid conflict. It is easy to see how a caring counselor can want to bend the rules for a student in trouble and, under other circumstances, that might even be appropriate, however risky. In this particular instance, however, the counselor is avoiding responsibility and is encouraging John to avoid responsibility in ways that will be destructive in the long term for both John and the counselor.

Robert Milstead

The positive relationship between John and his counselor is obvious by the openness of their discussion of the dangers from John's disclosure. The counselor has clearly dedicated a great deal of time and energy in establishing what has become a mutual caring, close relationship.

The counselor, as a school employee, is expected to comply with school rules and procedures. Failure to do so puts the counselor at risk of disciplinary action. The counselor is now in the unenviable position of potentially harming the relationship with John, being at risk of disciplinary action, and/or losing credibility with John's parents. Many people would interpret the counselor's decision at this point to do nothing other than offer suggestions as tacit approval of John's behavior.

If the counselor really has John's best interest at heart, specific actions should take place. The counselor should hold another conference with John, explaining the unease felt in the current situation. John should be told the counselor will schedule an appointment with the parents in about a week. John's grades and postgraduation plans should be the primary focus, but the drinking will also likely be discussed because it most likely affecting his school performance. The counselor should be explicit in telling John this will provide him an opportunity to tell his parents about this behavior in a supportive atmosphere. The counselor should encourage John to stop drinking and to remove the alcohol from school property. The counselor could supply John with the names of several treatment agencies either before or during the conference.

Although the conference with John's parents will not be easy, the potential benefits are enormous. John can earn the respect of his parents by admitting he has a problem and outlining what he has done to start dealing with it. He can also reaffirm the concern and respect of his counselor in helping John deal with his problem in a supportive atmosphere.

Supervision:
"I Thought I Was Off Duty"

CRITICAL INCIDENT

Background

Several years ago I was supervising counseling interns in the clinical phase of their program. One of my students was placed in a school counseling setting in her hometown. She had heard there would be an opening for a school counselor in the near future at that school and she had high hopes she would be offered the position on completion of her internship. The intern met in group supervision once a week with other interns at the university. As part of the course requirements, students were asked to turn in weekly journals describing their on-site experiences. During one such group meeting, as the students were sharing experiences from the past week, this particular student mentioned, as an afterthought, an encounter she had with one of the students that week at her school site.

Incident

The intern was outside the counseling setting but was on the school grounds having a casual conversation with a student as he was playing basketball by himself. She had not seen this student in her role as school counselor and was not acting in that capacity when she began a "friendly" conversation with him. The student was a white male, age 13. As the student continued to shoot baskets, he mentioned to her how unhappy he was at home and that he "hated" his parents. In fact, he said that he "wanted them to go away."

Because the intern had not related this encounter in her journals, I pressed her for further details trying to ascertain the seriousness of the boy's statements. She recalled the student stated he had read where other parents had "gone away" but did not all kids want their parents to "go away" at some time or another? The intern said the student planned to inject his parents with antifreeze while they slept, but then laughed about it as if it were a joke. As warning bells were going off in my head, I continued to pry details out of her, which she provided somewhat reluctantly. Among the details she remembered was she thought he was well liked at school but did not seem to be outstanding. I asked her if she had reported this encounter and conversation with the school counselor who was her on-site supervisor or to the principal. She stated she "had not done so" because this conversation was not part of a counseling session. She said she took the student's comments to be improbable and, because the discussion took place on the basketball court, it seemed like he was "letting off steam."

The supervision seminar occurred on a Thursday evening. Friday was a student holiday and the school would be closed. At that point, I decided to immediately consult with other counseling faculty members to get a consensus on the urgency of action with this dilemma. Was there a duty-to-warn situation here? After consultation, we were in agreement that this situation needed to be handled immediately and should not wait until school was in session the next week. An action plan was formulated that included (a) notifying the principal immediately (that same evening) of the threat, (b) notifying the school counselor (the intern's on-site supervisor), and (c) contacting the university attorney to get legal advice.

Discussion

The intern was hesitant and somewhat unwilling to make these calls because she was sure that "creating all this fuss" would somehow put her in a bad light at the school and jeopardize her chances for obtaining employment with the system. I told her I would be expecting a follow-up call from her letting me know what she had done. I also told her if she did not follow-up in a timely manner, then I would implement the action plan from the university level. She also asked me if she would still be responsible if her principal and counselor did not agree to warn the parents or did not properly follow-up? The principal and school counselor agreed to call the parents in for a conference, and they did tell the parents of their child's threat against them. However, the conference did not occur until Wednesday of the following week. The parents' response? They were reported to have just laughed and said, "Oh, he says things like that all the time!" "This is not the first time we have been warned about something like this." "Yes, we will speak to his therapist about this." Nothing more was heard about this situation. At the time I felt a little foolish that we had perhaps overreacted to this potential "foreseeable risk."

QUESTIONS

1. What would be considered a "timely manner"? Should I have been more direct with regard to a specific time?
2. The conference with the parents was not held until the next week. Should this situation have waited over a holiday weekend? Because the local school officials decided to handle the

situation, is the time of the conference any concern of university personnel?

3. Should the school personnel have gotten permission to discuss this with the child's therapist (no evidence was really given that he was in active treatment) themselves instead of relying on the parents to convey this information?

4. If the parents had not conveyed this information to the therapist and later there was a serious incident with other students at the school (a shooting or some violence), what accountability would fall on the school or university personnel for this oversight?

5. The student was left out of this scenario in the action steps. When and how could he have better been included in this process without causing him to lose confidence in the school counselor?

6. Should the counselor intern have called the parents herself about the conversations she had with the boy? Why or why not?

7. Was the action plan appropriate for the school counselor intern?

8. Was the university liable in any way? Before or after the action plan?

RESPONSES TO THE INCIDENT

Shoshana Hellman and Galy Cinnmon

This critical incident deals with the question of boundaries among systems and the issue of responsibility. A number of systems are involved in this incident: (a) the university—the counseling intern and the trainer-supervisor; (b) the school—the school counselor-supervisor and the principal of the school; (c) the family—the parents and the teenager; and (d) the private therapist. The main issue is the relationship between these systems and who is responsible for what. Also, we should examine who is the client of whom and what is the interaction between the parties, especially because of ethical considerations.

As to the issue of responsibility: The major responsibility in this case is of the school counselor (supervisor), who has the professional responsibility for the well-being of the students in the school and at the same time for the professional development of the student counseling intern. As a result, the boundaries between these two should be very open. The students should know that there is a counseling intern in the school, and also that there are cases in which information that they provide cannot be kept confidential. Causing harm to themselves or others is an ethical issue that should be brought up by the intern in her conversations with students and by the school counselor. It should be clear that there is an open dialogue between the intern and the school counselor about any matter concerning the school because of the responsibility of the school counselor.

The responsibility of the university (e.g., trainer) in our opinion was to notify the school as soon as the trainer heard about the case. Once the school was notified, it is the sole responsibility of the school (principal, school counselor) to decide on its course of action and timetable. It is not the responsibility of the university to act directly but to function as consultants to the school upon request.

The parents should have been notified as soon as possible. The parents have the main responsibility for the teenager, their son. The school cannot force the parents to meet early, but they do have the professional responsibility to clarify to them how serious the matter is. And because the parents mentioned the teenager's therapist, the school should have asked to talk to the therapist with the parents' permission. It is questionable whether the parents would have agreed to do so, but it is the task of the school counselor and the principal to request such a permission by emphasizing the potential consequences and the severity of the situation. At this point, the accountability of the school for the students and the possibility that serious incidents can happen at school should have been discussed with the parents. We think a group consultation of the parents, the two counselors, and the therapist with or without the teenager would have been useful. In our opinion, the connection with the therapist or referral to further treatment of the teenager is essential. Otherwise, because there were warning signs and the school did not do everything in its power to notify and seek for treatment of the student, it would be held accountable if something serious happens at school as a result of this lack of treatment.

As for the teenager, he should have been notified about the action plan as soon as his parents were notified. The school counselor is responsible for the students, and he should have known ahead about the ethical limitations. At the same time, because he did talk to the intern, she should continue to see the student with the proper consultation by the school counselor and the university.

Tom Hohenshil

This is indeed a difficult situation for all concerned, including the child, his parents, school personnel, the private therapist, and university personnel. The incident involves both ethical and legal issues. The first key issue involved here is a clinical judgment as to the seriousness of the student's threat to do harm to his parents. The following comments about the incident are based on the assumption that the threat is a serious one. Given that, the course of action is fairly clear.

Although talking with the student on a basketball court is not a typical counseling setting, the counseling intern should realize that she is a representative of the school counseling program and as such probably entered into a counseling relationship with the student even though it did not occur in a traditional counseling office. By confiding in the counseling intern, the student seemed to believe that such a relationship was created.

Once the counseling intern learned of the student's plan to cause harm to his parents, the intern should have immediately verbally notified her on-site supervisor and her university supervisor, and followed this up in writing. The appropriate action for the school then would have been to immediately contact the parents about the incident and also notify the appropriate law enforcement officials. Not to immediately do so could raise considerable legal and ethical issues for school personnel if the student committed violent acts to his parents or others in the future. In addition, it would have been advisable to get parental and student permission to share the incident with the student's therapist. Helping the student and his parents get counseling help should have been of paramount importance and a high priority for school and university personnel.

The fact that the intern did not seem to recognize the seriousness of the situation is a reflection on the counselor education program, her own judgment, or both. The fact that she was somewhat reluctant to either share the information with the university supervisor or make the necessary contacts raises additional questions about her judgment. If she was delaying taking professionally responsible action only because she was concerned about getting a job in the system, then the counselor education faculty should meet to consider appropriate remedial action regarding the student.

It seems that university personnel were following a reasonable course of action for the most part, although they should have required more immediate action. In addition, they should have recommended involvement of appropriate law enforcement personnel from the juvenile justice system. Consultation with colleagues was appropriate, as well as consultation with the university legal staff. In terms of general university liability in such a situation, faculty and the university are liable for assuring reasonable supervision of and action on the part of the counseling intern involved in the incident. This involves following the ethical principles of the profession, as well as applicable laws in the state where the incident occurred.

Terminal Illness: "I Can't Believe This Is Happening"

CRITICAL INCIDENT

Background

Our school was a small, rural school of 1,000, with students in Grades 1 through 12. Jason had always been a very active boy in our school. He kept good grades, played on several local baseball teams, and was well liked by his classmates. I had spoken with him on a couple of occasions because his parents had recently gone through a messy divorce. This situation led to a lot of animosity in the home and stress for Jason to choose one parent over the other. After a few visits and some time, Jason started to readjust. He

lived with his mother during the week and his father on the weekends. He had some issues with his stepmother and stepbrother, but
he seemed to handle these things in stride. Because he was the
only boy in his family, he felt more comfortable at his father's house
and did not let these things interfere with his relationship with his
father. All in all, Jason's life was much like that of any of his eighth-
grade peers. That is why everyone was taken by surprise. He
looked the same as everyone else. He laughed and played like the
others. He never seemed particularly frail.

One weekend while Jason was at his father's house, he told his
stepmother that his stomach was hurting very much. Thinking that
he was trying to avoid his chores, she gave him some medicine and
sent him out to mow the lawn. Although Jason protested, he went
outside and began to work. That afternoon when his father came
home, Jason was doubled over in the front lawn. He ran over to
see what was wrong and found a large swelling on Jason's
abdomen. They rushed him to the hospital. Jason had cancer, and
the large swelling was a tumor on his stomach.

Because the onset and growth of the tumor was so rapid, aggressive treatment ensued. Jason was sent to Children's Hospital, where
doctors operated to remove most of the tumor. Then he was subjected to chemotherapy and radiation until the cancer subsided.
These treatments caused him to be very weak, his wound from the
surgery healed very slowly, and he had lost all of his hair.

Incident

While Jason was in the hospital, both his mother and his stepmother (who were teachers) helped him to maintain his schoolwork. When the doctors released him, Jason went back to school.
He had missed his friends and was ready to be with them again.
Most of his classmates had made cards and written notes and sent
them to him in the hospital. They missed Jason and were ready to
have him back, too. What both he and his classmates were not prepared for was that Jason was not the same anymore. He had
changed; he was different. He did not look the same. He was bald,
so he wore hats all of the time. He had lost a lot of weight. He was

not as playful because he had to be careful when he ran. The children were afraid, and Jason was crushed.

I saw Jason in the hall a couple of days after he came back to school that spring. He was looking at the floor, walking by himself, and looking very sad. I asked him if he would mind talking for a minute and explained to his teacher that the conference might take some time. Jason said he did not understand. Everyone had been so nice and had written they wanted him to come back. Now they did not even wanted to sit near him and only his best friend spoke to him the first day, and now even this friend was making fun of him with the others. My heart went out to him while he cried and said in stuttering speech he wished he had not come back from the hospital and all his friends in this school were fakes.

I decided I should be an advocate for Jason. I decided his illness needed to be addressed in all his classes. All of his teachers and his little league coaches met with Jason's parents and myself. We all learned about Jason's new needs, his medicines, and his illness. Together we took this knowledge and tried to explain it to the children. Our plan was to tell the other children Jason was special. They could not catch the disease; it was not like chicken pox or the flu. Sometimes Jason would have to slow down and could not play running games. He was much better than before, but he was still pretty ill. We always waited until Jason was out of the room before we talked to his classmates. The students began to understand, things seemed to get better, and Jason looked forward to his ninth-grade year.

Discussion

Jason was made "special." Most of the kids were very considerate of him. When new classmates enrolled in school, the students would most often explain about Jason before the teacher would. His coaches made special positions for him, like "Official Ball Boy" and had jerseys made for him so he could be included with other players. His coaches would even let him participate in some of the drills when possible. Everybody wanted to help Jason.

Jason (in the 9th- and 10th-grade year) had a steady girlfriend, had decent grades, but still could not play baseball the way he once had. However, he and his girlfriend became increasingly close and this seemed to take Jason's mind off baseball. In Jason's 10th-grade year he suddenly took a turn for the worse, as traces of the cancer returned. Jason was readmitted into the hospital where he spent the remainder of his school year. That summer, Jason died of complications brought on by the reoccurrence of the cancer. He was 16 years old.

QUESTIONS

1. It is very disturbing to realize that a child might have a terminal disease. Although some intervention is needed to help the other people understand what is wrong, can it ever be too much?
2. Was it fair to Jason for others to make allowances for him without his asking? While people should be encouraged to be considerate, how did this contribute to Jason's feelings?
3. I have often blamed myself for Jason's lack of close personal relationships because of the frailty that we stressed to all of his classmates. How do you protect a child without limiting him or her?
4. While much time was taken to educate Jason's peers about his disease, we did not take special time to educate Jason about his peers' reactions. I look back and realize that my action lacked balance. What would have been a better way?
5. What was my role in helping Jason and his girlfriend understand the ramifications of such a serious relationship?

RESPONSES TO THE INCIDENT

John B. Stewart

There are two issues that I think frame this context: one is a crisis and the other is the role of an advocate. The crisis described here could be termed a situationally originated one, which influenced both Jason and his peer group. Jason viewed this crisis from the perspective of having been diagnosed with a potential-ly fatal illness, whereas his peer group's perspective was that one from their group had a potentially fatal illness. Jason displayed signs of helplessness and hopelessness, as well as discomfort and anxiety. His peer group displayed anxiety and, because of their lack of appropriate social skills to deal with this crisis, teasing behavior. The counselor chose to exercise the role of an advo-cate in resolving this crisis. How this role was conceptualized and the process implemented are critical issues in bringing this crisis to a successful resolution.

The counselor's motive for action was the desire to promote Jason's welfare in the hope of providing for positive personal growth and development as well as helping him reintegrate into the school environment. Furthermore, the counselor involved the fam-ily, teachers, and coaches in the development of a plan to promote these goals. When counselors act as advocates for their clients, they should represent their client's interests to another group. First and foremost, advocates must receive a clear mandate and directions from the client. A client must be able to give consent to the planned actions that ensue from the initial meetings with the counselor. In this particular example, the counselor did not consult Jason but involved his parents and other significant adults to develop a plan that addressed the negativity coming from Jason's peer group. Although the counselor acted appropriately to involve Jason's par-ents and the other significant adults, I suggest that Jason should have been involved in these discussions from the beginning. Such an involvement would give Jason the message that his perspective was important, as well as give him some sense of empowerment about how he conceptualized his illness and the attitudes he might have been portraying to his peers. However, the counselor appeared to have explored only the possible positive outcomes with this group and not the possible negative ones that might result from this form of intervention. Not all clients will think to ask about outcomes, and counselors must discuss with them the possible pos-itive and negative implications of any course of intervention.

Prior to initiating any action, the counselor should resolve a number of critical issues. First, the counselor should examine his or her motive for and role in the advocacy. Because counselors should represent the views of their clients, it is important for the counselor to view this issue from Jason's perspective and not lose sight of what Jason wanted as an outcome. In this particular context, the counselor appeared to have acted as a parent, and his or her desire was to have Jason's peers change their treatment of him. I suggest that this outcome was desirable but that the plan did not directly involve Jason, and consequently he was not likely to feel any empowerment or personal growth as a result of the individuals acting on his behalf because he did not have an active part in developing the plan. Counselors need to explore their client's interests and not just act in what they think is their client's best interests.

A second issue is the perspective taken on the outcome. In this context, the advocacy appeared to have a win–lose outcome: Jason did not have to change, his peers must. If indeed this was the perspective, it seemed to have elements of denial embedded in it. Jason could not deny that he had cancer and the treatment that followed that diagnosis, he could not deny his physical weaknesses that limited his involvement especially in recreational sport, and neither could he deny the effects of this treatment, particularly his loss of hair. I suggest that counselors need to give careful thought to the outcomes desired when dealing with this type of circumstance. Ideally win–win outcomes are desirable. Jason must accept his circumstances and be able to grow within these parameters; his peers must have the skills and the confidence to help them deal with the possibility of this disease affecting them and to deal with their interpersonal relationships with Jason.

A third issue concerns the skills of the counselor in implementing a plan with this population. First, the counselor must determine the skills Jason needed to deal with the nature of his illness and the parameters it set on his activities. Second, the counselor must determine what skills were needed by the reference group to help them deal with Jason. And third, the counselor must decide if he or she could provide these skills. I suggest that Jason needed help to deal with his grief and the emotions he would experience as a result of the illness and its possible implications for his life. He needed skills in being able to relate these feelings and discuss his thoughts and fears about possible outcomes. His peer group needed to be taught the social skills to deal with Jason on a one-on-one basis. Avoidance usually develops when individuals do not know how to deal with the situation. I suggest the counselor should help Jason's peers to reframe their negative feelings and attitudes into positive and supportive ones. Also, the counselor should help Jason to reframe how he viewed himself as helpless and understand the circumstances that have shaped him.

In this particular context, the counselor took the role of providing information about Jason to his peers and significant adults. Adults involved in Jason's life have a right to know how his illness would influence Jason's progress within their respective jurisdictions. I suggest that Jason should have been involved to give consent about how much information needed to be shared with these significant adults. One of the concerns here is how children and adolescents would understand the information and how they might construct meaning about Jason's illness. It appeared that Jason had been victimized as someone different, particularly as a result of his medical treatment. The counselor should not assume that Jason's peers would understand the information from the "inappropriate" perspective. Such an assumption should not be taken automatically, and I suggest that there might have been some checks included in the plan to assess how Jason's peers were understanding the information they were given. For example, Jason's peers should have been allowed to ask questions about his illness, and they should have been allowed the opportunity to paraphrase their concerns for Jason. Perhaps Jason should have been the one to tell his immediate peers the extent of his disease and why his behaviors were not as they were before his operation. I suggest that one of the goals of advocacy is to help individuals speak for themselves. Counselors need to understand the information-processing styles of the populations with whom they work and take precautions to provide the type and amount of information so that accurate processing will take place.

In summary, when acting as an advocate, counselors should begin by identifying the client's issues and interests, clarifying the client's concerns, developing a plan or strategy to address the concerns with fall-back options, and then evaluating the plan with a "reality check" to see if it meets the client's needs. Counselors need to give thought to their role in the advocacy, how they conceptualize the outcome, their skills in bringing about the changes that are deemed necessary, and make sure that their clients are directly involved in all aspects of the advocacy.

Linda Foster

The terminal illness of a child has profound and far-reaching effects. Families, friends, peers, and others are often devastated by the death of a young person. The question of when and how much intervention is needed is one for examination. In the case of Jason, the counselor believed a great deal of intervention, on his part, was necessary. The counselor's assumption of a very active role should be dependent on the wishes of Jason. However, because of Jason's status as a minor, his parent's permission and consent should also be taken into consideration.

The counselor's intention was well conceived but without guidance from Jason and his parents. The ethical issues of confidentiality and the client's best interests are paramount. Together, Jason, his parents, and the counselor must determine the amount and kind of intervention needed.

By the counselor's assumption of intervention, Jason's power was taken away, which in turn might have contributed to his feelings of helplessness and "being different." By not allowing Jason to be involved in his return to school, the other students only heard the counselor's perspective. Jason was not allowed to share his feelings and perspectives, thereby taking away his voice. If Jason was allowed to be involved in the intervention with other students, he would be seen as strong and given the opportunity to contribute to his welfare and treatment by others.

A concern of balancing the "specialness" of Jason so as not to accentuate the fact that he was different because of his cancer could be addressed several ways. One possible way was to have other children who have survived cancer come and speak to the students. This would enable the other students to see survivors and not victims. The survivor children would be given the opportunity to share their feelings and perceived treatment. This would in turn help students react to Jason in a sensitive manner, yet see his possible recovery and the return of the former Jason. Even though Jason had childhood cancer and adults often react from a nurturing parental viewpoint, childhood is a time of learning, not only for Jason but for the other students as well. Although protection of Jason physically and emotionally is of concern, personal growth and experience are tools for teaching and learning, not only about others but also about ourselves.

By talking with Jason before his return to school, the counselor could have determined what Jason was expecting on his return. An honest discussion with Jason about his appearance and physical condition needed to be addressed. Jason needed to be educated with regard to the other students' perceptions and their expectations of him.

If Jason were allowed to discuss his fears, concerns, and expectations about returning to school, some of the stigma attached to his appearance might have been lessened. Better preparation of his peers with regard to the changed appearance of Jason might also have helped the other students to recognize that only Jason's appearance and strength had changed. More dialogue among Jason, the counselor, and Jason's peers might have alleviated the concerns of all involved.

As a serious relationship began to develop between Jason and his girlfriend, the counselor could have helped Jason and his girlfriend understand the ramifications of a serious relationship during his illness. Issues of grief, jealously, sorrow, and longing could be discussed so that each of them would be more prepared for loss either by death or maturation.

In this incident, it appeared the counselor, in his zeal to ensure that Jason be treated fairly, might have compounded Jason's feelings of inadequacy, loneliness, and adjustment to his new role. Jason and his parents needed to be more involved in the discussions surrounding him and his cancer. Input from Jason and his parents could have addressed issues of importance and concern to them in facilitating Jason's return to the school environment.

Overall, the attempt on the part of the counselor to alleviate the anxiety of Jason's peers did not seem to be the most effective means of educating the students with respect to childhood cancer victims. A more effective way might be to help Jason feel "normal" in his school setting. A return to normalcy from his intense treatment for cancer would assist not only Jason but also his peers in seeing Jason return as a fellow student, not just as a cancer victim.

Transient Student: "All Alone and Scared With No One to Talk to"

CRITICAL INCIDENT

Background

As a school counselor in a large inner-city high school, I see students come and go throughout the school year. The high school in which I work is located next to a large government housing project. Approximately 95% of the 1,100 students enrolled in my school receive free or reduced lunches. They live in neighborhoods where violence and crime rates are high. As a result of the intense poverty prevalent in the surrounding community, families move frequently because of the loss of a job, inability to pay the rent, or trouble with the law. These moves are rarely anticipated and are therefore performed without notice to the school. Owing to the transient nature of the student population, it is often difficult for students to gain entrance into positive peer groups or form healthy and lasting relationships. The following incident is reflective of a problem faced by one student who entered this inner-city high school where he knew no one and had no support network.

Tarus, a ninth-grade African American student, enrolled at the high school in January shortly after the beginning of the second semester. He was from New York City and had been sent to live with his aunt and her children. In New York, Tarus and his mother lived in a high-crime area where gangs actively controlled the neighborhoods. Tarus, who was small for his age, lived in constant fear of the gangs. In school he was a good student and proved himself to be very articulate. After the violent death of his best friend, Tarus's mother decided to send him to a safer place to complete his education. Thus, she sent him to live with her sister in a large urban city in a southeastern state.

Tarus's aunt lived in the government housing project adjacent to the school. Unbeknown to his mother, Tarus's 15-year-old cousin was a member of a local gang. He began to pressure Tarus to join the gang. Tarus had been removed from one potentially dangerous situation only to find himself caught in one equally as dangerous.

Once enrolled in school, Tarus again proved himself to be a good student. However, he was laughed at and ridiculed for his willingness to participate in class. He was being pressured by his cousin and his cousin's gang members to join the gang or face the consequences. Being new at the school, Tarus had no peers to talk to, he could not talk to his aunt, and he did not want to worry his mother. The only friend he had was one of his teachers, Mrs. Abrams, whom he trusted.

Incident

One day during Mrs. Abrams's preparation period, Tarus appeared at her door and asked if he could talk with her. He told her that several gang members wanted to fight him at school because he refused to join their gang. Tarus was scared and had no one to turn to. Because the other boys had threatened violence toward Tarus, Mrs. Abrams suggested they go to the principal and inform him of the situation. When in the principal's office, Tarus began to tell his story. He became very emotional and began to cry. The principal said, "Dry your eyes and stop that crying. Be a man. Men don't cry. A man will face up to the situation and meet it head on." He told Tarus, "the best thing to do might be to tell the police or tell them you do not want to be in their gang. I can't watch you all day, I have a whole school to run."

Tarus was now terrified. Mrs. Abrams, in a desperate attempt to help Tarus, brought him to my office and told me the story. I looked at this scared child and told him "to cry." I assured him there was nothing unmanly about crying. Crying was an okay way to release tension. Tarus broke down and cried for several minutes. Once he gained control, we discussed his situation. I told him there were several avenues we could take in addressing his problem. I could request a conference with his aunt, I could call his mother and inform her of the situation, and I could intervene with the principal on his behalf. He seemed relieved that he had shared his burden with someone who accepted him without judgment and who appeared concerned about him and his situation.

Discussion

That afternoon I called Tarus's aunt and told her I needed to talk with her about Tarus. She told me that Tarus would only be with her for a short amount of time, and she was not really responsible for him. She had all she could handle trying to raise her own children. If Tarus had problems, he would have to deal with them himself. Tarus had asked me not call his mother because he did not want to worry her. He did not see returning to New York as an option. I talked with the principal, and he said he would try to handle the situation in the school. However, he could not be held accountable for what happened off the school grounds. In desperation, I contacted the Family Court probation officer who worked with the gangs in our area. I told him the story and he said he would see what he could do, but, until the gang members actually attacked Tarus, there was not much the law enforcement agencies and Family Court could do.

Several days after Tarus came to me for help, a fight erupted in the front of the school. Tarus was beaten up by three other boys. All of the boys involved, including Tarus, were suspended by the principal. Tarus's aunt sent him to his 70-year-old grandmother in another state. She and her children moved to another housing project across town. I never heard from Tarus again.

QUESTIONS

1. How can we help transient students build positive and supportive relationships in school when they know they will only be there for a short period of time?
2. What alternatives did this child have? What could I have done to be more helpful?
3. I felt the principal's reaction to Tarus did more harm than good. How could I, as a counselor, educate the principal in positive ways to deal with transient students?
4. Even though Tarus requested I not contact his mother in New York, should I have called her?

RESPONSES TO THE INCIDENT

Carla Mulkey

This story had a heartfelt message. Some of the most sad cases I've had in my counseling career have involved transient students, who are here today but gone tomorrow. Here is an analogy to contemplate:

How do you keep a plant alive that has very short roots, when it is constantly being transplanted into depleted soil that lacks nutrients, with little light and water available? It is no wonder that a student facing insurmountable odds and obstacles in his or her life might drift into despair, depression, desperation, or even suicide. Who or what will help the student to live a kind of life he or she deserves? The following come to mind:

1. Having a teacher who takes a special interest.
2. Having a hobby or sport to attend.
3. Having a synagogue, church, or place of worship.
4. Having a teen recreation center.
5. Having a weekly mentor or tutor, for academic, emotional, and spiritual support.
6. Having alternative placement settings through the help of a social worker.
7. Having the support of a law enforcement officer, or Juvenile Probation Officer.
8. Having a friend who has survived gang activity.
9. Having programs that find safe havens for juveniles in danger of joining gangs.
10. Having a relative who understands, even if the relative is over 70.
11. Having literacy programs, including bibliotherapy and library materials.
12. Having adult role models in the media and school who combat crime or immorality.
13. Having positive, alternative lifestyles and vocations to offer.
14. Having youth group traveling opportunities.
15. Having enough funding for youth programs.
16. Having more hiring of individuals in the helping professions.
17. Having legislators who care about youth programs.
18. Having communities contribute in raising our children.
19. Having local as well as global focuses on youth concerns.

What can be done in the meantime? I would tell this caring school counselor to do something that my sign on my school desk suggests:"Hang in there—Someone's not finished with you (or me) yet!" You may have lost the battle, but you have not yet lost the war. This young man has been battered and abused, but he is not down for good.

Remember the story of Rocky, the boxer? Sometimes when life gives you nothing but lemons, you have to somehow make lemonade. Perhaps the move to a new neighborhood will at least bring a change of scenery which, in turn, could help Tarus obtain a new lease on life. Often, with cases involving social services or law enforcement, there is no easy answer regarding placement. Still, we all know individuals who somehow struggled and "made it" in life, despite horrific circumstances.

Teach resiliency. Speak the truth. Coordinate with others. Gather the troops for support. Learn all you can about this student. Investigate alternatives. Lead by example. Never give up, yet learn when to let go. Remember past mistakes. Always think "What if ...?" Think, pray, or meditate on the "What ifs." Above all, take care of yourself and the little, inner person inside of yourself.

Many young persons have gone on to thrive after they have found nourishment through a providing, caring, persevering, steadfast, and loyal friend. School counselors should represent those kinds of care-giving friends for students like the example in this story.

Lawrence E. Tyson

As a school counselor in a large high school with a 50% turnover rate during the year, I realized the limitations (i.e., developmental services) of the counseling staff's services to the student body, particularly to students who were with us a short time. Our first act was to determine how to promote the ideals of positive and supportive relationships between students, and between adults and students. Our belief was that this issue affected students who remained with us, as well as our transient population. Our belief was not to promise (to students) what we could not deliver. We wanted to be seen by students as adults who would give truthful answers to their questions and who could be trusted to follow through on commitments. We also wanted to establish a program to ease the transition of our new students into our school community. We started an ambassador program aimed at new students. Student ambassadors were selected from each grade and participated in a workshop on communication skills and sensitivity toward new students. Upon entering our school, each new student was assigned a student ambassador for 3 days. Ambassadors helped new students acclimate to the school by providing a tour, meeting them after each class, eating lunch with them, introducing them to the key adults (i.e., principal, librarian, dean, coaches, attendance personnel, secretaries, club sponsors), and answering questions. The ambassadors were also required to call the new student at home at least once during the 3-day assignment. Also, once per month, the ambassadors held a social for all new students who enrolled during the month. Refreshments were served, ambassadors became reacquainted with the students who had enrolled during the month, and a faculty member who was a club sponsor, coach, or in charge of a student activity was invited to speak about their program. The ambassador program did more to help new students feel accepted and to ease their transition than any direct service we could have provided.

In this scenario, Tarus seemed to have reached out to those expected to help him. Everyone seemed to react in a timely manner and in Tarus's best interest. The conditions under which the child arrived and was living was out of the counselor's control. Sometimes, despite our best intentions, we do all we can do and it still is not enough. This appears to be the case with this counselor. This counselor acted appropriately despite the obstacles.

The principal's attitude toward the potentially dangerous situation concerns me the most. He does not appear to comprehend the danger to this student and to the student body. The language and tone of voice the principal used during the conference with Tarus was inappropriate and unethical. The principal's remark about not being able to watch Tarus all day could be interpreted as the principal not fulfilling his legal obligations toward students in danger. Tarus was the counselor's main responsibility. After the situation had been resolved, the counselor might need to evaluate if this is the type of administrator to work for.

After talking with the aunt to determine more of the child's history, and assuming the mother was the legal guardian, the counselor should have called the mother in New York. It is admirable that the child did not want to worry the mother; however, this was a case in which the counselor should have acted (called). The counselor should not have agreed not to call Tarus's mother. She has a legal right to know if her child is having difficulty adjusting to school, let alone in danger.

Values:
"I'm the Expert Here"

CRITICAL INCIDENT

Background

My own background includes going to college rather late in life because of economic reasons. During the Second World War, I worked in the shipyards to earn enough money to go to college, and then my college work was interrupted several times because of financial demands made by my own family. However, I finally got a Bachelor of Arts degree, taught for several years while attending graduate school at night, and received the my master's degree after 6 years of struggle. At long last, I was appointed a school counselor. I mention these items to indicate that I personally worked hard to get a professional education and to show that I believe that one should try hard to get ahead. Also, as a high school counselor, I have very often argued and pleaded with bright students who do not plan to go to college to do so, and I have helped several to find ways and means to get further education.

I believe that colleges should be training grounds for the intellectual elite, and not for everyone. Because half of the U.S. population has less-than-average academic aptitude, I believe that at least half of the population should not go to college. They will not get much out of it because college degrees will not mean much. Also, going to college for such kids is likely to be a disastrous experience. To put it simply, I think some kids should go to college whether or not they are interested or can afford it and some should not go to college. I believe that one of my functions, perhaps my main function, is to advise high school seniors and their parents about the wisdom of any child going to any college.

One of my counselees was Peter, who was below average in everything. We had complete records on him going back to kindergarten. He had taken about a dozen IQ tests and general academic aptitude tests over the years, as well as test of achievement, and not a single one of them showed he was above average. His grades were above average, however, which I assumed to be a function of his docility.

He was a good student who did what he was told and never got into trouble. He was a spiritless, mild, meek, and inadequate boy, with very little spunk, drive, or will. He always complied and tried his best, but his best was below average in every objective measurable respect. He had few friends and, to put it simply, he just existed. I had seen Peter several times on routine matters and found him to be more or less a lump. Whatever I would recommend, he would accept. He had no ideas of his own. His modal response to almost every question was to say, "Hudunno" (translated: "I don't know"). He was a scared rabbit of a boy.

The specific background relating to the incident has to do with a counseling session I had with Peter, which centered on what he should do when he graduated from high school. I asked him what he intended to do, and I got one of his "Hudunno" sounds. I asked him what his parents wanted him to do and was told "college." Peter had a habit, incidentally, of answering questions with one key word. When I heard that he was being encouraged to go on to college, I was shaken. I knew that, given his level of knowledge, he did not even deserve a high school diploma. I was certain that any college would soon throw him out and that this event would be a traumatic experience. I was certain that his parents would be quite upset were he to go to college and not succeed. I felt it might also be quite a financial, as well as emotional, burden for all concerned.

I then told Peter he should think over carefully whether he really wanted go beyond high school and to talk things over with his parents. I also told him to tell them I would be happy to talk with them about the matter. He seemed to understand. The next day his mother called and asked for an appointment. I set it for the first time I had available.

Incident

Both of Peter's parents came in, and the session started cordially enough. I told them I was interested in Peter and I felt the three of us should discuss what would be best for their son. I carefully went over Peter's tests and objective grades with them and interpreted his school grades. I then tried to explain to them what college was like. (Neither of the parents had gone to college, and there was none in this town.) I told them that, in my judgment, Peter had almost no chance to succeed in college and that going there would most likely be burdensome on them as well as possibly traumatic for Peter.

The father nodded from time to time in agreement with me, but the mother just glared at me, and I began to realize that she was upset. I continued, trying to be a neutral and yet as persuasive as I could, giving them all the information I had and trying to let them understand the whole matter from my point of view. I reminded them that this was "my opinion" and that the decision was "theirs" and that what was important was "Peter's welfare and happiness." But I felt I was not getting through to the mother. Finally, I finished and awaited their reaction.

The mother began to accuse me of not wanting Peter to go to college. She told me he had always wanted to go, and that when he had come home several nights before he was all shook up and disturbed about what I had told him. She said I had no right to say what I did. It was none of my business. My business was only to help him select the best college for him and not to influence his decision to attend college. This decision was the family's decision and not mine. Peter was now refusing to study or do his home-work. He would do poorly on the finals because of my discussion with him. I had not encouraged him. Where there is a will there is a way. If he had good grades in high school, he would also have good grades in college. What did I know about tests anyway? Which were better indicators of college grades, tests or high school grades? Did only people with high IQ have a right to go to college? Was college not supposed to help someone use his talents as best he could? What should Peter do now? Become a linoleum layer like his father?

To the last question I answered, "What is wrong with being a linoleum layer?" Her answer shocked me: "Better he should be dead." I realized at this point that I was not dealing with a rational woman, but what made this a critical incident for me was her next statement and request. She had thought it all out clearly. "Peter has a right to go to college and try. My husband and I have worked hard and saved money for this. We want him to enjoy himself at college and get a chance to learn something which may help him in life. You have now discouraged him. I want you to call him in and undo the harm you have done. Tell him you were joking, tell him you were mistaken. Tell him anything, but get him motivated to pass his examinations as well as possible."

Shaken by this scene, which had gone so differently from how I expected, I looked at the father, who shrugged helplessly. "I think maybe you ought to do what she says. After all, she is the mother. Peter is our only son. We want what is best. Both of us think he should go. Maybe you ought to go along with her. I see your point. Maybe you are right. But he should get his chance. Otherwise she will always hate you."

The incident occurred for me then and there. I closed my eyes and thought carefully. I knew I was right, and I was positive the mother was wrong. I knew that Peter should not go to college. I could see the whole thing. My problem was what to do. Should I stick to my guns, tell them this was how I saw things, and that right or wrong I would do what I thought was right, that I was a professional person, hired by the city to give my judgment on academic–vocational matters? Or, should I do what I thought was unwise, go along with the ambitious but unrealistic mother, and thereby harm the child? I knew I really did not know what the right thing to do was, that the matter might be seen differently by different counselors. But I could not pass the buck to anyone else. My decision was to go along with the mother. I agreed, called in Peter the next day, and more or less said to him what his mother wanted.

Discussion

Peter did get into college, and at the end of the first semester returned home and entered his father's business. I called a faculty member at the college with whom I had considerable contact in placing students and asked for information about Peter. I was told he had not adjusted well, that his grades had been very poor, that he had been on academic probation, that my judgment had been faulty in recommending him to them. In the future, he indicated, he would be much more skeptical about my recommendations.

I explained the situation, and the faculty member stated he understood my problem and that this was a fairly common problem for high school counselors. Probably about all that could be done, he felt, was to go along with parents.

QUESTIONS

1. Should a counselor operate only as a technician, doing what the "clients" (i.e., students or parents) want, rather than as a professional doing what he or she thinks is right?
2. In this instance, what would you have done that I did not do? Try to get another professional opinion or try to argue and convince the mother and refuse to change my opinion?

3. How should one handle such problems? Should one just refuse to get involved? Would this not be malfeasance?

RESPONSES TO THE INCIDENT
Rudolf Dreikers

One can understand the difficulties of the counselor in this particular situation when one considers his background. He was very correct in providing it; it explains his utter blindness in regard to the damage he did, as a consequence of the high standards he had set for himself. Because he worked very hard to get his master's degree, he became an intellectual snob, looking down on those who did not come up to his standards.

Tied to this general attitude is his exaggerated opinion about the significance of a college degree. He really believes that college is for the intellectual elite, from which the rest should be excluded. First of all, there is often no correlation between a college degree and competence in the field. The degree is reserved for those who have the ability to pass examinations. And we are becoming aware that many students who do not qualify for college are much more successful, even intellectually, than those who are admitted on the strength of test scores. When less intelligent students are denied admission to college, it deprives them of the opportunity to obtain better jobs; many students want to go to college only because their financial prospects will be significantly improved. But all this information is, of course, beyond the grasp of the counselor, who is fascinated by the importance of intellectual superiority. Unfortunately, the student had to suffer for it.

The fact that Peter's grades were "above average" did not impress the counselor. He took the achievement test average as a basis for his assumption that this student was "below average." It is obvious the counselor did not like the student by the way he described him. It never occurred to him to understand Peter's handicap—his discouragement, particularly in dealing with a demanding "superior" which he, the counselor, was. For him, Peter's peculiar behavior was apparently a sign of intellectual inferiority. His anticipation of Peter's inevitable failure was a critical variable and was much more harmful to Peter than the consequences of a certain college failure. It is obvious that Peter felt inadequate to meet demands, which may well explain his low performance on tests. Discouraged as the boy obviously was, the counselor did his best to discourage him further.

The interview that the counselor had with Peter's parents is a masterpiece of self-deception. The counselor was furious about what the parents, especially the mother, said and apparently was utterly unaware of what he himself did. It starts off with the statement that he tried to be as neutral as he could, while every act and sentence revealed his own prejudice against the boy and his reluctance to understand what the mother had to say. He stated that "the mother began to accuse me of not wanting Peter to go to college." For heaven's sake, was that not exactly what he tried to do? Then the mother described the boy's reaction after the counselor had told him he should not go to college, that "he was all shook up and disturbed." The counselor certainly was not disturbed by that, nor did he recognize the harm he had done to the boy who now refused to study or to do his homework. He could not see how correct the mother was in blaming him for the probability that the boy would do poorly in his finals as a result of the counselor's attack. She was justified in assuming that if the boy had good grades in high school, he may also have good grades in college.

But the counselor believed more in tests than in the actual performance of the boy. Peter's mother's evaluation of a college education was much more accurate than the distorted view of the counselor, when she said, "wasn't college to help anyone to use his talents as best he could?" Then the counselor even exceeded himself in his utter blindness to the situation. He was enraged that the mother did not want the son to become a linoleum layer like father. Why was the counselor not satisfied with working in the shipyards and instead worked so hard to get a college education? Was it not the same desire for higher status that motivated the mother? But the counselor could not see this issue.

In other words, it was not the mother who was irrational. She was correct in condemning the action of the counselor. The function of a counselor is to understand and to help, not to sit in judgment and to condemn. A boy who can make above-average grades in high school is entitled to get a college education. It would be up to the counselor to reduce difficulties. Instead he discouraged Peter, not only in regard to a possible college education but in his functioning at the moment. The mother was justified in demanding that he undo the harm he did and to "get him motivated to pass his examinations as well as possible."

Where did the counselor go wrong? All his professional training did not provide him with the ability to size up the situation. We have seen many cases in which, on the basis of tests alone, faculty evaluations have been made, and students have been discouraged from going to college who, when they ignored the advice, have gone and succeeded, sometimes even with top grades. Conversely, students who have seemed to be eminently qualified for higher education have failed miserably.

In this sense, the counselor was a victim of a system that will be increasingly recognized as faulty and inadequate. He compounded his mistaken evaluation of the situation with his personal concern with the elite, with intellectual righteousness. For him the question was whether he was "right" or not, regardless of what happened to the student. His description of his interview with Peter's mother showed his blindness in regard to the role he played in the boy's life.

To answer his question—the counselor is not obligated to do what clients, students, or parents want; but he should use better judgment in dealing with a touchy situation. It is not enough that counselors do what they think is right; it is more important they have a better idea of what is right. Finally, his performance, beginning with his critical and contemptuous attitude toward Peter, was not professional but highly subjective and personal.

What could the counselor have done? First, he would have to deal with Peter's attitudes—his overambition on the one hand and his self-doubt expressed by his inadequate social adjustment on the other. After reconsidering these factors, he may have been better able to call Peter's attention to the risks of academic failure unless Peter learned to function more adequately in general. The counselor overlooked the specific problems of this student entirely and merely acted on the basis of his psychometric findings. As long as our system produces counselors whose sole technique is to give and evaluate tests, such examples of an utterly inhuman approach to student counseling will continue to plague us.

Allen E. Ivey

The basic problem in this case lies not in the questions raised by the counselor at the close of the case but in the third paragraph, where his explicit statement of his own values makes clear his expectations of less-than-average students. We see here an intellectual elitism, a complete acceptance of the validity of tests and grades as the prime indicators of who should go to college (despite considerable evidence to the contrary), and a godlike attitude ("my main function [is] to advise high school seniors and their parents about the wisdom of any child going to college").

Until this counselor examines his own personal values and realizes the potential destruction that lies within them (Peter was "more or less a lump"), he will be of only minimal value to the students he serves. He will probably continue as the college "traffic cop" helping only the apparently bright and gifted individual to higher possibilities. Could it be conceivable that some of these individuals might be more effective salespeople than professionals?

A more open and encouraging posture to all students is required of the counselor. This does not mean the counselor should encourage Peter to go to college. Rather, it means the counselor should explore with Peter how he really feels about his future. Accepting the one-word answer "college" after "Hudunno" does not impress one as exploration, counseling, or perhaps even conversation.

In this case, it must be granted that the student perhaps has only minimal chance for success in college. A series of interviews might explore Peter's interest and future plans in some depth. It seems strange that no one ever really asked Peter what he wanted to do. The counselor should not neglect his values and opinions in this case, but there is no need to impose them on the student. The counselor might point out the problems inherent in college attendance, but he could also indicate that individual differences and personal motivation determine eventual success. Peter then could take the data and use the information in his own decision-making process.

Peter and his counselor could explore alternatives to college and whether or not college was the right decision. The counselor could then meet with the parents with an informed sense of Peter's position. Some additional preparatory work with the parents might be useful before a final decision session. What are the parents' goals and aspirations? Have they fully considered alternatives? If college is the eventual decision, a variety of alternative institutions can be considered where Peter's chances for success are maximized. By careful choice of college and an honest, truthful admission recommendation, the counselor's problem with the college admissions office could have been avoided.

In short, if the counselor had known Peter as a person before the session with the parents, the confrontation with the mother might have been avoided and a more compatible decision for Peter, the family, and even the counselor might have resulted. Unfortunately, the counselor remained a prisoner of his own values and was unable to listen to or see the situation he encountered. This case illustrates a problem all too common in counseling. The focus here is not on the child but on wishes of the parents and the counselor.